Written by
Montana Mike

COVER PHOTOS

FRONT COVER
View from MacDonald Pass lookout

BACK COVER
Top left:
Mike & Dana's Last Dance Together at Patrick and Lizzie's wedding
Top right:
Dana's Last Note to Mike

Bottom left:
Annie on Riley and Mike on Sonnet in Our Equestrian Arena
Bottom right:
Annie Singing to Grandson Carter James

Journey To
Life's Dance Ranch
A magical story ... in prose and poetry.

ISBN: 978-0-9990882-8-9

Copyright © by Michael D. Maixner

All rights reserved. No part of this book may be reproduced or transmitted in any form by any means, electronic or mechanical, including photocopying, recording, or by any information storage or retrieval system, without permission in writing from the copyright owner.

This book was published in the U.S.A. by Susan the Scribe, Inc.
www.susanthescribe.com

Edited by Andie Jackson

Book and Cover Design by Andie Jackson
Wonderdog Designs, Jacksonville, Florida
andiejax@att.net

DEDICATION

It is with love and enormous gratitude I dedicate this book to my love, **Annie Z**. The book never would have happened if it had not been for the constant love, support, encouragement and the countless hours Annie spent helping me. There were times I just wanted to forget about the book altogether. Annie wouldn't let me. There were times when writing about the past was very difficult emotionally for both of us. Yet, Annie consoled me and buoyed me up. There were times when I was just too tired. Annie gave me strength and helped me rest. All in all, it was mostly a joyful work together. Annie remembering vignettes she wanted me to write about, then using her superior memory to help edit my writings and keep them historically as correct as possible. It warmed my heart to hear her laughter or see some tears as she worked on the book. I am sure that God sent me Annie, my angel, to help me complete this mission. Thank you, Sweetheart, I love you more than I can say.

Dear Friend, Wonderful Writer, Wonderful Lady

Four months after I lost my wife, Dana, and started a company to raise money for ovarian cancer awareness and research, a delightful lady came into my life. She had heard of my loss and start-up business and wanted to write my story for the Jacksonville, FL newspaper. **Susan D. Brandenburg "The Scribe"** wrote a beautiful article, and in the process became a most wonderful and trusted friend. When I met and was dating Annie, she wrote another beautiful article for the newspaper and became a good friend of Annie's. When she heard my poems, she was the first to encourage me to publish and has continued to do so for over twelve years. It is my great privilege to have Susan as a friend and now as the editor and publisher of my book. Susan is a writer with enormous talent. But even more, she is a truly good, kind and generous person and friend. Thank you so much for your love and support to me and Annie.

A special thanks to sister, Marcy

When my spontaneous writing started and I was overwhelmed by what was happening, I would call my sister, Marcy, and read her my writings. She was patient, kind and encouraging. I often heard her say, "These writings are not from this world. They're coming from the other side." Perhaps she was right. For her constant encouragement, listening and tireless work with Butterfly Ballet, LLC, I can only say, "A million thanks and much love." Your brother, Mike.

My thanks to Andie Jackson

Many thanks to my enormously talented graphic artist and editor, Andie Jackson. Her imagination and creativity greatly enhanced the beauty, expression and readability of my book. I am so blessed to have her be a special part of this work.

Preface: My Prayer for this Book

The following is a compilation of writings which I felt compelled to start after I lost Dana, my precious ballerina wife of 26 years and then experienced the miraculous "Butterfly Dancer Dream" one mysterious night in early February 2007. The need to write continued through the journey of losing my amazing love, Dana, and then through my life after that tremendous loss. Today I see clearly what a wonderful and incredibly beautiful life I have been given; so many experiences with so many people of such diverse goodness. In gratitude for all lives who have touched mine, I want to share with you glimpses of them and their goodness, magic and miracles. I hope the songs, poems and my life's journey, which I felt divinely led to capture, contains for you the reader the beautiful nature and goodness I have experienced. It is my hope that some of these writings, as I traveled through loves and losses and love again, may bring comfort or new and different insights to those who read them. My prayer today is that God helps me in my autumn years to paint their portraits, write their songs and do justice to the gift of their lives touching and enriching mine. Thank you, Lord, for this glorious life and guiding my journey to "Life's Dance Ranch," my heaven on earth. Amen.

Montana Mike

Summer & Winter View of "Life's Dance Ranch" from Clausen Rd.

Table of Contents

DEDICATION	Love and Gratitude	i
PREFACE	My Prayer For This Book	ii
PART I	The Beginning of My Life & Loves	1
CHAPTER 1	First Life, First Love	3
CHAPTER 2	Schooling Begins	17
CHAPTER 3	Creation of My Something-Nothing-In-Between Theory	25
CHAPTER 4	Girls, Girls, Girls	33
CHAPTER 5	Decision Time	45
CHAPTER 6	Moving On and Miracles	51
CHAPTER 7	My Dancer Came to Me	61
CHAPTER 8	Ovarian Cancer Changed Our Lives	89
CHAPTER 9	Miraculous Dream of My Dana	117
CHAPTER 10	Dana's Butterfly Awakens	127
PART II	Life After Loss Comes Love Again?	139
CHAPTER 11	There are No Coincidences Only Miracles For Me	141
CHAPTER 12	The Courtship Begins	163
CHAPTER 13	Bumps in the Road	183
CHAPTER 14	And Away We Go, Go, Go	197
CHAPTER 15	My First Love and New Love Meet	211
PART III	Life's Dance Ranch	223
CHAPTER 16	Coming Home	225
CHAPTER 17	Life on the Ranch	249
CHAPTER 18	Animal Family	271
CHAPTER 19	My Family Blessings	289
CHAPTER 20	Ever Growing on Life's Dance Ranch	295
PART IV	Selected Poems	303
CHAPTER 21	On Nature	305
CHAPTER 22	On Sorrow	323
CHAPTER 23	On Darkness	349
CHAPTER 24	On My Life's Truths	369
CHAPTER 25	On Inspiration	421
CHAPTER 26	On Nothing	429
CHAPTER 27	On Life's Dance	457
EPILOGUE		464
MORE THOUGHTS		465
LAST POEM		467

Part 1:
The Beginning of My Life & Loves

FIRST LOVE

HE WAS BORN IN MONTANA
IN THE LAND OF OPEN SKY
IT WAS THERE HE GREW TO BE A MAN
IT IS THERE HE'LL GO TO DIE

BUT LIFE TOOK HIS HAND
ONE SKY BLUE DAY
SAID COME WITH ME
WE MUST GO AWAY

HE LEFT HIS TRUE LOVE
HE FELT HER CRY
THE RAIN CAME DOWN
AS HE SAID GOODBYE

HE KNEW HE'D ALWAYS LOVE HER
SHE'D STAY HIS TRUE BEST FRIEND
SOOTHED HIS SOUL, AND BACK WITH HER...
WAS WHERE HIS LIFE MUST END

Chapter One
First Life, First Love

I can't write about love without sharing with you my first love. Her name is Montana and it is from her I was born. It's she who called me back time and time again. At times, it was for joyous celebrations with family. At times, I desperately needed her to cradle me in her glorious landscape and sooth my deepest grief. It was to her that I turned to untangle the despair in my heart, releasing my greatest losses to her cleansing winds. Often, I've been far away and lonely for her voice, only to experience joy by allowing memories of her to fill my mind and heart. She sent me into life and I left her many times, but she always welcomed me back safe in her embrace. I would never have believed, having traveled the world with my career, that she would once again bring me home through the most unusual of circumstances. Now I know it is here in her mountain majesty that I will die, a blessed man. My love, my darling, my Montana – how grateful I am for the solid foundation she provided me in this life. You see, I came forth from her heart in Lewistown, Montana, and grew to be a man just south of there in Harlowton. I was born into a life of *"Magic & Miracles."* Open your eyes and your heart and return with me to the beginning.

A CHILD IS BORN

It was October 22, 1949, and winter had already arrived in central Montana. The "white-out blizzard" was worrying Dorene who was nine months pregnant, having frequent contractions, with the nearest hospital 55 miles to the north over a treacherous road.

Journey to Life's Dance Ranch

Doc got Dorene in the car and headed for the hospital in Lewistown. When he reached Eddie's Corner, a place he knew well, with only 15 more miles to go, he accidentally turned the wrong way toward Great Falls. Off the road he went and into a snowbank. They were stuck in the blizzard and it looked for sure like Dorene's second baby would be born in that car. Doc frantically rocked the car, putting it first in drive then reverse, over and over again. Suddenly, almost miraculously, the car popped out of the snowbank and back onto the road. Twenty minutes later they reached the hospital just in time for Dorene to give birth to a baby boy. When Doc laid eyes on his new son, Michael, his first words to Dorene were "He's kind of long and skinny, isn't he?"

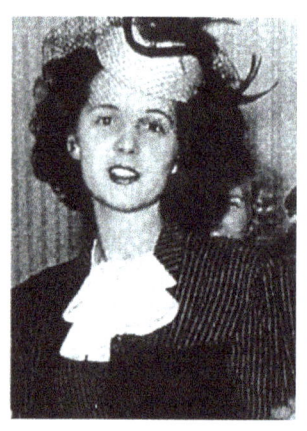

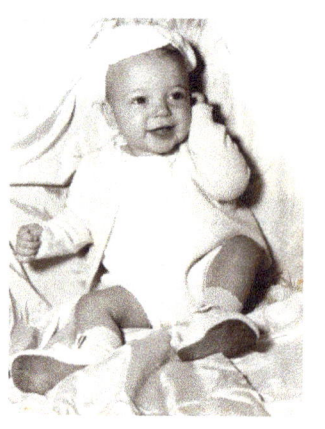

DORENE   **DOC**   **BABY MIKE**

And so began this life of magic and miracles. I believe that somehow with God's grace, I chose my family: Dorene, my gentle kind-hearted mother, Doc, the local small-town dentist, and my beautiful older sister, Mary Lou. Then, over the next few years, Mom gave birth to two more wonderful sisters, Marcy and Margaret.

We grew up in Harlowton, a little prairie town on the east slope of Montana's Crazy Woman Mountains. There are many legends about how my beautiful Crazy Woman Mountains came to be named, and no one knows for sure, but they are firmly in my boyhood memories of

Chapter One

growing up in Big Sky Country. Oh, Montana ... the most powerful love of my life.

CRAZY WOMAN MOUNTAINS

Early in life I was lucky to learn an important lesson ... that some things are time-based and don't last forever. We had glass baby bottles back then and I enjoyed milk from the bottle for almost a year. Then I discovered a wonderful game. I would grab the nipple and throw the empty bottle onto the metal heater grate on the floor beside my crib and, much to my delight, it would crash into a million pieces. Mom had thirteen bottles. As I broke another bottle, Mom would say, "Okay, Mikie, when the last bottle is broken, there will be no more." She was true to her words. So, I learned early that things come, things go and often leave one with a feeling of gratitude or loss or both.

The heating grate that I broke so many baby bottles on would remain a wonderful place of mine but for a different reason. When I was old enough to turn the heat on in the morning, probably about age five or six, I loved to get up real early while it was still dark. I would go into the living room and turn the heat from our nighttime temperature

of sixty to about eighty. Then I would grab a blanket and curl up over the grate. At first the air coming through the grate was cold, but it quickly warmed up and made a warm place to curl up. Unfortunately, my two younger sisters soon figured out how pleasant it was on the early morning heating grate. I was forced to get up earlier and earlier to beat them to my favorite grate. We had other grates, but the one in Mom and Dad's bedroom, was the most comfortable. I would probably still enjoy curling up with a blanket in the early morning darkness if we still had forced air heat. Ah, the wonder of youth.

Growing up in Harlowton had all the wonderful freedoms a kid could want ... including the freedom to get hurt. Kids had more casts, more stitches, more scabs on knees and elbows, more polio, more measles and chickenpox than kids today. We grew up with freedoms that children today can't imagine. We had no electronic devices, no television yet, so our imaginations were free to run wild and entertain us in the most magical ways. The spirit of life and love was crafted for me from this beginning. We played outside, never suspecting that the things we saw in the Dick Tracy comic strip would one day be our reality. Satellite cell phones and computers didn't exist. Life was so much simpler then.

One of the first things I loved about Montana was the wind. Lewis and Clark said the three curses of Montana were the wind, the cold and the mosquitoes! They were right about the mosquitoes, at least in Harlowton during July and August. The whistling wind helped keep mosquitoes and deer flies down and the first hard frost would rid of us of them until the next summer. Yes, we had cold and we had wind. In fact, Harlowton and the surrounding areas of Judith Gap, Big Timber, and Livingston are some of the windiest places in our nation.

Chapter One

THANKS TO MARK J. FEIST OF **LAME COW CARTOONS** FOR PERMISSION TO USE. MORE GREAT STUFF AT P.O. BOX 5924, HARLOWTOWN, MT 406-930-0509

    As a kid, the wind could literally blow me over. However, we learned to use the wind to our advantage. By opening our coats wide, we created a sail that allowed us to run so fast, it was as if we were flying! Exhilarating and oh so exciting! We also looked forward to the spring when the wind slowed down and we could fly kites. When the gentle, steady breeze showed up, Dad would help us build a kite out of paper and lath and a long tail from strips of old rags. We would head up the hill to the golf course. The kite string was made of cotton and wasn't as strong as kite string is today. Dad would help get the kite up to what seemed a mile in the sky. We would keep adding keys, ribbons, and other things on the string, and watch the wind push them up further into the sky. Inevitably, the string would break and then we would run for what seemed like miles to try and find what was left of our beloved kite.

    Mom was gentle, quiet, loving and strong ... our protector and teacher. She was a smart, common sense woman, a classy lady in every

sense of the word. She was exceptionally kind and generous, graceful and beautiful. Mom had undying love for her children and was always there for us. She was a spiritual woman who lived a true Christian life, always faithful to her Catholic religion. One affliction Mom suffered, almost to the end of her life, was migraine headaches. She would have at least a couple of migraines a month, depending on the stresses she came under. She usually made it through a big event, but immediately afterward, would suffer with three or four days of pain and vomiting. When Mom had a migraine, we kids were expected to be quiet and often were sent to our babysitters, Mrs. Ostrom or Peggy Fuchs. When Mom suffered, we suffered with her. It was difficult not telling her of our school happenings or seeking her help with our homework, but we supported her as she supported us.

Mom's gentle nature was often mistaken for timidity or fearfulness. Nothing could have been further from the truth. She was both physically and emotionally strong, and fiercely protective of her family. Mom was also a wonderful housekeeper. Our house was always neat, spotlessly clean and beautiful. She was also strong in her commitment to any civic job she undertook. I remember her being a chaperone at a school dance, after one of our high school football games. Two of the football players, both over 6'3" tall, started throwing punches at one another. Mom didn't hesitate an instant. She immediately stepped right in-between them, pushed them apart and said, "You boys can't fight in here. If you want to fight, you'll have to go outside!" They were so surprised that they ended the fight right then and there.

Mom was never petty, always considerate of others and their feelings, a genuinely good woman. Suffice it to say that I never heard my mother utter a swear word or an unkind word about anyone.

My father and mother were true patriots who flew the American flag every day. And every day we gave thanks to God for this wonderful country we live in. They were proud Americans who found magic and wonder in all people regardless of race, creed, color or political leanings. They were people of great character and deep love.

Chapter One

OUR MOTHER

She gave us life
She gave us love
She gave us joy and laughter
She gave us strength and honesty
And we hope that we'll take after
This woman of great goodness
A woman like no other
The one who's always there for us
To care for us, our Mother.

"Mom, Dorene"

Dad "Doc," the town dentist, was a ball of energy, extremely outgoing, with an insatiable need to learn. He had a brilliant mind, was a dreamer and much more outwardly loving to Mom than she was to him. I always wished that they could have had the kind of relationship Mom's parents or Dana and I had... loving, supportive, and mutually, outwardly affectionate.

WINTER WONDERLAND

Dad loved winter and Christmas and his best gifts were any new magic he could find in friends, nature, and his God. I believe the most poignant event I ever shared with my father happened with one of our town drunks, Dean Mays. On weekends Dean was always drunk and sometimes we would find him passed out in the street. Dad and I would take him where he could sober up and get back to the sheep he tended during the week.

The memorable event happened the year Dad was head of the American Legion. Every Christmas they had an end of the year Christmas party with a guest of honor, and when Dad informed the organization that this year's guest of honor would be Dean Mays, most of the members were horrified and thought Dad was nuts for inviting the town drunk to speak.

The day of the party arrived, and members started showing up and getting settled in their seats. I was sitting with Mom and Dad directly across from Dean. He wore a handsome western suit, milk chocolate brown with light brown pinstripes. He was clean shaven, sober and was wearing a beautiful pair of western boots and hat to match his suit. Nobody had ever seen Dean this way before. People smoked back then and many including Dean lit up. Then Dad asked Dean if he would please give the blessing. I'll never forget watching Dean stand up. The room went deadly silent. Dean took a drag from his cigarette, looked up in the air and slowly began...

Chapter One

> "I ain't much good at prayin' and You may not know me, Lord.
> I ain't much seen in churches where they preach Thy Holy Word,
> But You may have observed me out here on the lonely plains,
> A lookin' after cattle, feelin' thankful when it rains,
> Admirin' Thy great handiwork, the miracle of grass,
> Aware of Thy kind spirit in the way it comes to pass
> That hired men on horseback and the livestock that we tend
> Can look up at the stars at night and know we've got a Friend
>
> So, here's ol' Christmas comin' on, remindin' us again
> Of Him whose coming brought good will into the hearts of men.
> A cowboy ain't no preacher, Lord, but if You'll hear my prayer,
> I'll ask as good as we have got for all men everywhere.
> Don't let no hearts be bitter, Lord; don't let no child be cold.
> Make easy beds for them that's sick, and them that's weak and old.
> Let kindness bless the trail we ride, no matter what we're after,
> And sort of keep us on Your side, in tears as well as laughter.
>
> I've seen old cows a starvin', and it ain't no happy sight:
> Please don't leave no one hungry, Lord,
> on Thy good Christmas night
> No man, no child, no woman, and no critter on four feet
> I'll aim to do my best to help You find 'em chuck to eat.
>
> I'm just a sinful cowpoke. Lord – ain't got no business prayin'
> But still I hope You'll ketch a word or two of what I'm sayin'
> We speak of Merry Christmas, Lord – I reckon You'll agree
> There ain't no Merry Christmas for nobody that ain't free.
> So one thing more I'll ask You, Lord; just help us what You can
> To save some seeds of freedom for the future sons of man!"

No one in town ever looked at Dean the same way after that. My father had shown them the magic of Dean which everyone else had missed for so many years. Only my father had found the magic in this man, who while out on the prairie tending cattle and sheep had memorized hundreds of beautiful poems. This was probably one of the best gifts my father ever gave me about loving, knowing, and caring about your fellow man. I still read this prayer and tell the story every Christmas dinner and it still brings tears to my eyes.

*In December 2013 the S. Omar Barker estate let us know that this poem is now considered in the public domain

Journey to Life's Dance Ranch

Life can send you magic and miracles, or perhaps they are there all the time if you take the time to see them. My parents taught me how to find them and perhaps even manifest them. Magic and miracles are so integral to my memories of growing up – especially the Christmas memories with Dad. Every year, it was Dad who organized a Christmas tree and greens excursion, to get the boughs needed to decorate the Nativity Scenes at churches around Harlowton. This was always a special event with many families participating. Dad would arrange to have a big truck, thanks to Wojtowick Motors, and families would head toward the Snowy Mountains. When we reached our destination, the fathers and kids would head out into the forest in search of the perfect tree. All tree hunters had a saw, axe or hatchet. Dads would help kids with cutting trees and greens and dragging them back to camp, where the mothers were waiting around the campfire with hot chocolate, coffee, marshmallows, and graham cracker s'mores. It was a wonderful Christmas tradition that my father created and perpetuated for years.

MAIXNER FAMILY CHRISTMAS

When it was time to decorate our church, Dad, the Maixner kids and my friend Walt Scotson would go upstairs to the choir loft where the Nativity scene was stored, bring it down to the front of the church for the day-long set up of this beautiful Christmas scene.

Another wonderful winter tradition that Dad always loved was waiting for the first big snow and then getting our two big wooden toboggans and several sleds out of the garage and heading with

Chapter One

neighborhood kids to our sledding hill. Dad would lay down on the biggest toboggan with a couple kids on his back and down the hill we would race. Dad, the biggest kid of all, had more fun than anyone. The town kids just loved Dad.

Another of Dad's winter traditions was "Moonlight ice skating." He would wait for a full moon clear night, then load as many kids as he could into our 1949 Studebaker and head for the airport pond, with wood, marshmallows and hot dogs in the trunk. We would start a campfire and then put on our skates. Out on the ice, the magical moonlight guided us around the pond. Dad, an exceptional skater, raced around the pond at high speed, forward and backwards. I was not a good skater especially in the oversized hockey skates I was expected to grow into. I could only skate for a short while before my weak ankles would almost be sideways on the ice.

I remember going down on the ice and seeing Dad flying in my direction skating backwards. I couldn't get up and out of his way, so I curled up in a fetal position and hung on. Dad hit me hard and went flying, landing on his head and practically knocking himself out. Though I loved the moonlight, fire, and the hotdogs, those oversized hockey skates kept me from enjoying the skating. I never grew into those skates and my ankles were never strong enough to allow me to enjoy this activity.

As I am sure you have figured out by now, Dad enjoyed traditions of any kind, especially Christmas traditions. One of his most fun traditions for his family and friends was making what he called "Bing Cherry Bounce." Near Kalispell, Montana, some of the best black cherries in the country come into season every August. During that time, Dad would always buy a big box of these cherries. He would get several glass gallon jugs and fill them one third full of the cherries. Then, he would fill them the rest of the way with whisky, usually, "Old Grandad." He would add one cup of sugar for every fifth of whisky and cap all the jugs.

On Thanksgiving Day, he would open a jug and each of us would be given a small glass prior to dinner. The jug was then re-capped and not re-opened again until just before Christmas. When Christmas neared, Dad would open a jug and take it down to the street corner with a sleeve of paper cups under his arm. There he would stand and as cars went by, he would offer each of them some Christmas cheer, a cup of his "Bing Bounce." I can still see him with the jug over his shoulder, pouring drinks for all his passing friends and wishing everyone a Merry Christmas.

Dad loved showing me the wonders of nature found in my beloved Montana. Many a time he would awaken me in the middle of the night, we would get in the car and head up the golf course hill. There we would watch the dancing northern lights, a lightning filled thunderstorm, a raging white-out blizzard, or a beautiful moon dog. Of course, during the day if Dad saw something beautiful like a sundog, he would never miss the chance to point them out and share them with me.

Music was one of my father's joys and I loved listening to him and his barbershop quartet buddies, Don Swanz, Bill Dysart, and Cal Ness. They sang in four-part harmony with a most wonderful honky-tonk piano player, Mary Lodie, accompanying them. Dad not only started the quartet, but also put together a Dixieland band which performed for Harlowton's people every year at their minstrel show. He also used his beautiful tenor voice to sing Christmas solos at all the churches in town.

Our family always attended midnight mass at the Catholic Church. Dad and the choir sang Christmas carols from 11:30 until just before midnight. I was an altar boy from third grade on, so was always back with the priest and other altar boys waiting for the mass to start. At midnight the church became deathly quiet as the organist played the prelude to "Oh Holy Night." When Dad started to sing the solo, I always got shivers going up and down my spine. It remains a special Christmas memory for my sisters and me.

Chapter One

Hunting season brought more lessons. I remember Dad coming to my bed before sunrise and saying "Mike, do you think there are any ducks out on those ponds?" I would jump out of bed and we would head for our first pond. It was always on the hill above the pond where we would share innumerable beautiful sunrises. I was just a little guy with a single shot .22 caliber rifle with little birdshot bullets. The chances of actually shooting a bird were extremely small but for Dad and me, our hunting was more a "learning about nature trip" than hunting. Dad would talk to me about the various grasses, shrubs, trees, clouds, and wild animals. I eventually graduated to a shot gun and Dad and I walked the fields, sneaking up on duck ponds or flushing out pheasants. Usually, we would get distracted talking and the birds would fly up, startle us and be long gone before we could take a shot. We were pitiful hunters. In all the years we hunted, Dad brought down a duck and I a pheasant. We cleaned them, stuffed them with wild rice, cooked them and they were delicious!

Childhood friends can be some of life's greatest blessings. Such was the case with me. I had three who impacted my life in very special ways. Billy Jones, was my mom's best friend, Scotty's, son. Billy was a wild and free ranch boy. I spent much joyful time with Billy on the Jones Ranch and at our home in Harlowton. Johnny Johnson was my bodyguard. John was a big strong good kid and great friend who protected me from bullies and was a great playmate. And Walt Scotson, who lived just two houses away from ours and became the brother I never had and part of the Maixner family. They are all great friends to this day.

Chapter Two
Schooling Begins

At one point, Dad decided he wanted to try a dental practice in Pasco, Washington. I went through summer kindergarten and then first grade at a parochial school. Soon Mom and Dad became lonesome for Montana and their mountain friends, and after a little more than than a year, we moved back to Harlowton. The Montana school system would not let me start 2nd grade because my birthday was too late so I was put back in first grade. Now school was a challenge for me because I was bored. Now I had to decide what was most important…paying attention to the teacher or lying my head down and taking a nap on my desk. The need for a nap usually won out. Many a time the teachers would call Mom and tell her to come get her little boy, he had fallen asleep on his desk again. Mom would come over to the school and take me home to rest. There were many times I would even prefer taking a nap to going out for recess. I did eventually outgrow this or should I say by necessity had to stay awake. It wasn't until the third grade that I began to learn new materials and I felt I would rather stay awake and start learning again. I must admit I still enjoy a good long nap to this day.

As a child I also enjoyed daydreaming. I had a vivid imagination and could entertain myself for hours. I loved playing outside. Cowboys and Indians was one of my favorite imaginings and I always wanted to be the Indian. We had a tree in our yard that grew sideways and I would pretend it was my horse and ride it holding on to a string (my reins) I had tied around the tree.

Journey to Life's Dance Ranch

Dad and Mom were out of town to a wedding and Mrs. Ostrom was baby-sitting us kids. In my imagination I had escaped the cowboys but my hands were tied behind my back so I had to ride with the reins/string in my teeth. Oh yes, I had tied a knot in the string to keep the end from fraying. One of my sisters came out of the house and yelled for me to come in for supper. Just then I imagined getting shot and rolled off the tree. Unfortunately, I forgot to let go of the reins in my teeth. When I hit the ground, my permanent front tooth was hanging by a thread and I was bleeding profusely. Mrs. Ostrom took me down to Dr. Ashberry, one of the town physicians who finished pulling the tooth, gave me some gauze to bite on and put the tooth in an envelope. When Mom and Dad got back the next day and Dad saw what had happened, his words were, "Oh Mike, couldn't you have just broken an arm or leg?"

MIKE ON A REAL HORSE "NO STRINGS ATTACHED"

I was lucky to have a dentist as my dad. He would make me many front tooth appliances before I was old enough to have a permanent bridge made. He even did a tooth transplant from my sister Mary Lou to me, a procedure that was unheard of in those days. Mary Lou needed some teeth removed for orthodontic purposes. Our blood types were the same and Dad thought our tissue types might be close enough. The transplant was successful. Dad put a crown over it and I wore it for several years until diving into the side of the Harlo swimming pool. You guessed it, it hit right on that tooth and knocked it out. That tooth has continued to be the target of unwanted force over the years. Through traumatic episodes, I have been forced to have the beautiful

bridge Dad made for me remade several times!

One of my great struggles throughout life was my vision, or should I say, poor vision. Mom had great vision but Dad's visual acuity was far beyond any one I have ever known. His close vision was very good, but his distant vision was so far beyond anyone else it wasn't even close. Unfortunately, my sisters and I did not inherit Mom and Dad's exquisite vision. In fact, in today's standards, as a child, I would have been close to legally blind. I did pretty well until I was mid-way through the first grade because I listened and could visualize and solve problems in my head. I attended parochial school for one year, my first-grade year. By mid-year we were starting long addition, long subtraction, multiplication and division. I was seated midway back in the classroom, couldn't read the chalkboard and wasn't able to visualize and solve these math problems in my head. My grades started dropping fast! My teacher was not sure what was going on and talked to Mom and Dad about the problem. Eventually it was decided to have my eyes checked. Sure enough, I couldn't see! Thus, began my life with glasses. I discovered a whole new world.

For me glasses were a great help in seeing the world but also a great nuisance at times. I hated smudged or dirty glasses so was constantly cleaning my glasses. As an active kid, while playing, I would get bumped in my glasses, they would bend or break and I was always going to the Optometrist to get them fixed or replaced. Contact lenses did not really come to the market until I was in 8th grade or a freshman in high school. These were hard contact lenses. There was no such thing as the soft comfortable contact lenses of today. My sister, Mary Lou, was the first in our family to get contacts which she tolerated quite well. My sophomore year in high school, Mom and Dad let me get contacts. My vision improved a bit, especially my peripheral vision which was great while playing basketball, but the new lenses were never comfortable and wearing them for more than eight to ten hours became extremely painful. My eyes always felt like I had sand in them when I was wearing my contacts. I couldn't wait to get them out as soon as I didn't need them at school or a basketball game.

When I graduated from high school, I decided I'd had enough. I was going back to glasses and so once again my life became reaching for my glasses first thing in the morning, having someone help me find them when I misplaced them, cleaning them, defogging and repairing. Such was to be the case for me until 2001 when I had Laser Surgery correction. Fortunately, the surgery has been a tremendous success and my vision has been 20-20 since then. It took months before my first move in the morning was not reaching for glasses...old memories die hard. Perfect vision has been such a joy. I feel truly blessed to be living in a time where technological advancements continue to improve our lives in so many ways.

MY ALL TIME FAVORITE JOB!

It was the summer of 1970. At age 21, I had secured a job working for my hometown, Harlowton. This was a job not many wanted, and most people seemed to have a disdain for. The job started very early in the morning, but you were done by early afternoon. This allowed me to slip off to the golf course in the afternoon which was a definite plus. I worked with a wonderful old man named Sig Amundson, Harlowton's longtime garbage man.

I think we both made life better for each other. Back then everyone in town had 50-gallon barrels, supplied and maintained by Sig. We used the barrels to put trash in and everyone burned the trash in their barrels. You always knew when your barrel started to rust, it wouldn't be long until Sig replaced it with a new barrel he had retrieved from the city dump. In those days we did not have a landfill. All garbage, trash and unwanted junk was taken to a spot just east of town. Huge mounds of stinking garbage, old junked cars, refrigerators, washers, (not many dryers, as most people dried their clothes on clotheslines), old magazines, rusted barbed wire, just about anything you could imagine.

As kids we would often walk to the dump with our BB guns. It was a magical place to shoot bottles, cans and a myriad of wondrous things, including some girlie magazines! I had my first look at a photo

Chapter Two

of a naked woman at the Harlowton dump. So, in the summer of 1970 it was my privilege to work with the man who had built this place. It would become my favorite job ever. Sig wanted to help me dump barrels into the back of the garbage truck, but I was young and strong and told Sig if he just drove the truck, I'd be glad to handle the barrels.

After several days on the job, I told my Grandma Mary that she would be surprised at what people threw away and how awfully stinky and dirty the garbage of some Harlowton residents was, and the following day (and every day thereafter), when we stopped to pick up Grandpa's and Grandma's garbage, I found it in brown paper bags neatly tied up with ribbons and bows.

One of the wonders of being a garbage man with Sig was seeing how excited he got finding copper pipe, copper wire or brass of any sort, especially spent rifle shell casings. One day I came across a barrel too heavy for me to lift alone and I asked Sid for his help. There was a tiny bit of trash on top of an almost full fifty-gallon barrel of brass bullet casings. "Max, we've hit the jackpot!" shouted Sig with glee, "and I'll share it with you!" I declined his offer, saying he should take them. I was happy for him.

Perhaps the most magical part of my whole experience of working with Sig was when he asked me to his house to meet his wife. As I entered, I noticed there were LP and 45RPM records neatly stored on shelves throughout the house. As it turned out, Sig had the largest record collection in the state of Montana. Another delightful surprise was meeting his lovely wife. He informed me that she had been a concert violinist in their early life. Magic and miracles were to be found in a small-town garbage man and his beautiful wife.

ANIMAL LOVE

The first pet we had was a stray cat. It was a gray brown striped cat the we initially named Tiger Kitty. We were moving back to Harlowton after a little over a year in Pasco, Washington. We had only

had the stray with us for two or three weeks before it was time to move. Mom told Dad she didn't want a stray cat moving with us if it was a female that might have kittens. Dad assured her the cat was a male and we all moved back to Harlowton. Not too long after our move, Mom went to get her laundry basket and there was Tiger Kitty with her baby kittens. Tiger Kitty and her babies were taken down to the basement and placed in a box with soft rags. We quickly renamed Tiger Kitty – "Mother Kitty".

Mom wasn't thrilled to begin with but all us kids were. The whole family eventually fell in love with all the kittens. When the time came to give them away, Mom and Dad let us choose one to keep. We chose one that looked much like Mother Kitty and we named it Tiger Kitty. Little did we know that months later Mother Kitty would deliver another batch of kittens. And much to our surprise, Tiger Kitty would deliver her first litter of kittens at the same time. Tiger Kitty wasn't really sure what to do with her kittens. She and Mother Kitty were down in the basement in different boxes. Mother Kitty proved to be not only a wonderful mother but a wonderful grandmother. After nursing her babies, she would go over to Tiger Kitty's box, get in and put her paw over Tiger Kitty and help her learn to be a good mama.

I don't think it was too long after that when Mom and Dad took both cats to Doc Holloway to have them fixed. Mom came to love our two cats very much and even forgave Dad for telling her Mother Kitty was a boy. Mom was to suffer one of her saddest moments when she accidently backed over Mother Kitty sleeping in the shade behind the car. It wasn't until many years later that we actually learned what happened to our dear Mother Kitty.

I loved the cats but my desire for my own dog began early. A little black cocker spaniel named Cindy was my next pet. I worked an entire summer - mowing lawns at 25 - 50 cents per lawn - to save up the $25 to purchase Cindy. Dad was adamant that Cindy would be an outside dog, so we built her a doghouse with a canvas flap door and a lightbulb inside to keep her warm in the cold Montana winters.

Chapter Two

I remember going outside to feed and walk her, and clean up the dog poop she left in the yard. I always prayed that one day she would be able to come in the house with us. We didn't have her spayed right away, and since she was an outdoor dog, as soon as she came in heat, all the male neighborhood dogs were there to get her pregnant. In early spring she delivered four puppies, three black (like their mother) girls, and one blond boy. We kids were sure she had done that so she could be like our family – three girls, one boy.

A wonderful priest, Fr. John Morressetti, lived in the rectory next to the church across from our house. He fell in love with Cindy. While we were away to school during the day, Cindy would go over and be his rectory dog. When we came home from school, Fr. John would send Cindy home. She always arrived with a hot dog sticking out both sides of her mouth, waiting to eat it until she was with us.

Dad finally acquiesced, and Cindy became an indoor dog. He came to love her very much. Dad and I always figured Cindy would become a great hunting dog. We were so wrong. The first time we took her hunting, a pheasant flew up. Dad and I took shots at it and missed as usual. When we looked around for Cindy, she was nowhere to be found. We found her quivering under the car. It was her one and only hunting trip. We also discovered that the 4th of July was her worst nightmare. Kids used to start popping off firecrackers on the 3rd and continued through the 5th and beyond. Cindy spent those days under the bed shaking.

I still remember her standing at the top of the stairs when I came home. She would be wiggling her back end and I would say, "Cindy give me a smile." She would pull her lips back and smile. When I went away to college, Cindy became Dad's and Fr. Morressetti's dog.

Every night Dad took her for a walk around town, always stopping at one of the town gas stations where he'd get a box of black licorice nibs for himself and a Baby Ruth candy bar for Cindy. During my junior year in college, Cindy was discovered to have cancer.

 *Journey to Life's Dance Ranch*

The vet recommended we put her down to end her suffering. I can still remember the time I spent at the Vet's in a small room, holding her, telling her how much I loved her, and how much I'd miss her. I let her know how grateful I was to have had her as my dog and, yes, I remember too well the look in her eyes when the vet came to take her. That day, I couldn't ask her to smile for me one last time. I could only cry. I still miss her.

Chapter Three
Creation of My Something-Nothing-In-Between Theory

My parents were devout Catholics who endeavored to have their children be the same. As a young child, I often questioned things I was told to believe that just didn't seem to make any sense to me. Even before my first communion, I was questioning this thing called God and the story of Jesus. I was told that we were made in the image and likeness of an all-good God, to know him, to love him and to serve him in this world. But, from what I could understand, this all good, all knowing God that created us would love us only as long as we followed certain rules and didn't screw up. One big mortal sin, and if we were unfortunate enough to die before we found a priest and made a good confession, this all good, all loving God who created us, would condemn us to hell for all eternity. For a kid, that's forever and forever which never goes away. The priest we confessed our sins to, we were told, was actually Jesus Christ in the priest's body. My first inkling that this might not be true was after making a confession. When I was done, the priest told me to say three Our Father's, three Hail Mary's and try to be a good little girl. Jesus Christ across from me in the confessional wouldn't have made that mistake! I knew Jesus knew I was a boy!

Other things started to bother me. How could an all good, all knowing God (omniscient) knowing everything, past, present and future, create creatures he would condemn to hell. This was explained to me by the concept of free will. We are given free will and if we screw up, it is for the "all just God" to punish us. But my question was always, if God knows all, past, present and future, how can we be given free will? Either we can do nothing that he does not already know or he really isn't

omniscient. My question always ended in the same final argument and the same answer from my parents and the church was "it's a supernatural mystery" and you must have faith. However, that wasn't good enough for me. I had to know my God, and not a God who was just a bigger version of man. A God who could be all loving, but as I also saw, all hating for those who used their free will to go against him. No, this couldn't be God! God had to be something more if God was to be the loving source of creation. What about all this God the father, God the son, and God the Holy Ghost? There had to be some way to make sense of this.

    I knew my parents accepted and believed the Catholic doctrine. And, I knew they were wonderful Christian people in the best sense of the word. They were kind, generous, looked out for the poor and the sick...for their friends and family. They loved our "Big Sky Country" and rejoiced and gave thanks for the blessings of living in our small Montana town. I had an incredible relationship with both my parents, but if I wanted to make my father angry or my mother sad, all I had to do was start questioning my religion. Where was my faith? So, for the most part, I kept quiet, but my mind didn't. I thought, if this religion didn't make sense to me, was there one that did? Or was there another way to look at this religion that helped it make sense to me? There were so many good, honest, kind people who had faith and believed. Perhaps I was wrong. Could they all be wrong? Could they be right, and I just wasn't smart enough or faithful enough to accept all that Christianity and perhaps even more, what the Catholic Church professed? I had to find a way to reconcile my views with those of my parents, sisters and friends. I had to find something acceptable that was not in conflict with their religion or any other, for that matter.

    I don't know when it came to me, but it was sometime before I got into high school. My thoughts were that perhaps they were thinking backwards, or I needed to think backwards to find my truth without losing theirs. That's when my "Nothing Theory" came into view. Somethings ... all creation ... had to come from where? The creation of somethings came from nothing, through the in-between to be something

Chapter Three

and then back again in an ever-pulsing energy which I called no-thing. Obviously, I was not using the traditional dictionary meaning for nothing which means absence of anything. But rather I viewed No-thingness as a sacred state of eternal creation, it was all inclusive of everything, past, present and future.

I was a simple boy who came to this concept with very little external influence but rather it came from my internal spiritual connectedness to nature, love and life. As an older man I find comfort in knowing many philosophers, scientists, religious experts and spiritualists over the centuries have all expressed beliefs also contained in my "Nothing Theory." My theory seems to be a blending of several, including occidental, Western – (being or thingness) and Oriental (no-thingness).

Whereas Japanese philosophy asks and focuses on, "What is Nothingness?" as fundamental to their existence. Western philosophy asks and focuses on, "What is Beingness?" as their central question for life's meaning. To me they are simply different aspects of an eternal pulsing energy constantly moving from *No-thingness* to *Something* and back again through the *In-between*. A never ending, flowing energy that pulses between the yin and yang of our existence. All part of the eternal One. This I kept in my heart for many years.

As a young boy, it helped me finally make sense of Christianity and the Catholic Church. I could then see God that *"Great No-thing"* as The never-ending flow of pulsing, energy, the potential of all existence and creation, past, present and future. The *"Something"* is Jesus and all humans as children of God and all variety of creatures and creations. The Holy Ghost, is the *"In-between"* as existence spins from *"Nothing"* into *"Something"* and back again. Existence changes and cleanses through the *"In-between"* phase as it prepares for its new role at either end of the spectrum.

 *Journey to Life's Dance Ranch*

I carved a stone one day which depicts symbolism of my and other's beliefs of their personal eternal understanding of this thing I call God.

"Eternity"   "Yin and Yang"

"Infinity Above Pyramid Below"

"The Cross with eye's pupil looking from below"

"Pyramid with eye looking into cross"

Chapter Three

VOILA! There was no more conflict for me except perhaps some man-made dogma that for a multitude of reasons attaches itself to all formal religions. Even the concept of good and evil seems in many ways defined by humans. Is there such a thing as good or evil? Certainly, but often it's defined through the eye of your point of view, which is relative to your place in existence.

This theory has so greatly influenced my life that it was the theme of the very first poem I felt spirit inspired to write, after falling into deep despair, upon losing my beautiful Dana in 2006. It appeared upon the page effortlessly as if God were reassuring and steadying me for the tasks ahead: life without my ballerina and a journey back to my first love... Montana.

IT'S ONLY GOD, YOU SEE

...AND PART OF YOU AND PART OF ME
AND PART OF EVERY OTHER
...THE "NO-THING" THAT WE SPRING FROM,
IS ONLY GOD, YOU SEE...

WHEN I WAS YOUNG, I REMEMBER,
I REMEMBER I WOULD SAY
"NO-THING" EVER HAPPENS HERE
AND I WAS RIGHT IN MY OWN WAY

FOR IN THE INNOCENCE OF YOUTH
I'D UTTERED SIMPLE WORDS OF TRUTH
"NO-THING" EVER HAPPENS HERE
BUT "NO-THING" ALWAYS DID
"NO-THING'S" WHAT YOU COULD NOT SEE
"NO-THING" ALWAYS HID

BUT "NO-THING" MADE UP EVERYTHING

IN MY SMALL TOWN, YOU SEE
AND IT WAS ALWAYS THERE
TO SOMEHOW, COMFORT ME

AND WE LIVED WITH GODLY "NO-THING"
IN THIS TOWN OF ONLY FEW
YET "NO-THING" GAVE US EVERYTHING
THE MOUNTAINS AND THE VIEW

AND I SEE THAT WHAT I SAW
ON THAT SEE-SAW AS A CHILD
WAS THE VERY BEST OF "NO-THING"
IN A SMALL TOWN IN THE WILD

IN A PLACE THAT TAKES ITS NAME
FROM THE HUGENESS OF THE SKY
IN PLACE WITH OPEN PRAIRIE
THAT IS SOFT UPON THE EYE

IN A PLACE WHERE "NO-THING" HAPPENS
AS A CHILD I COULDN'T CARE
THAT WHEN SWEET "NO-THING" HAPPENS
IT'S A BLESSING TO BE THERE

SO, LIKE MOST OTHER CHILDREN
I WENT AWAY TO SOMEWHERE
OR WAS IT NOWHERE? JUST THE SAME
TO BE WHERE SOMETHING HAPPENS
TO PLAY IN GROWN-UP GAMES

BUT LOOKING BACK TOWARD "NO-THING"
AS TIME, NOW LETS ME DO
I SEE I MUST GO BACK
BEFORE MY LIFE IS THROUGH

TO MAKE AMENDS WITH "NO-THING"
FOR LEAVING "NO-THING" BLUE

Chapter Three

FOR CHASING AFTER SOMETHING
THAT'S ONLY HALF THE VIEW

WHEN I GET BACK TO "NO-THING"
THEN ALL THINGS WILL BE RIGHT
I'LL BE WITH GOD
I WILL BE FREE
MY SOUL WILL HAVE ITS FLIGHT

...AND ALL OF YOU AND ALL OF ME
ARE PART OF EVERY OTHER
DISTINCTION GOES AWAY WITH DEATH
AND "NO-THING" BECOMES CLEAR

IT'S THEN WE SEE ETERNITY
IT'S THEN WE LOSE OUR FEAR...

Chapter Four
Girls, Girls, Girls

As I was growing up, contemplating my beingness and no-thingness, I was also very interested and distracted by the opposite sex. I knew what I wanted in a relationship and exactly how I would love a woman. Unfortunately, I also held the unrealistic belief I could love any woman and live in a happy, loving relationship with her. This did not prove to be the case in all my relationships! At one time or another I fell in love with virtually every girl in our class. But I was much too shy to let on, and, once we got into high school, all the other upper classmen dated them. I always thought, "Why would they want to date me when they could date the older, better looking, more experienced guys. I was always shy when it came to girls and then women. I wanted so badly to be one of the cool guys.

Sometimes when you are a kid, trying to be cool can be painful. My best guess is I was probably in the third or fourth grade when a new kid moved to Harlo and into our neighborhood. He, I don't remember his name, was only there for a year or so before his family moved away. He quickly became someone who was looked at as being very cool. He was a good athlete, good looking, a good student and lots of fun to play with. We all wanted to be like this kid. One of the things we found cool about his looks was his prognathism, i.e. his lower jaw stuck out beyond his upper jaw. Since we all wanted to be and look like this kid, we all started going around with our lower jaws protruding. I am sure many people must have thought we looked silly, but we thought we looked cool like our friend. However, it didn't take us long to realize that looking cool would get painful after a while. Just try holding your jaw in an unnatural protruded position for any length of time. One of life's lessons in just being yourself.

Another example of how susceptible I was to what I considered cool had to do with my fingernails. The boy I admired was several years older than I, handsome, a good athlete with a cool hair style and very neat, with extremely short fingernails. Wanting to be like him, I started cutting my fingernails very short, often to the point they would be too short, bleed and be very sore after trimming them. Ah, the price you pay for being what you think is cool! Years later I realized that he didn't cut his fingernails to keep them short. He chewed his fingernails. To this day, I still trim my fingernails very short. No, I don't do it to be cool. I just like them short and clean. And as a dentist, I wanted them to look good when patients saw the hands that would be in their mouths.

I did not seriously date until well after my 16th birthday, but I did get caught by Lenna Sue Morse for the Sadie Hawkins dance. She was definitely way smarter (valedictorian of our class) and I just knew if I said anything at all it would probably sound stupid to her. I had just gotten my driver's license the day of the event. I begged Dad to let me drive the Buick, it had a radio. Instead, Dad let me drive the Old Red Studebaker Lark. No radio and certainly not the coolest car in town. But that night it might have been the quietest. We didn't talk much, and I was too shy and naive to try anything else.

The first girl I ever asked on a date was a friend of my younger sister, Marcy. It took me weeks to get up the courage to call Gail Wojtowick and ask her on a date. We dated for over six months and I really wanted to kiss her at the end of our dates. My sisters and Mom would ask each time if I had kissed Gail goodnight. My answer was always, "No...gutless wonder." Mom and the girls would tease me, saying, "You're going to be sweet sixteen and never been kissed." Finally, it was the night before my birthday, and I summoned the courage and kissed her goodnight! I am sure Gail laughed when she went into her house. It was undoubtedly the fastest, sorriest example of a kiss, as I barely touched her lips to mine.

Chapter Four

We did kiss much more after that and she was a wonderful sensuous girl. We dated for many months after my first kiss and I really enjoyed being with Gail. She was beautiful, smart and athletic. I was broken hearted when we broke up. It really wasn't my idea, but I wasn't strong enough to stand up to my sisters and mom who were all telling me I needed to get more experience dating different girls before I went off to college. I'll never forget the evening we were in the car and I suggested to Gail that maybe we should try dating others. She immediately slid to the far side of the car. The car felt like ice to me. She was sad and I was devastated. Gail and my sister Marcy came to Carroll College a year after I did. Gail was a cheerleader there and met a wonderful handsome good guy named Dean Leary. He was a linebacker on the football team. They made a handsome couple, were eventually married and had three beautiful daughters.

At one time, my sister Marcy was dating a guy from Roundup. He asked her to their Junior Class Prom. Mom and Dad were not thrilled with the idea of Marcy driving 70 miles down the road to the Prom and then to a special post-Prom Drive-in movie theatre and breakfast, before heading back to Harlo. My parents only agreed when Marcy and I came up with the idea to ask a mutual friend of ours, Kathy Vicars, who was a Roundup cheerleader, to go to their prom as my date. That way we could, ostensibly, safely go on a double date. The dinner and dance were great. Marcy and her date got in the front seat and I was in the back with Kathy. The front seaters appeared to be enjoying themselves respectfully so, but there was absolutely no action taking place in the back seat.

Yep, you guessed it, I was still too afraid I would not measure up to the Roundup guys she had dated! Years later, serendipity brought us together. Kathy was with her husband, a US Navy attorney in Charleston, SC. I was a young Navy Dentist with my wife and kids. My commanding officer lived in the same sub-division as Kathy and they were friends. He told me about her and thought it would be great if we got our families together for a visit. We were able to visit, and I told her she must have thought there was something wrong with me. She said that for years she thought she must have done something wrong. She

was a really nice girl. Darn, another missed opportunity.

Finally, in the latter half of my senior year in high school, providence smiled on me with a beautiful transfer student named Caroline Cheshire. She was new to the school and I summoned up the courage to ask her to dance at a youth center event. We hit it off, started dating and began looking forward to the upcoming summer we could spend together. We walked together at our high school graduation. However, as you may guess, I still had not kissed her or told her I loved her. That same nagging shyness kept holding me back. The morning after graduation the phone rang. It was Caroline and she was crying. Her father, a talented crane operator for the Alaska pipeline had just informed her they were moving to Standford, sixty miles northwest of Harlowton. Their trailer was hooked up and they were leaving in an hour.

I was broken hearted once again. I drove over and spent the last hour talking with her. Did I kiss her goodbye? I wanted to so badly, but …she grabbed me, hugged me and gave me a kiss I'll never forget. And then she was gone. I had not been this broken hearted since Gail. My parents knew how much I cared for Caroline and when I asked if she could come down to Harlowton for a week to visit, they agreed. The plan was to drive to Stanford, pick her up, and then drive twenty some miles to Lewistown where I would take her to a nice dinner and then to a drive-in movie. Yes, this was actually going to be my second experience at a drive-in theatre!

So, I had another chance with Caroline and I did not want to mess up this time. After a wonderful dinner with her at a Lewistown restaurant, we headed for the drive-in. Everything was going great. With one kiss under my belt I felt ready. I tried to present myself as suave and debonair, but it was just an act, about to come to a crashing end! When we got to the drive-in theater, we pulled up a few rows and parked on the elevated dirt ramp so we could have the best view of the screen. I hooked the speaker with its cord on the inside of the car window and then rolled the window up to hold it in place. So far so good, everything

Chapter Four

was going as planned. Now it was time to put my arm around her shoulder and give her a little kiss. Unfortunately, disaster struck!

Just as I was closing in on her waiting lips, I simultaneously let my foot off the brake. The car rolled back off the dirt ramp snapping the cord on the speaker and bending the speaker pole nearly to the ground. Cars behind us started honking. The movie hadn't started yet and I got out of the car to try and straighten the pole and replace the now broken speaker and cord. Horns were still honking as I moved up a few rows and picked another spot and safely put the car in park. It went on to be a steamy wonderful night.

If I hadn't been brought up with the idea you must wait on sex until your wedding night, I would have been honored to lose my virginity to Caroline. She was a great kisser, a beautiful, sensual woman. I wish I had told her I loved her but that was another thing you saved for the woman you were to marry. Time and circumstances and a college curriculum which was all I could handle pulled me away from her. It was I who stopped writing. I'll always be ashamed I didn't have the courage, decency or consideration to tell her I couldn't be in two intense relationships at once …school and love. I still keep her in my prayers and hope she found someone to treat and love her in the way she deserved.

Aside from my love life, high school proved to be a successful experience for me. I was a good enough athlete to be offered a basketball scholarship to a few Montana colleges and I achieved my goal of winning the Harlowton golf championship as a high school junior. School came fairly easily to me, which was unfortunate in a way because I never really learned how to study. When I got to Carroll College and enrolled in the pre-med program, I had a rude awakening. Learning how to study took me almost a semester.

THE 4 M'S : MIKE, MY SISTERS, "THE GIRLS" MARY LOU, MARCY, AND MARGARET

In high school I had sailed by in the wake of my high achieving older sister, Mary Lou. She was a straight A student, valedictorian of her class, a cheerleader and involved in every school club and activity. She went on to Carroll College ahead of me and was once again the #1 student in her class, a cheerleader and voted "Campus Sweetheart." I think teachers at both our high school and Carroll College expected me to be as bright, gifted and dedicated as my sister. However, I was just a B+, A- student, who loved science and math but struggled with reading, English, history, foreign languages and typing.

MARY LOU

SHE IS MY OLDER SISTER
SHE WAS OUR MOTHER TOO
SHE HELPED ME GROW TO BE A MAN
MY SISTER...MARY LOU
SHE WAS A HIGH ACHIEVER
WHO SHOWED US ALL "THE WAY"
SHE GAVE US LOVE AND KINDNESS
AND STILL SHE DOES TODAY
LIKE OUR DAD
A BRILLIANT MIND
A GENTLE SOUL (GIFT FROM MOM)
WE RARELY FIND
TO HER GOD
HER FAITH IS TRUE
SHE IS OF LOVE
OUR MARY LOU
AND WHEN LIFE'S JOURNEY
FOR ME IS THROUGH
I'LL WANT HER THERE
DEAR MARY LOU.

Chapter Four

Actually, all three sisters, including Marcy and Margaret, would outshine me at school. And being smart, like Mary Lou, they were also beautiful. Both were cheerleaders, and Marcy was chosen homecoming queen at Montana State University from which she graduated with a degree in dietetics. Margaret designated the "Spirit of Harlowton High School" started at Carroll College and then transferred to University of Washington graduating with a dental hygiene degree. She went on to teach at the University of Minnesota where she received the award as the dental school's "most outstanding educator" which had previously only been awarded to dentists.

As you can see, growing up, I was surrounded by high achieving women! It's because of my relationship with my mother and sisters, I learned to love and respect women. I believe my relationship with my siblings helped me with many of my future relationships and ability to relate to women. I also credit my sisters, particularly Mary Lou, with creating a life-long habit of mine. It might interest you to know (or not) that I have slept with a pillow over my head since I was age seventeen. And I must say, through no fault of my own. This one I blame on a crazy fad. We moved into a new house Mom and Dad had just built. It was a beautiful house on an acre lot above a beautiful stream and only a block away from the high school. I was blessed to be given the downstairs bedroom just below the living room and have my own bathroom next door. But as it turned out, not everything was a blessing. There was a weight loss fad that was going around Carroll College girls had fallen prey to. Mary Lou was a very slender beautiful girl and I thought it was crazy for her to succumb to such lunacy.

The fad was supposed to reduce the size of your buttocks, as if Mary Lou needed that. What they were told to do was bounce on the floor on their bottoms for a half hour or so to reduce butt size. I can only imagine the laughs whom ever created this scam must have had. What does this have to do with me sleeping with a pillow over my head you may be asking? I always liked to go to bed earlier than the girls and Mary Lou liked doing her bouncing in the living room just after I went to bed. It sounded like thunder above my bedroom and I started putting

pillows over my head to try and dampen the pounding. No, her bottom never got smaller, it was small as it was and needed no bouncing. As for me, sleeping with a pillow over my head has remained a sleeping habit to this day.

"THE 4 M'S" (MARY LOU, MIKE, MARCY, MARGARET) AT CARROLL COLLEGE AND LATER AT LIFE'S DANCE RANCH

MY BROTHERS-IN LAW

My sisters have given me many gifts over the years but none better than the men they married. Mary Lou would start with her late husband who would pass away at age 28 from colon cancer six months after diagnosis and 4 days before their first child, a daughter, Sarah Lisa, was born. Pat Walsh was a big handsome Carroll College basketball star, a businessman and headed for law school in California. He was a good, kind man. He was blessed to have Mary Lou and his baby daughter with him at the end. We all loved Pat and the large Walsh family he came from.

Chapter Four

MARY LOU AND PAT

MARY LOU AND SARA LISA

Sara was a beautiful happy baby who would help all of our family heal from the loss of her father, Pat. She also helped me in getting through my failed first marriage by being a wonderful niece to dote on. She was a blessing we all needed at that time in our lives and continues to bless us to this day.

Though it took some time, Mary Lou was to find love again with another wonderful Carroll College man she had dated. We were all thrilled to have Gene Mallette back in our lives and with Mary Lou again. According to Gene's Economics professor, Gene was the smartest business mind he had ever taught. Gene wasn't just smart, he too, was an incredible athlete. He was a Carroll College Hall of Fame football player. He also had tremendous boxing skills. His first year as a boxer Gene won the Montana State Golden Gloves Boxing tournament in the light heavyweight division. He then went on to win the Northwest Region Golden Gloves Tournament. And finally, at the National Golden Gloves Tournament in Reno, Nevada, he lost a split decision to the

Journey to Life's Dance Ranch

National Runner Up. Not bad for a Shelby, Montana boy competing in his first year as a boxer.

Gene's grit would serve him well in his business endeavors. Starting with virtually no money, he acquired a small cargo/mail airline and airplane leasing company which he turned into the number one rated business of its class in the United States. He was selected Provo Utah's "Business Man of the Year" and afforded many other honors over the years. Mary Lou and Gene have been a great team and are two of the most kind and generous people you would ever want to meet.

GENE AND MARY LOU

After selling his airline business, Gene and Mary Lou built a truly beautiful rock home on forty-five acres with Ten Mile Creek flowing through their property. We love having them so close. Gene still flies his P-51 Mustang and it is great seeing him do a barrel roll as he flies over our ranch. When Gene and Mary Lou moved back to Helena, Carroll College asked Gene to sit on their board of directors. He and Mary Lou have been very active in Carroll College events and fund-raising.

Marcy would bring another terrific and exceptionally talented man into our family, Kelly McMullan. Kelly was born and raised in Boone, Iowa. He was "Mr. All-State" in basketball, football, baseball and

Chapter Four

and track for all four years in high school. In college, he was an NCAA all American shortstop and was drafted to play professional baseball. He decided against playing baseball in the professional ranks and instead was a highly successful teacher and high school basketball coach for a couple years. He then decided to pursue a masters degree at Montana State University in Bozeman, Montana. There he and Marcy would meet, fall in love and eventually marry at Montana's Big Sky Resort Chapel. Kelly would go on to work for Roche Pharmaceuticals while Marcy worked as a flight attendant for Northwest Airlines out of Minneapolis, MN. It was a God send to have them in the area while I was going to dental school at the University of Minnesota. I was a lonesome small-town boy and it was great support and comfort having family there with me.

Kelly and Marcy would eventually move back to Boone, Iowa, where Kelly, an accomplished businessman, would successfully work at his father's business until it was finally sold just a couple years ago. He and Marcy became stalwarts of their community and their church. Kelly, with his quick mind, common sense thinking and delightful sense of humor was a source of much joy and laughter and sound advice. Kelly has been a wonderful brother-in-law and great friend to me, our family and all who are blessed to know him.

MARCY & KELLY

KELLY & MIKE'S RUN TO THE "TWO DOT BAR"

Marg would bring us Vern Maddock. Vern was one of the smartest guys I ever knew. I only wish I could have had even a fraction of Vern's knowledge and skill sets. Considered the best welder in the state of Montana by his fellow pipe fitters, Vern could weld at the highest, most technical level. He was also an accomplished mechanic, plumber, builder and could fix anything. Perhaps Vern's greatest gift to us all was his love and care for our dear mother. We all consider Vern and Margaret as the angels who gave our mother that love and care twenty-four hours a day in their home for so many years.

Chapter Five
Decision Time

When it came time for me to head to college, Dad asked me what I thought I wanted to study. I told him I wanted to study music. He said, "No Mike, it's a tough life and you'll never make a living at it. You need to go into medicine or dentistry." I respected my father so much and was really not strong enough to stand up to him and say no. Even though I would have liked to study music, philosophy, or archeology, I resigned myself to becoming a physician.

Just about the time I was to apply for college, the Viet Nam war was raging and the government instituted a draft lottery. My lottery number turned out to be 100. It also happened to be the lowest number drawn for our county and our county's quota to send to the military was one. Guess who the first one to go would be...me. I was ready to go serve my county but then a friend I had grown up with, Howard Nelson, volunteered. He wanted to become a Marine and go fight in Viet Nam. That filled our draft board's quota and the county granted me an education deferment. Howard became a Marine, went to Viet Nam and was killed in action. I've always felt that Howard died so I could live. I give thanks for him every day.

I was off to college with a decision not to accept a basketball scholarship, but instead to focus all my efforts at becoming a doctor. I knew that would make my parents proud and I could make a good living and be a respectable professional like so many in my family. The thought of not being accepted into medical school never crossed my mind. I became an A- student in pre-med programs. Dr. Manion, the legendary

head of the program, offered me a work study position as one of his lab instructors. My confidence was high.

After I finished my sophomore year at Carroll College, I went back to Harlowton to work on the Milwaukee Railroad for the summer. I started to date Jan. Yes, she was also a cheerleader and close friend of my baby sister, Margaret. Jan was beautiful, smart, and athletic. It was not long before I was in love again. She was a very good kisser and I'm proud to say we kissed often! But with her in high-school and me in college, it was a long distance (132 miles) relationship and I was still consumed by my studies.

During summer breaks from Carroll, I worked for the Milwaukee RR as a section worker, then as a switchman and brakeman. I loved working, especially for the RR and I had a wonderful summer romance with Jan, but we saw each other infrequently during the school year, when most of the romance was by phone or letters. Yes, we actually wrote love letters in those days. After she graduated from high school, she enrolled in the University of Montana in Missoula to study art, dance and acting. We got to spend time together in Harlo during the summer break and have an occasional rendezvous in Deer Lodge where her grandparents lived. It continued to be a long-distance relationship, and I continued to focus hard on my studies while juggling the relationship with Jan.

My senior year, I submitted several applications to medical schools, including Colorado, U of Washington, Washington University at St. Louis, and others. Then the wait was on. One by one, my friends and fellow pre-med and pre-dent students received letters of acceptance. And one by one, I received letters of rejection from every school I had applied to. Dr. Manion recommended I take some post-graduate study at Montana State University and reapply the following year feeling certain I would be accepted in my second try.

Chapter Five

READY FOR MARRIAGE OR NOT ????

My relationship with Jan continued to develop and yes, I actually told her "I love you." She was the first girl I ever said that to. It was a gift which would lead to a proposal of marriage in the Church on a beautiful softly snowing Christmas Eve in 1971. She accepted. I knew she would not only be the first woman I'd say that to, I honestly believed she would be the last. Never did I imagine this relationship would turn out to be what I was to consider the greatest failure of my life.

I graduated from Carroll in June of 1972. Jan and I were married on July 22 that same year. Our honeymoon consisted of a trip to Denver to interview at U of Colorado Medical School. Then we drove to her grand-father's family cabin on Rock Creek Lake outside of Deer Lodge. We made love, rowed a boat on the lake, picked huckleberries and made more love. Life was romantic and yes, sex was wonderful. During that summer we lived in Harlowton in a little apartment above Bain's Department store. There was one bedroom, a living room and tiny kitchen with a refrigerator just big enough to hold a quart of milk, a jar of mayonnaise but not much else. It was an old apartment, no AC, very hot in the summer months and very noisy being on Main Street. But we were young and in love. We played golf, made love, played more golf and made more love.

That year Jan won the ladies city golf championship and I won the men's, for a second time. We were happy and decided to go to Bozeman where I would train and get certified as an orderly and work evenings to help pay for school. We were lucky to get an apartment in some brand-new married housing on the University Campus. I did some graduate work in immuno-biology and hematology and applied again to several medical schools.

The fall after Jan and I were married I had the opportunity to go deer hunting with my dad and Jan's dad. My dad had gotten permission to hunt on a rancher friend's property. We arrived early and there were multiple deer standing on the rancher's front yard. He invited us in for coffee then drove with us to a place he had often seen many deer. As we drove through his property, I remember passing through a beautiful canyon with more bald and golden eagles than I had ever seen in one place. Finally, after a bumpy drive over very rugged terrain, we reached where he felt we would find deer. Sure enough, there they were.

My father-in-law immediately shot a buck, two to three hundred yards up a mountain side. He and I went up to retrieve it. When we reached the deer, he realized he had forgotten his hatchet and knife which he normally used to dress out the deer. Undaunted, he said he could dress it out with his pocket knife. I was on the upslope of the mountain holding the front legs. Below me, he was working his way toward me as he gutted the deer. Since he had forgotten his hatchet which he usually used to open the brisket, he needed to cut the esophagus and trachea and then reach under the brisket and pull all the guts out of the abdominal cavity. As he was struggling to cut the esophagus and trachea, suddenly the knife cut through and continued up into my right wrist. We immediately put a handkerchief over the cut, wrapped my belt tightly around the wrist and I headed down the mountain.

When I got to the bottom my dad asked what had happened and I told him I had had a knife run through my wrist. Dad said, "Let me see." As I exposed the wound and the spurting blood, Dad told me, "Mike you got an artery and we've got to get you back to town for care." I assured Dad that I would be fine, I would go back to town, get treated and be back to continue the hunt that afternoon. That would never happen.

Dad, the rancher and I headed back over the rugged terrain to the ranch house. Dad and the rancher were in the front seat, I in the back of the rancher's jeep. I was talking to Dad and the rancher and all of a sudden, I felt my lap getting warm. I looked down to find a pool of blood. When Dad and I had taken the belt off to look at the injury, I had simply put the handkerchief over the wound and applied pressure. What I didn't realize was the wound went completely through my wrist.

Chapter Five

As I held pressure on the front of the wound, blood was pouring out the backside of my wrist. I repositioned the handkerchief and tightly wrapped the belt around it once again.

When we reached the ranch house, I saw that the rancher was "pure white" and obviously scared to death about my condition. He had a big Oldsmobile and told Dad he would get me to the hospital and Dad could follow us. That was probably the fastest wildest ride I have ever taken. The trip was thirty-five miles over a narrow hilly road. Once we hit the highway, he never was below 120 miles per hour and as we went over hills his car would literally go airborne. What a ride!

When we arrived at the hospital, on seeing the injury, the physician immediately took me to the operating room. I was extremely lucky that he had done a fellowship in vascular surgery. I asked him if I could watch as he sewed the radial artery back together and he agreed. After anesthetizing, he did a cut-down on the wrist and skillfully sewed the artery back together. He told me there was probably some tendon damage but that was surgery for another day. As the day went on, I soon realized there was no function with the thumb and two forefingers on my right hand.

Three days later, it was off to Billings to have surgery to reattach the tendons in my injured hand. I was placed in a cast and told I was to return to Billings in six weeks to remove the cast and be followed up. I left in pain but with plenty of prescription narcotics. Jan and I went back to Bozeman where I would try and catch up on the post graduate course material I had missed. The pain never stopped, even with meds. It was difficult to sleep, to study and just a difficult time period. When we finally got back to Billings and the cast was taken off, the pain immediately stopped. The pain had not been caused by the surgery but rather a pressure point, from the cast.

The surgeon told me I would be lucky to get fifty percent function back. He could see slight movement in all the affected fingers although I could not. He suggested I purchase a portable bathtub water jet device.

He told me to start with a nerf ball using water as hot as I could stand. Through diligent and what seemed unending therapy with the hot water jet, I gradually started to get function back. Every tiny increase in movement became a milestone. Perhaps the biggest milestone after months of painful rehab leaning over the bathtub was touching my thumb and two affected fingers to the palm of my hand. It was then I felt certain I would get most if not all function back and I did. I am still grateful for the orthopedic surgeon, a Dr. Yoder, who gave me the opportunity to work my hand back to nearly full function and eventually work as a dentist. I've been blessed.

     Our marriage seemed idyllic for those looking from the outside, but early on I sensed things going wrong. We had some struggles while at MSU. I was again rejected from all Med schools to which I'd applied. We decided to go back to Harlowton for a year. I would work for the railroad and she would work as an assistant in our local physician's office. Meanwhile, I applied to several Dental Schools and received an early acceptance letter from the University of Minnesota. Things were looking up, but not so much in our relationship. Things became more and more difficult, then intolerable for me and I finally asked her for a divorce. After the divorce, I was so ashamed; I spent three lonely years not dating anyone.

Chapter Six
Moving On and Miracles

Accepted to dental school, but in a state of desperate sadness and feeling of absolute failure as I awaited my divorce from Jan, I traveled to Minneapolis where my sister Marcy and her husband, Kelly, lived. Marcy and Kelly were a great help in looking for a place I could rent while attending dental school, but everything seemed so expensive. I had no money and was going to have to borrow all the money to pay for my dental schooling. We looked all over for a place close enough for me to walk to school. Miracles have a way of happening to me at some of my darkest times. Such was the case with an address … 1414 S. 3rd Street, Seven Corners, Minneapolis, Minnesota, one mile from the dental school.

It was a three-story apartment building with almost all the apartments being efficiencies, very small but just what I was looking for. It had a beautiful indoor swimming pool, sauna and exercise room. At one time the University had owned it and used it as VIP quarters for special guests, lecturers and University big wigs. I told the manager it was a great place, but I just couldn't afford it. Then he said, "Would you be willing to refinish the deck around the pool, clean and maintain the pool, sauna and exercise room? If you would, we could give you abatement on your rent." I said yes instantly! The manager and I became good friends and I would eventually be a groomsman in his wedding.

It was back to Harlowton to pack up my stuff. I didn't have much. The divorce went through on July 22, 1974, exactly two years to the day after Jan and I had married. With spirits at rock bottom, I got

in my car and headed toward Minnesota. It was a long lonely ride. Marcy and Kelly met me at 1414 S. 3rd Street. I unpacked my stuff and then we went to look for some furniture. An oak barrel to put my cow skull on, a wooden spool for a table, a single bed and mattress, a cheap couch that folded down into an uncomfortable bed, a couple of stools for the kitchen bar and that was it. All the time we were there, we saw no one else in the building. When Marcy and Kelly left, I was as alone as I'd ever been... away from my true love, Montana, a small-town boy in the big city, starting school and knowing no one. For two weeks, I attended classes, came home to my apartment, and didn't see a single person. No one to say hello to, no one to get to know, no one at the pool, sauna or exercise room. I was lonesome, unhappy, ashamed and sure I would go crazy in this place.

But miracles do happen ... and one happened to me just in time. It was a beautiful sunny Saturday morning in September when they started to arrive – a bevy of beautiful young women! I'd never seen so many pretty women at one time. They were all second and third-year nursing students from St. Olaf College in Northfield, Minnesota, doing their two-year hospital service at Minneapolis hospitals, and the miracle ... St. Olaf College rented virtually every apartment in the building as dorm rooms for the nursing students. My spirits immediately elevated.

I would get to know many of these beautiful women. In fact, it was they who first gave me the moniker "Montana Mike!" If I hadn't been so ashamed of my failed marriage (the first ever in my family), I would have loved to date some of these wonderful girls, but I just wasn't ready to tell anyone about my failure and venture into another relationship. I'm sure some of them must have thought I was gay, because I never asked any on a date. There was one, however, a special sensitive woman who sensed my pain and fear. Sarah Schunaman would come to my room every day to see how I was and how my day had gone. I would wait anxiously for the knock on the door, and she always brightened my day. Finally, I worked up the courage to tell her of my marriage and divorce, asking her to please tell no one because I was too ashamed.

Chapter Six

It was Sarah "Sal" who really saved my life in many ways. We have kept in touch over the years. She married a wonderful man, Craig Arnold, a choral director; they had two beautiful boys and have had a wonderful life together. I am so proud of her. She is no longer "Nurse Sarah" but now Dr. Sarah Arnold, having recently completed her Ph.D. in nursing administration. I will be eternally grateful to this caring woman and all of her fellow nursing students who enriched my life so.

LET THE DANCING BEGIN!

It was around this same time that dancing entered my life and it fortunately has never left. Reflecting back, I have come to believe everyone needs to seek their own life's dance, their unique purpose for being, metaphorically as well as physically. As the country song goes, "Life's a dance you learn as you go, sometimes you lead and sometimes you follow." Music and dancing have had a profound impact on my life, and sometimes I have led and other times I have followed. I am so grateful for all my partners over the years who took the chance to dance with me.

My first actual dance steps came rather reluctantly ... Sometimes thinking you know more about your best friend than you actually do can be rude awakening, a blessing or both. Such was the case with my best college friend, Bill Tacke or as I called him "Tac." Tac had just come to Minneapolis to do a residency in Physical Medicine. He was able to get an apartment in my complex just down the hallway from me. It was great to have my old undergraduate buddy back around again. One afternoon I heard a knock on my door and when I opened it my sister, Margaret was there with a proposition for me. She said, "Mike, how'd you like to take a ballroom dancing class with me, I'll pay." My response was, "Are you nuts, no way, even if you pay!" Of course, she countered with, "Ah come on, Mike, it would be a lot of fun!" "No way Marg, I'm not taking a ballroom dance class or any other kind of dance class either," I said.

She pleaded, and pleaded and when I continually objected, she

played her trump card. She said, "I'll bet Tac would do it." My response was, "Are you kidding me? There is no way in hell Tac would take ballroom dancing!" She came back with, "Well if Tac will do it, will you you?" "Oh yea, if Tac will do it, I'll be glad to do it because I know for absolute sure he won't!" Her quick response was "OK let's go down to his apartment and ask him." "You bet, Marg, let's go, I know he'll say no! Maybe hell no!" So off we went and knocked on Tac's door.

When the door opened, Marg immediately asked, "Hey Tac how'd you like to take a ballroom dance class?" His quick response, "That sounds fun!" I was crushed and said, "Tac, how could you?" What was done was done and Marg, Tac and I started taking ballroom dance. It turned out to be great fun. We learned foxtrot, slow waltz, quick waltz, Mazurka, rumba, cha cha, tango, lindy swing and many others. Minnesota is known for its big band ballrooms and dancing. Minneapolis had quite a number of big ballrooms where big name bands would come to play. We had grown to be good friends with the dance instructors, and they told us if we came an hour early to the dances, they would give us a free lesson before the show began. We had a blast and went almost every weekend we could. It was where Tac met his dance partner to be, Barb Teaburg. They were to become dance partners for life. They have been happily married now for over forty years.

HO, HO, HO, OH NO!

Life can teach you some brutal lessons at times. Such was the case when I came home for Christmas my second year in dental school. Shortly after arriving home after a train trip from Minneapolis, my mom asked me to do a favor for her. We had some friends in town that needed someone to dress up in a Santa Claus outfit and come to their homes to bring gifts and a Merry Christmas for their young kids. Mom had already told them I would do the job. I wasn't very thrilled and really didn't want to do it but finally agreed. Mom said I might need a little drink to loosen me up and get me in a jollier mood. She brought me a glass of peppermint schnapps and I drank it, though I really didn't care for it.

Chapter Six

Then Santa, my sister Marcy and her husband Kelly were off to visit the children. When we arrived at the first house, Santa was immediately asked what he was drinking. I said, Peppermint Schnapps, and they poured me a strong one. I Ho Ho Ho'd and gave gifts to the children. The friends thanked us and gave me a Peppermint Schnapps for the road. Fortunately, I wasn't driving and Marcy and Kelly took me to my next performance site. As we entered these friend's house, they immediately asked what Santa was drinking and were quick to bring me another Peppermint Schnapps. I was starting to feel no pain and was becoming much jollier.

After we were finished at the second friend's house, Marcy and Kelly suggested we go bar hopping. I had never been in any of the bars in Harlowton, let alone gone barhopping. There were seven or eight bars in our town and our goal was to have Santa appear in all of them. I don't remember much about that night; however, I do remember having a lot of bartenders saying, "What will Santa have to drink? Peppermint Schnapps? It's on the house!" My memories of most of that evening are very foggy but I do remember dancing with someone's boxer dog in the Stockman bar. We made the rounds and finally finished up at the Argonaut Bar.

There, I started to feel a bit green, was beginning to lose my composure and felt I might get sick. I told Marcy and Kelly to please get me out of there and take me home. I barely made it to the house, made a stumbling dash to my bathroom, kneeled down, grabbed the toilet and proceeded with a long night of vomiting. I do remember Mom coming down while I was hugging the toilet and telling me how sorry she was. Laughingly I told her it wasn't her fault and I would be OK. After several hours, I was finally able to let go of the toilet and stagger to my bedroom with trash can in hand and lay down in bed. The entire room kept spinning as I laid there on my back with one foot on the floor.

When I finally arose early the next morning, my head was exploding, I felt nauseated and there was absolutely no where I could find any relief. No question, it was the most painful Christmas of my

life. To this day, I cannot even think of Peppermint Schnapps without getting a queasy stomach. This experience is a perfect example of the old adage that "No good deed ever goes unpunished". Of course, it was my own fault, but I have been told I entertained and helped a lot of people feel jolly that night.

NEW MONTANA LOVE

Then, 3 years after my divorce, I met a new love. It was she in whom I first had the courage and trust to share my feelings. And miraculously, she knew and understood. After all she was a Montana girl born of the prairie's wind and she understood my soul. It was the Montana in her that I loved and trusted. Our relationship was always long distance except when I would come back to Montana from dental school during breaks.

We would spend wonderful times on her folks' ranch enjoying the beautiful Montana outdoors mending fences, cleaning barns, doing midnight calf watches during calving season and watching muskrats swim across their lake at sunset. Occasionally we would drive to Billings to pick up ranch medicines and supplies, donate blood to the Red Cross, go to dinner and be back to the ranch in time for our calf watch. After our calf watch we would head back to the ranch house and she would make a delicious breakfast of eggs, sourdough pancakes and side pork.

Chapter Six

MONTANA GIRL

I SEE HER STILL, IN THE BEAUTIFUL BLOOMING DAFFODILS OF SPRING,
AND WE'RE NOT JUST FRIENDS, WE'RE SO MUCH MORE
THOUGH LOVERS WE COULDN'T BE
OUR SOULS WERE LOCKED IN LOVES EMBRACE
FOR ALL ETERNITY

YES, LIFE HAS CROSSED OUR PATHS AT TIMES
WHEN MY HEART WAS LOST IN PAIN
SHE RESCUED ME WITH HER GOOD HEART
TO GIVE ME MINE AGAIN

THOUGH WE WEREN'T MEANT TO BE
THERE IS NO QUESTION OF...
WE SHARE A COMMON DESTINY
WE SHARE A DEEP TRUE LOVE

CALL HER MONTANA

THIS LOVE WAS CALLED MONTANA
IF YOU HAVE TO KNOW HER NAME
OR YOU COULD CALL HER DAFFODIL
TO ME THEY ARE THE SAME

WE WERE TWO KITES WITHOUT A TETHER
WE SOARED SO HIGH, WE FLEW TOGETHER
AND AS TWO KITES WITHOUT A STRING
WE FOUND THE PLACE WHERE EAGLES WING

OUR MINDS WERE LOVERS FROM THE START

AND SOON OUR HEARTS WERE TOO
WITH ME SHE SHARED A COMMON SOUL
CONNECTED TO MY MIND
SHE UNDERSTOOD WHEN OTHERS DIDN'T
SHE SAW WHERE THEY WERE BLIND

SHE ALWAYS LISTENED PATIENTLY
TO WHAT I HAD TO SAY
THEN DISTILLED IT TO ITS ESSENCE
HELPED ME GET TO GOD THAT WAY

I NEVER CAN REPAY HER
FOR THE GIFTS SHE GAVE TO ME
OR SAY HOW MUCH I VALUE HER
AND I LOVED HER AS A BABY
AND I LOVED HER IN MY YOUTH
FOR I FOUND IN HER GREAT GOODNESS
AWESOME BEAUTY AND PURE TRUTH

AND AS A MAN IN DESPERATE GRIEF
SHE WAS THERE TO COMFORT ME
"NO-THING" ALWAYS HAPPENED
WHENEVER WE WERE TOGETHER
AND IT ALWAYS WILL.

Following in my father's footsteps, I completed dental school, but instead of going into private practice, as planned, I entered the Navy. The railroad had closed down in Harlo and the town just could not support two dentists. The Navy was there for me and I was initially stationed in Orlando, Florida. Our long distance, safe relationship, was just what I needed at the time. After my move to Florida, I felt it was time to ask my Montana girl to come down to be with me and see if the relationship might develop into something more.

Chapter Six

I sent her a one-way ticket. Illness in her family and the need to be home to help take care of the ranch, kept this from happening. Time and distance and then meeting Dana kept the relationship from developing into anything more than just a beautiful friendship. Looking back, that was fortunate for both of us, for I don't see how the relationship away from Montana could have lasted. She loved Montana too much to become a Navy wife moving every couple of years to mainly near ocean duty stations. I left her in Montana where she belonged, as life took me in another direction.

Chapter Seven
My Dancer Came Dancing to Me

    Once in Orlando, I was busy learning to be a dentist at the Navy Recruit Dental facility. I was blessed to serve with many skilled senior dental officers and learned an enormous amount from them. It was a great way to start my young dental career. I found an apartment complex with a swimming pool and tennis court and rented a small one-bedroom apartment which was much larger than the little efficiency I had rented during dental school. Life as a young Navy dental officer consisted of working, playing and generally enjoying life. My dear friends, Jim McCutcheon (a Navy lieutenant who entered the Navy the same time I did) and his fiancee Susan also lived in the same complex. We spent many great times together sitting poolside, playing tennis, going to the beach, canoeing and barbequing. It didn't take me long to get to know almost everyone at the complex. Life was good, but my love life was in a stall.

    Then one day I got my first vision of a beautiful girl with a basket of clothes heading to the laundry room. I decided it was time to do my laundry. When I got to the laundry room, she was gone, but I had taken a book to read while I waited for my laundry and for her to return for hers. She came back, I introduced myself, she said her name was Dana and we talked a bit. She was delightful, intelligent, well spoken and incredibly beautiful. I could tell, however, there was a sadness about her. Just before she went back to her apartment, she told me she was in the process of going through a divorce. I felt sorry for her, remembering the deep sadness and struggle I had gone through with Jan and my divorce. I had read several books which had helped me cope

after my divorce and thought they might help her. I went and got them and by process of elimination figured out which apartment was hers. I knocked, she came to the door and invited me in. It was February the 4th, 1979. She was making cake for her little sister's birthday. We visited a bit and I left.

DAMAGED BIRD

SHE WAS DAMAGED WHEN SHE FIRST ARRIVED
BUT HE LOVED THE FACT THAT SHE'D SURVIVED
THE BRUTAL JOURNEY THAT SHE MADE
AND HE KNEW JUST WHAT HE HAD TO DO
HE'D FIX HER WITH SOME LOVER'S GLUE
FOR HE HAD HAD SOME DAMAGE TOO
BUT KNEW THAT DID NOT MATTER
IT ONLY MADE WHAT NOW SURVIVED
MORE SPECIAL AND MUCH MORE ALIVE
AND MOST WOULD NOT HAVE MADE IT
BUT HERE SHE WAS, THIS INJURED BIRD
HE'D LIFTED TO THE BRANCH
ONCE MORE SHE SANG SO SWEETLY
THANK GOD, SHE GOT THE CHANCE

Chapter Seven

After that our relationship developed into a friendship of talking with one another. I would always sit on one side of the couch, she on the other. No, I never sat close, never held hands and of course, never kissed her. Although separated from her husband, she was still a married woman. I respected her too much to have the relationship be any more than that until her divorce went through. But, as our friendship deepened, we did many fun things together: meeting for lunch, riding bikes, sitting by the pool, going to the beach with Jim and Susan, and attending art shows and musical events around the area. Though I was falling in love with her, I wouldn't let myself get closer while she was still a married woman. I continued to sit on one end of the couch and she sat on the other. This relationship went on for over nine months.

Near Christmas I had to have a surgical procedure on my side and was allowed to go home to Montana to recover. When I returned to Florida, the first thing I did was knock on her door. No one answered. Thinking she may have gone to her parent's house, I rode up the bike path and knocked on their door. Her little brother answered the door and told me she had moved to Texas to try and reconcile her marriage. I was saddened but hopeful she would be able to reestablish a loving relationship and happy life.

So once again, though living a great life, I felt lonesome and longed for a more permanent relationship with a woman. There was another girl I had dated a few times my senior year in dental school. It never became serious. I never kissed or held her. And of course, I never told her I loved her. But she was a lot of fun, beautiful, smart and could always make me laugh. Though she was in Michigan working as a nurse, I thought it would be fun to have her come to Orlando for a visit. I called and asked her to come and she said yes. This was to become a wonderful romance which would turn me head over heels in love with her. We had a magical week together in Orlando. Yes, I did tell her I loved her and before she left to go back to Michigan, I asked her to marry me and have our babies together. She wasn't ready to commit. After all, we had only been in a romantic relationship for a bit over a week. She must have

thought I was nuts. Our relationship became long distance. Again, time and distance interfered. I made a trip to Michigan and we had another great week together but she still didn't consent to marry me. We continued our relationship from afar.

Then one day my life would change in a way I could never have imagined. I was in my apartment reading when there came a light knock on my door. I wasn't sure I had even really heard a knock but went to the door to check anyway. There to my utter surprise was Dana. She asked me if I would like to go for a ride and talk. I grabbed my bike and we rode to a spot near a golf course where we could sit and talk. She told me her dad had driven her and a trailer full of her stuff to Texas where she hoped to repair the relationship with her husband. Unfortunately, when they got there, her husband was having another affair with a different woman. They simply turned around and drove back to Orlando. She told me it had taken all the courage she could muster to come to my apartment and knock on the door. She said had I not answered she would have never come back. Our friendship renewed, we started spending time together.

But I still had not told her I loved her, kissed her or held hands. I was honest and straightforward about my Michigan love relationship. Dana continued to drag her feet in pushing for the divorce to go through and our relationship continued as it had been. But I could tell I was falling in love with her. In love with my Michigan girl, still caring for my Montana girl and now in love with Dana; life had become incredibly difficult and complicated for me – loving man that I am.

One night, Dana asked me to go with her to an art show near a lake in downtown Orlando. After the show, we walked around the lake and stopped to sit at the outdoor theater. I looked her in the eyes and told her that I would really like to see if our relationship could be more, but as long as she was married it wouldn't happen. Then in a rather blunt way, I said, "So if you think you might like a more intimate relationship, you'll have to 'Go or get off the pot' with your divorce." It was exactly what Dana needed to hear. Within a couple weeks, her

divorce went through and she took a chance on me. Yes, I did sit next to her, held her and told her I loved her.

I was at my wit's end; in love with two women, either of whom I would have felt blessed to have as my lover and best friend for life. As time went by, my relationship with Dana became more intense, but she always told me if I decided to marry my Michigan girl, she would back out of the picture with no hard feelings. But I loved her too much and knew I had to call my Michigan girl and tell her I had fallen in love with another woman. My Michigan girl flew down to Orlando to see if she could make our relationship work. When I picked her up at the airport, I hugged her, kissed her and told her I loved her. She stayed several days with me and we talked. She told me she was ready to marry me and have our babies. Perhaps the most difficult thing I ever had to do was tell her my relationship with Dana had gone too far and I was going to ask Dana to marry me. She cried. So, did I. I told her I would always love her. Saying good-by as I put her on the plane was one of the most brutal moments of my life. I still think of her often, still love her and pray that she found a wonderful man and has had a beautiful life. The day after she flew back to Michigan, I went to Dana's apartment and asked her to marry me. She told me she would have to think about it. I said, "OK you've got sixty seconds." She immediately said yes.

We drove in my Volkswagen Beetle convertible with the top down in the rain to a jewelry store to pick out an engagement ring. I wanted to get married the next day, but Dana wanted to have a small wedding with her family there. And so, on the 6th day of September, 1980, we were married in the Navy Chapel on the Orlando Navy Base.

WEDDING DAY   SEPTEMBER 6, 1980

LIFE WITH MY DANCER, MY DANALEE

My life with Dana started with both of us taking a chance on love again. We had each been through marriages that failed and devastated us. Were we sure that this marriage would work out? No, but we both wanted to take the chance at love again. Dana was a beautiful 28-year-old professional dancer working for Disney World as an entertainer and choreographer. She was also going to the University of Central Florida working toward a master's degree in Speech Therapy. She was kind, brilliant, beautiful and as grounded as any person I had ever known. I was a 31-year-old Lieutenant in the Navy, fresh out of dental school. We knew we loved each other for far more than just what seemed the most perfect physical relationship either of us had ever experienced and one that would continue through our entire marriage.

Chapter Seven

I moved out of my apartment and into Dana's about two weeks before we were married. From the first moments I was living with her, I felt as comfortable and happy as I had ever been. She was a meticulous housekeeper, a wonderful cook and though we had cardboard boxes covered with cloth for end tables, cinder blocks and boards for our bookcase and an oak barrel with cow skull which I contributed to the new household, Dana had a way of making everything look beautiful. I gave all the rest of my furniture away. She had a very comfortable California King bed, probably our best piece of furniture, and a nice area rug. With me, she got very little except my undying love and $65,000.00 in student debt. Still, she was willing to take a chance on this simple Montana boy.

With every day I was with Dana, I loved her more. She was so beautiful both physically and personally. At the end of every workday, I knew I would always find love, support, my best friend and joy when I came home. That never changed except to keep getting better until the day she died. She was so strong, so sensible, so pure, so good. She made every day a good day and I knew as long as she was with me, I would always be where I had to be. Her mood was constant. She never showed any fluctuations during that time of the month. She was always kind, gentle, and loving to all. Dana was the perfect partner.

Dana had studied Ballet and other dance forms from the time she was ten years old and was the consummate professional. Growing up with Ballet, as with most aspiring ballerinas, she loved performing in the Christmas Nutcracker and danced many of the parts. She continued her dance training and performance while attending college with a professional dance company in Orlando, Florida and after she graduated secured a job with Disney World the first year it opened.

She was one of the first dancers and choreographers for the Diamond Horse Shoe Review at Disney World. Dana enjoyed her work as a professional entertainer. She loved the dancing! Everyone loved dancing with Dana because she was not only a terrific dancer, she was a wonderful friend to everyone she worked with. I did get to see her

dance for a huge convention at Disney World. I remember afterward we had dinner together in one of the Disney Hotel restaurants. She was still in costume with heavy makeup, false eyelashes and her wonderful smile. I was so proud to be seen with this beautiful ballerina dancer.

DANA DANCING "THE NUTCRACKER" IN HIGH SCHOOL

DANA (FAR LEFT) DANCING AT DISNEY WORLD IN THE DIAMOND HORSESHOE REVIEW

A NAVY LIFE

However, when we got married, I would take her away from all that with a Navy career which we started in Guam half way around the globe. Even in Guam she continued dancing and teaching others. She would put on dance shows with her students that wowed our Navy community. She would go on to perform and teach at every place we were stationed. She performed professionally with the Robert Ivey Ballet Company when we were stationed in Charleston, SC and with the Mark Spivak Ballet Company during our tours in Jacksonville, FL. She also taught ballet for both of those ballet companies. From her earliest years of dance, she performed in the Nutcracker every Christmas possible. At every duty station she never tired of performing in that joyful celebration of Christmas.

Chapter Seven

From the start, Dana was the perfect wife, lover and friend. She was also the perfect Navy wife, which is no easy life. Dana also earned a degree in Floral Design and Marketing, and she loved her floral design business. She blessed my Navy career. I am absolutely certain I would never have been promoted to Captain had it not been for the strength, grace, counsel and the undying love she gave me every day. There were two things I never failed to tell her at the end of every day "You're the best and I love you."

My Love's Portrait

If they asked me how I loved you
I would hope they had the time
To watch me paint your portrait
On the canvas of my mind
And use a brush I found
Within a recess of my heart
With the color your love gave my life
Upon my brush, I'd start
And memories of the passionate
Yet tender, love we shared
Would be the brush's first strokes
And they'd show how much I cared
How much to me, was given
The canvas must be vast
To try and paint a love so deep
Is such a daunting task
But still, I am quite certain,
It is something I can do
For the hand of God will help me
The hand that gave me you

Journey to Life's Dance Ranch

I'll never forget a day seven months after we married that she came to the clinic and tapped me on the back. I excused myself from my patient and went into the hallway with her. She put her arms around my neck and whispered in my ear "We're pregnant." I was overwhelmed! Her due date was the 15th of November 1981. The wind was taken out of our sails a bit when we got a letter from my future boss and sponsor on the USS Proteus (AS-19), a submarine tender stationed in Guam. He welcomed us to the island, told us much about duty there and at the end of the letter said, "Oh yes, and we are scheduled to deploy to the Indian Ocean for six months on (you guessed it) the 15th of November." It appeared that I just might miss the birth of our first child and Dana just might be alone halfway around the world on a tiny island in the Pacific Ocean. Dana took it all in stride as she did everything. So, in mid-May we started our journey westward; first a stop in Montana to visit my family then on to San Francisco where we would board a plane for Guam.

FLOWERS FOR MY DANA

BURST OF COLOR

SCENTED JOY

STEMS OF MAGIC

HE'LL DEPLOY

GIVEN WHEN

SHE LEAST EXPECTS

WARMS HER HEART

HIS LOVE REFLECTS

BEAUTY GIVEN

BRINGS A LIFT

FLOWERS ARE

TRUE LOVE'S GIFT

SO...

Chapter Seven

GIVE HER LOVE
GIVE HER ROSES
GIVE HER DAFFODILS
IN SPRING
GIVE HER DAISES
JUST FOR FUN
SHOW HER SHE'S
THE ONLY ONE

After we got to Guam, we were given housing in a place called Apra Heights on a street called Neye Lane. We ended up sharing a duplex with Barry and Camille Smith who would become our best friends. We had one other house on little "Neye Lane" where Tom and Tammi Weiman lived. They also became great friends. The six of us became known as the Neye Lane Gang. We became like sisters and brothers. Dana was four months pregnant and the coming baby became the primary focus of all our lives. We truly were a family of six, waiting, excited about number seven. We became comfortable going next door, or having Barry or Camille just come over, opening the door and asking to borrow a cup of sugar or just to come visit. This open-door policy did backfire on us a time or two. We were all at our hormonal high points in life.

One day I went next door to borrow something, tapped on the door and went in, calling Barry and Camille. I heard a somewhat muffled response and so I continued further, saying "Barry? Camille?" Then I heard a loud, "Go away! Go away!" I retreated quickly and went home to tell Dana. The four of us had a good laugh about it later. They had been having a passionate moment together and didn't want me interrupting. After that, I started waiting for them to actually come to the door rather than take a chance on coitus interruptus!

Journey to Life's Dance Ranch

THE NEYE LANE GANG MINUS ME

Barry and Camille would eventually become Patrick's God parents. Tom and Tammi were also with us for the baptism, along with my boss Tom and his wife Ginny Carlson. We could not have been more blessed in our Guam family.

Sometimes good fortune can come to you by way of misfortune and such was the case for me on Guam. A few weeks prior to a deployment that would have taken me to the Indian Ocean for 6 months and would have kept me from being with Dana for Patrick's birth, I ruptured my left Achilles tendon playing racquetball with my boss and the ship's supply officer. Fortunately, for me there was a dentist at the base dental clinic who volunteered to take my place on the ship. I was able to do his job at the base clinic. Three days after the injury I had a surgical repair and was put in a long leg cast for three months. This was a "mis-fortunate" blessing which allowed me to be with Dana for Patrick's birth.

Just before the ship was to deploy, they had a traditional "Dining Out" party. This was similar to a "Dining In," which was only for ships officers. However, with the "Dining Out" party, the officers were required to bring their wives. These were quite formal affairs with dress uniforms for men and formal attire for women. It is a time for poking fun at each other and bringing to the attention of the Commanding officer what might be considered "breaches of decorum," punishable by fine. Dana was a few weeks away from delivery but looked beautiful in her pink formal maternity gown. I was wearing my formal wear for the first time and of course had my long leg cast with a black sock covering my toes.

Chapter Seven

It didn't take long for my boss, Tom Carlson, to point out to the Commanding Officer that I had committed, "a great breach of decorum." I was wearing my cumber bund upside down... it was the first time I'd ever put one on, after all. The Commanding Officer said, "Lt. Maixner would you please stand and defend yourself." I awkwardly stood up with my crutches, pointed to my cumber bund and my leg and said, "Sir, I would like to defend myself, but as you can see, I don't have a leg to stand on." The Commanding Officer and everyone roared with laughter. The Commanding Officer said, "Well put Lieutenant, you may sit down, there will be no fine." It was a fun evening of levity, friendship and camaraderie.

FORMAL NAVY EVENT WITH BARRY AND CAMILLE

PARENTING BEGINS

On the 15th of November 1981, Dana woke me at five AM all excited; she had just had a contraction. I wasn't surprised. She always had perfect timing. We both knew our baby was coming on its due date. Unfortunately, that was the last contraction she would have. Two weeks later, her doctor decided it was time to induce. After fourteen hours of brutal labor without progression, it was decided to take the baby C-section. Our next shock was when the doctor came down the hall with a bundle in his arms and said, "Congratulations, Dr. Maixner, you have a new baby boy!" Whoa, we were expecting a girl! We hadn't even really talked about boy names. And so, I took the bundle with our new son to

the nursery to help give him his first bath. There were lots of beautiful babies there, but Patrick certainly wasn't one of them. His head was pointed, and his face was bright red from all the labor he had gone through. I remember thinking, "We're going to love him to death, but I hope Dana isn't too disappointed. He's the ugliest baby I've ever seen." I went up to recovery to see Dana, then drove home and got a few hours of sleep. When I got back to the hospital and went to the nursery, a miracle had happened. Patrick's head had rounded up, his face was pink like the rest of the babies...he was beautiful.

As young parents Dana and I had the naïve belief our babies would be the best babies because we would be the best parents. When Patrick was born, he did nothing to shatter that misconception. He slept through his first night. Dana and I didn't. We thought something must be wrong, babies are supposed to cry and wake you up in the middle of the night. He really was the perfect baby. He had a wonderful, happy disposition, rarely crying or fussing. Patrick did everything early, walked at nine months, talked early, and was potty trained by age three. When we would go out to eat, while other babies were crying, spitting food out, throwing crackers on the floor, Patrick sat quietly, ate all his food and smiled at all who admired him. Dana and I knew we had parenting down. How else would our child be so good and so easy?

We got pregnant again and had Andrew at the hospital at our new duty station, Camp Pendleton, California. Suddenly the reality hit us that maybe it wasn't our great parenting that had created the perfect baby/child Patrick. Andrew started life crying and continued to cry for two and one-half years, or at least it seemed like that. Early on, the first year, he was colicky and then he started a seemingly endless string of ear infections. He would stop crying only to eat and during his rare hours of sleep. His ear infections would continue until he reached age two and a half years, then joyfully, he grew out of them.

Andrew waited until two days after his first birthday to sleep through the night. Dana and I weren't there to experience this milestone. My father had passed away one day after Andrew's first birthday. Dana,

Chapter Seven

Patrick and I had flown to Montana on December 29th, 1985 for the wake and the funeral. We were blessed to have a wonderful elderly lady, Mrs. Minio, who was our saving angel. She loved Andrew and would hold him and walk as he cried. She was so patient and kind. She was such a blessing in our lives. I'm sure she is in heaven and smiles now to see what a wonderful man Andrew has become.

Last visit with boys and Dad

Dad left this world in 1985 at the age of seventy-two by way of congestive heart failure. I still see him every day in so many ways and I miss him today as much as I did the day he died. I couldn't have been more blessed with any other father. So much of what I am came from him, and I try to live my life in a way that would make him proud.

ODE TO DAD

It's a feeling of fullness pulsing through me
It's kept me from sleeping
It's almost three thirty-three!
Barely an hour since
I went to bed
The energy's there
And it's moving the lead.
I can't stop the pencil
It has something to say
It wants to keep moving
It will have its own way

Journey to Life's Dance Ranch

Right now, it's just writing
The energy's there
The channel is open
There is spring in the air
I see a green meadow
With flowers in bloom
I smell the sweet fragrance
Of mountain perfume
I'm watching the sunlight
As it moves through the pines
I'm feeling the wind blow
It's not in my mind
It's happening somewhere
Or maybe it's not
Maybe it's nowhere...
Or some other spot
But I know it is real
I can feel the breeze
I can hear in the meadow
There's a lark with its song
The grass moves to and fro.

I'm there with my dad now
We're climbing the hill
We climb the next rise
And then to the top
He has something to tell me
When we come to a stop
...about something he was
When that something was Dad
But now he's stopped walking
He's crying instead
And I feel my own eyes

Chapter Seven

> AS THEY FILL UP WITH TEARS
> HE'S ALWAYS BEEN WITH ME
> AND HELPED THROUGH THE YEARS
> THOUGH HE LEFT IN THE WINTER
> AS MOST OF US WILL
> LIFE LASTS ONLY SO LONG
> 'TIL WE MEET THE GREAT STILL
>
> HE JUST WASN'T READY
> WHEN HIS TIME RAN ITS COURSE
> WHEN THE TRICKSTER LET GO
> WHEN HE LOST THE GREAT FORCE
> AND THOUGH HE LOVES "NOTHING"
> HE KNOWS HE MUST BE
> BE SOMETHING AGAIN
> 'TIL HE'S FINALLY SET FREE
> HE HAS TO COME BACK
> IN A PHYSICAL WAY
> I WANT HIM TO TELL ME
> BUT NOW HE WON'T SAY
> OH DAD, I MISS YOU SO
> THIS I KNOW YOU KNOW
> I DREAM OF THE DAYS WHEN
> WE'LL FLY KITES ONCE AGAIN

After our tour at Camp Pendleton, we moved to Bethesda where I had been accepted to do a residency in comprehensive dentistry. I was getting very little sleep, and often when I'd get home from school, Andrew would be crying and had been all day for Dana. Andrew would immediately reach out for Daddy. I spent many nights with Andrew lying on my chest, crying until it was time for me to go back to school, or until his eardrum would rupture. Once his ear would drain, he would stop crying and drop off to sleep. However, this lack of sleep was beginning to affect me in many ways. I was living in a constant state of sleep deprivation.

Finally, for the sake of Dana, Andrew and Patrick - and my own health and sanity as depression grabbed hold of me - I decided to withdraw from the residency program. The Commanding Officer at Bethesda brought me into his office and told me this would probably end any chance I would ever have to be promoted to a higher rank. I told him that may be the case, but my family needed me more right then. I was content to be a Lieutenant Commander in the Navy and let be what would be. Fortunately, the officer's harsh warning did not stop my career advancement over the years. I am not sure when I wrote this note to Dana, but I believe it was on her birthday during our difficult times at Bethesda, Md.

My Love,

For the beauty you bring my life each morning when I look across the pillow,

For the joy you always give …being such a good friend to come home to,

For the strength you have for both of us when I'm not strong enough myself,

For the patience and gentle love you constantly give to your three difficult boys,

For the CLASS which can't be taught or learned but which you have so naturally,

For the home which you keep so well and make such a wonderful beautiful place,

For the goodness, kindness and fairness which you give to us all,

For the way you see the world and help me when I need some common sense,

For that most precious gift….your trust……………………………………

I love you more than I am capable of saying,

Happy Birthday. Je T'Aime   Mike

Chapter Seven

Life teaches you lessons in many ways which can be humbling. We had the perfect child in Patrick. Andrew was a wonderful kid who took us through a long and difficult struggle early in his life. Patrick would continue to be a kind, gentle child and a good big brother. Andrew was wild, funny and fun. We were blessed in our boys – so different from each other, yet best friends to this very day.

I always tried to be a good father to our boys, but sometimes I would just screw up. I remember a time when Patrick was 2 1/2, we were stationed at Camp Pendleton, CA and lived in on base housing. Our house sat above a canyon where we would see deer, rabbits, rattlesnakes, road runners and coyotes. We had been warned about the coyote attacks on small dogs and even small children. Dana had an appointment in Oceanside and I was babysitting. The phone rang and I went to answer it. I was only gone a minute, but when I went back to Patrick's room where he had been playing, he wasn't there. I ran through the house calling for him, looking for him. He was nowhere to be found. What if he had gone outside! I ran out and looked around the house. What if coyotes had got him? I was starting to feel a frantic desperation. I ran back inside, searching with no success. Back outside I went, frantically calling Patrick's name. I searched everywhere, even looking in the canyon...no Patrick.

I ran back inside and again searched every room and closet in the house. I finally ended up in the Master bathroom and there in a little nook I had overlooked was Patrick. He had found a tube of toothpaste and emptied it on his hair and all over his face and shirt. I reacted poorly and scolded him for not answering me when I called. If I could only do it over, I'd tell him not to move, I'd get a camera and take a picture. I'd tell him toothpaste was for your teeth, not your hair. Then I'd give him a hug, tell him I loved him and put him in the bathtub to get cleaned up before Dana got home, or maybe leave him for Dana to see. She would have had a good laugh.

Journey to Life's Dance Ranch

PATRICK

HE WAS A GENTLE BABY
WITH THE GOODNESS OF HIS MOTHER
HE ALWAYS WALKED BEHIND
AND LOOKED OUT FOR HIS BROTHER

THE BROKEN BIRD
WOULD FIND HIS HAND
WITH LOVE'S EMBRACE
'TIL WING WOULD MEND

THEN GENTLY HE WOULD SET IT FREE
RELEASE IT TO ITS DESTINY
GIVE THANKS TO GOD FOR GIVING HIM
THE CHANCE TO HELP IT LIVE AGAIN

HIS EYE AND HEART COULD ALWAYS SEE
A NEED TO RESCUE... FROM MISERY
AND WITH HIS GENTLE GOODNESS CARE
BRING COMFORT THAT WAS NEEDED THERE

ON GUAM BEACH WITH DANA

PATRICK HOLDING ANDREW

BIRTH OF DANA'S BUTTERFLY

For her birthday on June 7th, 1984, I was inspired to design in wax and cast in some old dental school gold, a Butterfly pendant with three ballerinas in its wings and body. The dancers were not obvious to the eye at first, but once spotted by the viewer, they often gasped in delight. She was the only ballerina to wear it for over twenty years. Little did I know then, that this butterfly, or perhaps it was the soul of my creation, would change the course of my life many times over.

DANA'S ORIGINAL PENDANT

When we were serving our second tour at Camp Lejeune, N.C. and living on the base housing, a stray cat showed up one day. He was a beautiful yellow tabby, whom we named Sunshine because of his color and his personality. He was a very affectionate cat. Every evening when I would come home from work, he would be waiting. When I sat down on the front step to remove my boots, Sunshine would jump up in my lap for some loving! Dana was allergic to cats, so he was an outside cat, except at night, when we would put him in the garage and he would sleep on top of our Dodge Caravan. I'm not sure where or how he learned to give hugs, but one night I went out in the garage, saw him on top of the Van, and for some reason I said, "Come here Sunshine, give me a hug good night." To my utter surprise and delight, he came to me, put one paw on each of my shoulders and nuzzled me, then laid back down.

From that day forward, it became a nightly ritual to get a hug from Sunshine. Many people were delighted to see Sunshine give me my hug at night. We had Sunshine for only about a year before he developed cancer. He quit eating, was losing weight fast and though I tried feeding

him with a syringe he continued to decline. The vet had advised us that it was probably time to euthanize him. Dana and the boys were in Florida visiting her family. So, it was up to me to take him to the Vet, tell him I loved him, and tell him goodbye. Just like my little dog Cindy, I'll never forget the look in his eyes. Fortunately for me, I wasn't to see that look again, until a day or two before Dana died. I saw it in her eyes too. They all knew how much I loved them.

Kids and life can teach you so much if you just take time to watch and listen. And, sometimes give you a reason to laugh at your own naivety or stupidity. Such was the case one evening when I was babysitting the boys. Dana had asked me to give them a bath before putting them to bed. At the time, Andrew was three and Patrick six. Just after I got them in the tub the phone rang. Trouble can happen in life if you step away for even a moment. Just before I ran downstairs to get the phone, I made one of the dumbest statements of my life! I said, "Boys I'm going to answer the phone and when I get back, I don't want to see a drop of water on the floor!"

They must have thought I'd lost my mind. Anyway, I wasn't gone longer than a minute or two. When I got back to the boys, the floor was awash and the water level in the tub was down significantly. Once again, I reacted poorly with anger, rather than laughter. I told the boys. "OK, standup." Then I gave Patrick a very light swat on his bottom. His lip began to quiver and it looked as if he was going to cry. And then I gave Andrew the same swat. He quickly looked at his big brother and said, "That didn't hurt me!" We all laughed.

About the same time frame, Dana and I had taken the boys to the beach. I know they saw the same thing at the same time, but their reactions reflected their personalities. A buxom young woman in a small bikini passed by us revealing a thong bikini bottom and a lot of bottom. Patrick had no noticeable reaction, but Andrew's little head and eyes followed her as she walked on down the beach. After she was about 10 feet passed us, Andrew let out a big, "whoooeeee!" And so, it was with the boys, Andrew the wild bold little firecracker, Patrick a gentle caring big brother.

Chapter Seven

Patrick would on occasion tease his little brother, just to make him mad. He knew Andrew hated anyone walking ahead of him. Andrew always had to be in the lead and if Patrick got in front of him, Andrew would do anything to regain the lead spot. This actually became one of Andrew's defining characteristics. When Andrew was about six years old, we had signed up for a charity three-mile fun walk. Just before the start, an announcement came over the intercom that the runners should go to the starting line and would be sent off first followed by the walkers. Andrew, Patrick and a friend of Patrick's immediately asked if they could do the run. I initially said no, since we weren't really dressed to do the run, but the boys persisted, and I finally gave in. Knowing Andrew, I was sure he would go out as fast as he could, ahead of the pack, but would probably get a side ache in a hundred yards or so and then we would have to stop and walk.

I was exactly right. At the gun, he went out like a little rocket and after about a hundred yards or so, I could see he was hurting. I told him, "Andrew, we don't have to run all the way. We can stop and walk a bit and then we can run a bit." I'll never forget the look of determination on his face as he turned to me and said, "Dad, I'll never quit, never quit, I'll never quit!" and he never did. He kept running until he caught up with Patrick and his friend, ran by them, then ran past every other kid in the event and finished in first place.

As it turned out, Andrew didn't just love racing, he loved running, period. He wanted to compete in every 5K and 10K event we were near. Before we would start an event, he would go to the awards table to see what the prize was for placing first in his age group. Then he'd say. "Dad, I'm going to win that!" I would tell him not to be over confident, that he didn't have take first in every race. And he'd always say, "No Dad, I'm going to win it." And he always did. He continued to develop and get faster and finished his high school running career by winning two gold medals in Hawaii's State Track Championships and his high school's Athlete of the Year Award in 2003. He was recruited by a number of Division One schools including Tennessee, but eventually settled on the University of North Florida where he was given a full ride

athletic and academic scholarship with stipend. He did not disappoint UNF, becoming their track athlete of the year as a sophomore.

Both of our boys were born free spirits and having a Dad in the Navy with the military regimented lifestyle was probably difficult in many ways for both of them. They both moved to the tunes of different drummers, certainly different from any drummer I ever heard in Harlowton. While I did not understand this at the time, I now realize this was probably more so for our gentle strong older son. Andrew started his own regimentation when as a young boy he fell in love with running. He soon realized it took discipline and a certain amount of routine to achieve his goals. He loved the outdoors just like his older brother and Andrew found great freedom in running free and fast.

Patrick was an incredibly kind, gentle, strong big brother. He was always there for Andrew and for the most part set a wonderful example. Andrew wanted to be everything his big brother was and do everything Patrick did. Patrick was a brilliant student with an incredibly keen and inquisitive mind. He thought deeply but often kept his deepest thoughts to himself. In school, he was always top of his class in courses he had an interest in and middle of the class in subjects he found no merit in. He was and still is an exquisite physical specimen and a natural athlete in virtually every sport he tried.

However, though he was very fast he didn't care much for running. While he was an amazing tennis player, he too gave that up one day and walked away from the sport. His main interest in school was drafting, engineering and nature especially scuba diving and marine biology. He had little fear of anything and was confident in himself and his abilities. He and his little brother were great risk takers. The more challenging something was, the more they both wanted to do it and become the best at what they did.

Chapter Seven

HAWAIIAN DUTY

Perhaps our biggest mistake with Patrick was forcing him to move to Hawaii with us after he graduated from high school in 2000. He had done very well at Neese High in Jacksonville in a special Program that focused on engineering, drafting and Marine Biology. He wanted to stay in Florida with his high school friends and attend Florida Southern University and study Oceanographic Engineering. We didn't feel comfortable leaving him half a world away and after much coaxing he finally acquiesced and went with us. Hawaii Pacific University was a very fine expensive school with one of the best Oceanographic Engineering and Marine Biology programs in the country. He was accepted and decided to enroll in their Marine Biology program.

We got him settled in the dormitory with one of the most stunning views on the Island. He took a part time job at a local dive shop where he took all his dive certifications except one needed to become a Master Diver. I never felt safer than when I was diving with Patrick. No matter what went wrong, he was always cool as a cucumber and never flustered. We assumed he was attending classes and doing fine in school. Unfortunately, at the end of his first semester his grades told us a different story. We then found out he had been diligently studying Marine Biology from the top of a surfboard or diving under the deep blue sea. Though his grades were poor, he had become an accomplished surfer.

Dana and I decided to give him one more semester to get his education act together, and he did...he became an even better surfer! Faced with his poor performance at Hawaii Pacific and lack of desire to do anything but surf, we decided it was time for him to have his way and go back to Jacksonville where he could go to work and hang with some of his high school buddies. We got him set up in an apartment, helped him with a used car, told him he would need to maintain automobile and health insurance and he was on his own.

SON GOES

HE WAS THE FIRST TO LEAVE THEM
FROM THEIR LIVES...TO DEPART
HE HAD TO MAKE HIS OWN WAY
BUT IT TORE HIS PARENT'S HEART
HIS MOTHER FELT SHE'D LOST HER SON
HIS DAD SAID... "HE'LL BE FINE"
FOR HE HAS HIS MOTHER'S NATURE
AND A LITTLE BIT OF MINE

Our flight back to Hawaii was lonesome and difficult, even though we knew he was working two or three jobs, all minimum wage. He soon found out that minimum wage was not really that, with taxes, social security and other automatic deductions. None of his jobs had any benefits or real potential for advancement. As parents we both felt we had failed him in some way.

I remember the morning Patrick called from Jacksonville at four in the morning. He said, "Dad, turn on your TV, one of the Trade Center buildings in New York has been hit by an airliner." We turned on the TV just in time to see another plane fly into the second building and watch both buildings go down.

After 9-11 the economy went bad everywhere, Jacksonville was no exception. Patrick had been the last person hired just months earlier and so was the first to be let go. Things got tough for him. Shortly after his jobs went away, he called Dana and told her he didn't have a job and he was just about out of money. Dana was expecting him to ask for money and perhaps a ticket back to Hawaii. But then he said, "And Mom, I have joined the Coast Guard." We were totally taken aback but were immensely proud of him for taking responsibility for his own life and happy he had joined the Coast Guard. He continued to make us proud as he has become a kind generous man, a hard-working and devoted husband and father to his beautiful family. And yes, he is still the gentle giant of goodness to us and his little brother.

FLICK FAMILY

One can choose whom he or she will marry but you don't get to choose the family that comes with the marriage. With Dana and my Annie Z, I could not have asked for better families to marry into. Dana's family are all very smart and extremely talented in the arts. Dana's dad, Bob, is a retired Emeritus English professor, her Mom Annie, a retired art teacher, brother Guy, a talented vocalist and pianist, sister Belinda, a theater arts and accomplished potter, and brother Dan, another musician, recording artist and teacher at Rollins College.

GREAT YEARS WITH THE FLICK FAMILY

For thirty-nine years I have been blessed to enjoy their friendship, goodness, talent and generosity. Dana and I always enjoyed getting together for family visits in Winter Park, FL or having family come visit us where ever our Navy travels would take us. I was very happy that we were all able to get together enough to have our children and those of Dana's sibling's children spend many wonderful formative times together. Dana and Belinda were very close.

 *Journey to Life's Dance Ranch*

Belinda's husband, Tom Glennon, another extremely smart musician and computer specialist, played acoustic base for several symphonies on the East and West coast. They had three beautiful girls, Kaitlyn and Kerry, talented vocalists and Kelsey, a ballerina.

Guy and his wife Annalee had two beautiful children, Robert Nichole, also very talented in the musical arts. Dan is a professional musician, playing violin, viola, guitar and virtually anything with strings. He is an exceptional teacher and has his own recording studio. Dana and I also felt blessed to have her Grandma, Ida and Grandpa Guy and Grandma Docia with us so we and all the children could enjoy those dear people. Suffice it say that our time with the Flick side of the family gave us much joy and many happy times together and still does.

Chapter Eight
Ovarian Cancer Changed Our Lives

Some moments in life you never forget. 9-11 was one horrendous day, branded into the heart, mind and soul of Americans across the country. We were no different in this regard. I also experienced another event, where the hot iron burned my heart and mind with such devastation and vivid detail. As I reflect back, I can still feel the burning embers and need to catch my breath. At the end of August in 2003, I received a phone call from Dana at four a.m., in my room at the Bachelor Officer Quarters, Kaneohe Bay, Hawaii. Dana and Andrew had left the island early to get back to our house in Jacksonville, receive our household goods shipment, get the house set up and get Andrew ready for college. I had stayed behind to do a turnover of my position as Marine Forces Pacific Dental Officer with my replacement. I was due to fly back to the mainland in just a few days. We had our Dodge Caravan shipped to Seattle and the plan was for Dana to fly there and meet me. We would pick up the van and then take several weeks to drive back to Jacksonville stopping along the way to see family, friends and this beautiful country of ours.

When I answered the call a man on the other end said he was calling from the Naval Hospital, Naval Air Station, Jacksonville, FL. He said my wife was there and needed to talk with me before they could release her. She took the phone and was crying as she told me she had gone for a follow-up visit to one she'd had just three months earlier. At the previous visit she received news that an MRI, taken of her abdomen, showed no signs of pathosis. She was given a clean bill of health but told she should have a follow-up visit in three months if the symptoms she had persisted.

The symptoms had persisted and included bloating, an unusual feeling in her pelvic area, a feeling she wasn't able to eat as much as she used to yet she was gaining weight. She also had a constant feeling that she had a urinary tract infection but when checked, didn't. I could feel her tears and mine as she told me they were quite certain she had advanced ovarian cancer. I couldn't believe it. I didn't want to believe it. She had had the symptoms for over a year. She had done everything right. She had gone to her primary care physician who had sent her for a plethora of tests. The only abnormality found had been diagnosed as an ovarian cyst which she was told would probably go away after menopause.

Her MRI report three months earlier was said to be clear...no evidence of cancer or abnormality. My head was spinning, how could this be? I told her how much I loved her, that we would get through this together and things would be ok; that I would talk with my commanding general and be on the soonest flight off the island home. As I hung up the feeling of desperation was greater than any I had ever experienced. I was praying to God that a mistake had been made, but deep down knew we were in serious trouble.

The bottom was dropping out of my life. The love of my life was in trouble and I was halfway around the world unable to hold her, to support her. I had so much to do before I could leave for home. Overwhelmed, I got dressed and packed all my stuff into the rental car. I cleared my room so it could be inspected before I left. I had a portable air-conditioning unit I had to remove from the window. I had promised to give it to a friend when I left. I carried it down three sets of steps and as I set it down outside, I remember cutting my hand and thinking I can't take this right now. I tore a piece off the tee-shirt and tied it around the cut. I headed to the BOQ office to let them know I had vacated and why. They said don't worry about the inspection, consider yourself passed, just go do what you need to do so you can get home.

It was probably around 5:30 a.m. as I got in the car and drove across the island to Pearl Harbor and up the hill to Camp Smith where

Chapter Eight

I worked. Things were becoming surreal and I was struggling to think of all the things I had to do before I could leave the command. I believe my first move was to inform the Chief of Staff and ask him if the General was in and if I could see him. He said yes, he was, and he took me right to him. I can't even begin to say how kind the General, Chief of Staff and all my fellow staff officers were. The General told me to do whatever I needed to get home as soon as I could, everything would be taken care of and I would be detached from the command that day.

I remember I went back to my office to let my replacement know I would be leaving. That day, his kindness was overwhelming. As I recall, I then went down to the administrative office to do needed paperwork, turn in my electronic badges and top-secret clearance. They had orders for me, checked me out on leave and I was finished with Camp Smith except to say goodbye to my fellow officers, enlisted Marines and Sailors, all friends. Before I left, I had to thank each of them for the privilege of serving with them. We had gone through 9-11 and two wars with each other and I admired and respected all of them enormously. The compassion and kindness I received that day before I was able to leave is something for which I will never be able to thank them enough.

After I left the command, I went to the airport and asked for the earliest flight and best connection to Jacksonville. The earliest flight wasn't until the next day. I purchased a ticket, got back in my car full of stuff and headed for the BOQ at Pearl Harbor. I was able to get a room for the night. The car was loaded to the top. I went to the nearest UPS store, got four big boxes and packed all the stuff in the car for shipment to Jacksonville. I don't remember for sure but I think after that I went back to Makalapa, the base housing area where we had lived and still had friends to say goodbye but I can't be sure.

I barely remember going back to my BOQ room and remember nothing else, not even getting to the airport, or the flight to Seattle or the long layover. I don't remember getting to Jacksonville, what time, what day or even meeting Dana (and Andrew?) at the airport, though I know I did. The earliest memories I can bring back now are of being with Dana in a hospital exam room with Dana's oncologist surgeon, Doctor Benrubi, at Shands Hospital. He had another MRI done on Dana and had performed a physical exam. To our relief he said he didn't believe it was ovarian cancer!

His palpations had been of a somewhat soft mass and with ovarian cancer he would have expected a much firmer mass. He said he couldn't tell for sure and needed to see the MRI first but felt pretty certain this was not ovarian cancer. This was a Tuesday. He said he would have the results back by Thursday and had an appointment made for us that day. Dana and I left the hospital with a great sense of relief. On Thursday when we returned, Dr. Benrubi's news robbed us of our newly found hope. He said he had read the MRI results and was now certain that Dana had a large ovarian cancer tumor and she would need surgery as soon as possible.

We both felt like we had been kicked in the stomach. We had gone from the highest high with hope to the desperate and helpless feeling when you or a loved one is told you have cancer. Here again, my memory disappears until I see myself sitting in the waiting room outside the surgery suite with family members, I think just Dana's family. But then, I don't think anyone else would have been able to get to Jacksonville. I'm thinking the surgery was just a day or so after we saw Dr. Benrubi, but I just don't remember. I do remember praying in the waiting room that Dr. Benrubi would come out of surgery with some good news.

As he came through the door into the waiting room, he came directly to me and said Dana had stage IV ovarian cancer that he was able to get most of it but some was inoperable. He was hoping chemo would take care of the rest. He also told me prognosis for stage IV ovarian cancer was not good, often less than three years. He put Dana on an immediate course of chemotherapy, her first session in the hospital and then every three weeks for six months, maybe a year – I just don't remember. What I do remember are the drives to Shand's

Chapter Eight

Hospital climbing the stairs to the Chemotherapy Unit, Dana lying down in one of the recliners, having IVs started and waiting for her chemo bags to arrive from the lab. She was given meds for nausea and some to help her relax or sleep during the three hour chemo sessions.

I remember the other ladies who were there as well, some alone some with husbands or families. All of us were hoping beyond hope this treatment would cure and save our loved ones. A nurse named Rita Carstens was one of the kindest, most supportive persons I've ever known and was an enormous help to all in her care in the Chemo Suite. Thank God she was there to help us through the process. They told us after that first session, that Dana would feel pretty good for about twenty-four hours and then she would start feeling the ill effects of the chemo. They suggested if there was any specific meal she would like, to go ahead and have it ready because she wouldn't feel like eating, once she started feeling the chemo effects.

The effects started mid-afternoon the next day. Though they had given her anti-nausea medication, she was still so sick and uncomfortable for the first couple of days that she mainly just stayed in bed and ate little or nothing. Then she would start coming out of it and want something to eat. We soon learned there were very few things she could stomach. She wanted a specific soup from Panera's and she could tolerate mashed potatoes. From then on when she would go through a chemo session, I was always ready to make a trip to Panera's or make mashed potatoes for her.

Perhaps one of the most difficult parts of going through chemo happened after the second session. She had not lost any hair to that point. She had just come through the session, was feeling better and felt the need to wash her hair. Dana always washed her hair in the bathroom sink. I just happened to walk by the bathroom and saw her standing in front of the mirror crying, holding a wad of hair in her hand. I went in, put my arms around her, told I loved her and she was just as beautiful as ever to me. She decided it was time to shave what was left of her hair, put a head scarf on and go to a wig shop. We went together

and found a couple of wigs that looked pretty good. She hated wearing a wig. She found wigs hot and uncomfortable and didn't really like the looks of them either. She bought some scarfs and chemo caps she wore around the house.

With each successive treatment, the recovery got longer and more difficult. By her last session it was taking almost a week for her to get through it. She never complained but she did try to think of what she might have done in her life that could have caused her cancer and how it could have been missed. Until her cancer diagnosis, Dana, without question, was and still is the healthiest person I have ever known. Aside from one day with flu-like symptoms, early in our marriage, she was never sick.

The boys and I would get sick but Dana never did. She never even had a cold. She was a terrific cook and made sure we had healthful, delicious meals beautifully prepared and served every day. She took great care of us and herself. She was a beautiful woman who kept herself in perfect physical condition with her dance and other exercise. She lived the perfect healthy life. She did love her dark chocolate and I would buy her boxes of Giardelli dark chocolate wafers. Her self-control was amazing. She never had more than one, maybe two wafers a day, usually at night after dinner.

She didn't want me or anyone seeing her with her bald head. I told her she was just as beautiful to me with a bald head as ever and if she was more comfortable going bald, I was fine with that. She would have none of it and even slept with a light sleeping cap until her hair started coming in after her last chemo session. When her hair did come back in, it came in very curly and beautiful salt and pepper color. Still, it was several months before she felt it was long enough to go without a scarf or wig.

All through finding out about the cancer, her surgery, chemo and recovery, I only saw Dana cry once and that was when her hair was coming out. I had made a promise to myself that I would not cry in front

Chapter Eight

of Dana. I felt I had to be strong for her and not have her worrying about me. I did cry though, almost every day. I would go for long runs, often ten miles or more and when I could run no more, I would walk home and cry. I imagine Dana knew. She probably saw it in my eyes, but she never said anything and neither did I. It was my coping mechanism for dealing with the intolerable hurt of seeing the love of my life go through hell. It was something I could do when I felt there was nothing I could do. It was my place to grieve.

REMISSION RELIEF

After she finished her rounds of chemo, her follow-up exams and MRIs showed no signs of cancer, thank God, she was in remission. She still had to go in for frequent exams and CA-125 blood draws but for now she was in remission. We knew what we had to do, live every day as if it were our last. And we did. It was an absolutely joyous time. We made love, made trips and rejoiced in each other.

One thing that brought Dana great comfort and peace was meeting Lizzie and Tessa. When Dana and I found out Patrick, who was in the Coast Guard in Ohio, was living with his girlfriend and his girlfriend's three-year-old daughter, we were both concerned to say the least. We called and talked to Patrick and he said we should come to Ohio and meet them. Dana was in remission from her cancer and was feeling well, so we made a trip to go see Patrick, this girlfriend and her daughter. On the drive from Jacksonville, Dana and I both talked about what we might find when we got to their apartment. When we were just outside of Lorain, Ohio, we called Patrick and he told us to meet them in a parking lot outside a restaurant.

When we got there and they were getting out of their car, we saw our son with this beautiful Indian maiden and her beautiful Indian daughter. The minute we met them we knew it was right. They said we were going to watch Tessa perform in a pre-school show after which we would go to a favorite restaurant for dinner. It was a perfect night.

Dana and I fell in love with Lizzie and Tessa, and Dana welcomed the possibility of a grand-daughter. We watched Patrick teaching Tessa to ride a bike and seeing Patrick and Lizzie being such good parents for Tessa, we were ready to head back to Jacksonville. But, before we left, I took Patrick aside.

I told him how impressed we were with Lizzie and what we hoped would be our first granddaughter. I told him this little girl was calling him Daddy and if he was really in love with Lizzie, he should give them the protections and benefits of the Coast Guard by marrying Lizzie and adopting Tessa. Patrick never really enjoyed taking advice from his father, to say the least. But this time, God bless him, he did the right thing. They were married by a clerk of court on August 5, 2005 and were planning a wedding ceremony to be held in Alaska exactly one year from their initial wedding date. We were ecstatic and so proud of them. Dana finally had the grand-daughter and daughter-in-law she had always hoped for.

From that wonderful visit we went to Charleston, Illinois to see where Dana was born. To Chicago to see our dear Guam friends, the Smith's, to Iowa to see my sister Marcy and her husband Kelly, then to Louisiana to see our best friends, Maria and Chuck Fairchild. Finally, we were back home in Jacksonville enjoying our beautiful home on the golf course. Life was as good as it had ever been. Dana was thrilled with Lizzie and Tessa. We had made plans to go back to Ohio for Christmas. Lizzie's family was coming from Ketchikan, Alaska and we were excited to be meeting them for the first time.

Back in Jacksonville, we were able to attend all of Andrew's collegiate track meets and get to know his track buddies. We were also able to make frequent trips to Winter Park for special family events or just to see our loved ones there. The year of remission that Dana and I had was as wonderful a time together as we had ever experienced. Life couldn't have been better.

Chapter Eight

RELAPSE

Through her first surgery and chemo treatments, Dana continued to encourage me to finish my career in the Navy which meant four more years. After Dana went into remission, she continued with that sentiment. We were so much enjoying her being in remission and back in good health. I decided I would go ahead and retire early so I could be with Dana full time. I was granted permission to retire early and we set the date for October 1, 2005. We were having a wonderful time together and though the worry of remission was always there it is amazing how much you can put that out of your minds and feel certain you would have a long healthy life ahead of you.

At that time some of my "widow maker," heart issues surfaced. I had tests which revealed I needed a bypass. I had an appointment with my cardiologist to talk about the timing for the surgery and Dana and I were going to see him on a Friday. We did go to my cardio appointment and the cardiologist said he had scheduled my surgery for the following Tuesday. Dana just happened to have her routine CA-125 blood test the Tuesday before and on Thursday when the results came back her numbers were elevated. Dr. Benrubi wanted to see her the following week to do a physical exam and perhaps order another MRI. We were both very concerned that her cancer may be back. My immediate reaction was to tell my cardiologist there was no way I could have surgery the following Tuesday; Dana's CA-125 was up and if her cancer was back, I couldn't be in a compromised state if she had to go through more treatment. My heart surgery would just have to wait until we learned more about Dana's condition. Fortunately for me the cardiologist ran more tests and decided the situation was not as serious as it had looked on the angiogram and because of my extensive history of distance running, I had excellent collateral heart blood circulation.

I wrote the following note to Dana just before we found out her cancer was back. As I read the words, I realize I was just repeating what she had said to me so many times.

> Sweetheart,
> As we await the results of our next CA125 test and experience all the stresses and anxieties that go with it, know that I am with you always. No matter the results, we can continue to live, to love and to deal with this part of our lives together. Every moment with you is a precious gift for me. We must continue to enjoy the goodness that life still sends us and never dwell on our difficulties (easy for me to say, huh?). But even without the threat of a shorter life expectancy with cancer, life is too short not to enjoy the good times when they are there and to live the life we are given to its fullest. I love you in sickness and health more than I can say. You are and always will be the <u>BEST</u> part of my life.
>
>   Mike

The following week we went to see Dr. Benrubi and his exam revealed a new abdominal mass. It was an emotionally devastating moment. He ordered more tests and in less than a week Dana was going into surgery to have two thirds of her liver removed. Dr. Benrubi had more bad news for us. The tumor had metastasized not only to her liver, but to her diaphragm and parts of her spine, both inoperable areas. It was back to chemo as our only chance to overcome her cancer. She was started immediately on a regimen identical to what had knocked the cancer down before. It soon became apparent that this regimen was no longer effective except at causing hair loss. Dr. Benrubi said it was time to try a new but more toxic form of chemotherapy. We were thrilled when the new chemo seemed to be working and her hair started growing back. We began preparing for my retirement ceremony.

Chapter Eight

DANA'S TWO BEST FRIENDS, MARIA AND JEANNIE,
GAVE JOY AND SUPPORT THROUGHOUT

RETIREMENT

The wonderful dental officers of the Navy Dental Center at Naval Air Station Jacksonville were incredibly helpful in the planning and execution of the retirement and reception. They also purchased as their gift to me a stunning traditional retirement shadowbox displaying my different ranks achieved, my awards, our various duty stations and my Navy sword. The event was flawless and beautiful, full of US Navy military tradition. Dana was there looking as beautiful as ever, however, she was not happy she had to wear a wig since she was still going through chemo. Patrick was in his Coast Guard Uniform with Lizzie and

Tessa. Andrew was in his Air Force Cadet Uniform. I was so proud and thankful for all of them and their enormous contributions to my Navy career.

I was particularly thankful that the two Dental Officers I had most admired throughout my career, Admiral Lewis Libby and his lovely wife Sarah and our best Navy friends Captain Chuck Fairchild and wife Maria, agreed to speak for my final Navy ceremony. All my family had flown in from Montana and Iowa and Dana's Florida family were all there as well. We also had many dear friends we had made over the years show up for my ceremony. I must say I was overwhelmed with emotion. Upon retiring from the Navy, I also let go of my "Titles." No longer would I be called Captain or Doctor. I just wanted to be Montana Mike and focus all my attention on the love of my life.

NAVY FAMILY

We had so many dear friends we met in the Navy the following are just a few pictures of our dearest friends.

Chapter Eight

SHADOW BOX & SWORD

ADMIRAL LEWIS LIBBY & WIFE SARAH

DANA & MIKE WITH DEAREST NAVY FRIENDS, CHUCK & MARIA FAIRCHILD

Dear friends who weren't able to make the retirement but added so much to our Navy lives included the Carlson's, the Brandt's, the Lynch's, the Certosimo's, the Kitslar's, the Wagner's, the Skipper's, the Gottstein's, the Canaans and many others. We were so blessed in our Navy family.

DEAR FRIENDS, BETTY ROGERS, CARMEN MESA, DARIN ROGERS & NATALIE ROGERS

FARLEY & MERCEDES SIMON WITH ANDREW

JOHN & ALLISON LEWIS

DANA & I ON FORD ISLAND, HAWAII CELEBRATING PEARL HARBOR DAY WITH CHUCK & MARIA FAIRCHILD, MARIA'S MOTHER CARMEN & GOOD FRIEND KENT KNUDSEN

Chapter Eight

After retirement we faced a cruel reality. The chemo knocked Dana's immune and blood numbers so low she would have to discontinue chemo, until her numbers came back to a level where they were allowed to give it to her again. As I remember, this usually took about a month. Fortunately, this new chemo didn't make Dana as ill. However, each time she would get the chemo again, her numbers would go lower and it would take her longer to recover and get her blood numbers up again. Dana's chemo was not working and we were running out of possible chemo options. Our cruise around South America and Patrick and Lizzie's up-coming wedding ceremony in Alaska were the positives we tried to focus on.

OCEAN CRUISE

We had planned a two-week ocean cruise around South America with our best friends Chuck and Maria Fairchild and some other great Navy friends, Marty and Carla Gottstein. It was March 2006. Dana knew she would have to stop chemo if she were to go on the cruise and risk life threatening infection because of her depressed immune system. She didn't hesitate and made the decision to make the trip. I was worried sick and to make matters worse I was the one who got sick and had to stay in our hotel room for a couple of days while we waited to board the cruise liner. I was also the first person to the ship's sick bay for treatment.

I completely broke down in front of the physician and told him how afraid I was that I would give Dana what I had. I spent the first few days in our state room too sick to go out. Finally, I got over it and was able to join our group. Ironically, half the people on the ship got sick with something but Dana never did. Aside from her cancer, she never got even the slightest cold and such was her life until the end. The cruise turned out to be everything we could have asked for including a time of the highest seas the cruise liner had ever experienced. Most people were sea sick but not Dana or me and we truly enjoyed our time even with the rough seas.

Journey to Life's Dance Ranch

KARLA & MARTY GOTTSTEIN, CHUCK & MARIA FAIRCHILD, DANA & MIKE ENJOYING DINNER ON OUR SOUTH AMERICAN CRUISE

Once we got back to Jacksonville, we knew what we were in for, more chemo. Dana's blood numbers had recovered and she was restarted. Unfortunately, her blood numbers went low more quickly and she had to come off the chemo sooner and sooner. Finally, Dr. Benrubi told us it was no longer doing any good and there were no other courses of action. Then I could no longer keep my promise to not cry in front of Dana. Dr. Benrubi told us there was nothing else that could be done; we had perhaps a month left and we should get things in order. As we looked at each other and took one another into each other's arms, for the first time together, we both cried. It was the most helpless either of us had ever felt. The reality of what was coming was overwhelming.

Chapter Eight

ALASKA WEDDING

We were both discouraged when all chemo and treatment was discontinued but Dana had another mission which I really believe kept her from dying sooner; Patrick and Lizzie's wedding ceremony in Alaska. She had promised to do all the flowers for the wedding and she didn't want to miss the ceremony or the reception. Maria flew in to be with her and help her find the right dress for the occasion. They found the perfect dress the first store they shopped in. It was a beautiful pink dress that fit Dana perfectly and she looked gorgeous in it.

We flew into Ketchikan a couple days early so we could tour the island and Dana could make needed arrangements for the wedding flowers and reception centerpieces. No one there would have ever suspected that Dana had terminal cancer and was suffering greatly. But when she got back to the hotel room in the evenings she would collapse. I really don't know how she was able summon the strength to put up a happy façade but I do know she did out of her love for Patrick and Lizzie. Dana's family also flew out for the wedding and were a great support always.

Lizzie's father, Joe, is a highly respected member of the Tlingit Indian Tribe in Ketchikan, Alaska. Lizzie's mother, Susie, is an Irish/Scottish nurse and teacher. Lizzie is a beautiful mix of the two cultures. Lizzie's father, Joe, petitioned the Tlingit tribe to allow Patrick and Lizzie to be married on the beach at the original Tlingit settlement site on the Alaska mainland. There had not been a ceremony of any kind there for over 120 years. Joe was granted permission and preparations began for the big event. Joe secured a large catamaran which held about 150 people to transport the wedding party and guests from Ketchikan Island to the mainland settlement site. When we arrived, we were ferried in small skiffs to the beach.

 *Journey to Life's Dance Ranch*

Chapter Eight

It was a misty cool day. The kids were dressing for the wedding in a tent on the beach; Lizzie in her stunning doeskin dress with black beaded raven on back (made by her mother) and Patrick in his white linen suit. Both were barefoot. Joe was in full Indian regalia, walking with wooden staff with bald eagle feathers. Just before the ceremony started the clouds parted and the sun shined brightly on all of us. Andrew was Patrick's best man and Lizzie's brothers were groomsmen. I believe everyone there found this wedding to be one of the most spiritual magical events they ever were blessed to be part of. After the ceremony, Lizzie's brothers took all the guests around the site to see the original foundations and where many Totem poles once stood.

After the tour it was time to reboard the catamaran and head back to Ketchikan for the reception. Joe and his son, Joe Joe, were the last to leave. Where there had been sun for the wedding, the clouds and mist were once again closing in on us. As Joe lifted his staff and walked for the skiff, a feather rose from the sand behind him and climbed upward riding on the new breeze. I remember it sent chills up and down my spine as I watched. As Joe and Joe Joe boarded the catamaran a soft light rain began falling. Beautiful, just beautiful, every bit of the ceremony, pure magic.

At the reception, Dana visited with everyone, danced with Lizzie's father, with me and with our boys. It would end up being the very last time I would dance with my Dana. It was just impossible to comprehend that our beautiful life's dance may be coming to an end. Her stunning floral designs graced every

OUR LAST DANCE TOGETHER WAS AT PATRICK AND LIZZIE'S WEDDING

table and her joyful presence brightened the room. No one ever suspected the suffering she was enduring or that her life would soon be ending. I really believe that once she made it through the wedding, Dana was at peace and ready to be home and get ready to go to the other side. For me the last weeks were some of the most difficult but also a time I felt it was my greatest privilege that she wanted me to be there and let her go.

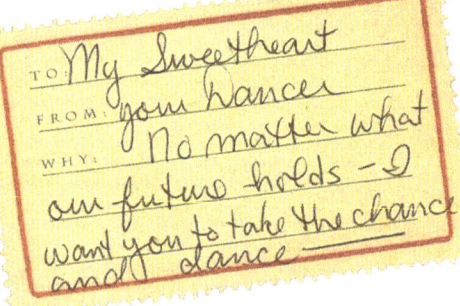

TO: My Sweetheart
FROM: your Dancer
WHY: No matter what our future holds – I want you to take the chance and dance

THE FINAL CURTAIN

Dana was an incredibly unselfish and thoughtful person. Shortly before she died, she asked me to sit down with her. She had a gift she wanted to give me. It was a book with the lyrics and a CD with Leanne Womack's beautiful song, "I Hope You Dance." She told me I had too much love not to love again. She wanted me to take the chance, love again, and dance.

Perhaps one of the most difficult times during Dana's illness happened just a couple of weeks before she died. I took her to the emergency room at Shand's Hospital where she was treated for her cancer because she was bloated with fluid, so uncomfortable, and had started having black stools the sign of internal bleeding. It was a Friday night. They told us the physician who could do the procedure to drain the fluid off Dana's abdomen would not be in until Monday morning. I was frantic, livid and felt completely helpless. Dana was admitted to Shand's Hospital where we suffered what was to be the most brutal and longest three days of our lives. Finally, the physician was there and able to drain many liters of fluid from Dana's abdomen. With Dana's intense discomfort relieved by the draining, she quickly fell asleep. Her mom and dad had come to the hospital to stay with Dana while I drove back home to shower, eat and try to get some rest.

Chapter Eight

It had been four full days since Dana or I had slept. I had never felt such a state of exhaustion. As I was driving home, I called my friend Darin Rogers, who was the Administrator for the Naval Hospital at Naval Air Station Jacksonville, and asked him if he could arrange to have Shands move Dana to a private room. I could barely talk and I remember him asking me if I was going to be able to make it home alright. I told him I only had about three miles and I felt sure I could make it. Thank God I did. When I got home, Andrew was there and immediately said, "Dad are you OK?" I told him I thought I just might need something to eat since I had not eaten for four days.

Andrew took me to the kitchen table, sat me down and then went to make me a sandwich. When he brought me the sandwich, I could no longer function, I really didn't know what to do with the sandwich. Andrew was saying, "Dad, Dad you need to eat the sandwich" but I couldn't move. He grabbed me, helped me to the bedroom and lifted me into bed. All I remember is closing my eyes and my brain exploding in what seemed to be the most intense electric storm I had ever seen. It must have gone on for a half hour or more before I was able to open my eyes and start thinking again. I got up, took a shower and put on fresh clothes. When I came out into the kitchen, Andrew was there and asked me. "Dad are you OK?" I told him I was going back to the hospital and I'd be OK. He said, "Dad, can I drive you?" And I told him no, I had to go alone.

When I got to the hospital Dana was in a private room. I'll always be eternally grateful to my friend, Darin Rogers, for making that happen. I know he had to pull some strings for me. There was a chair next to Dana's bed which folded down into a sleeping couch. I folded it down, grabbed her sleeping hand and fell into a deep sleep. When I awoke Dana was smiling at me feeling better and wanting to go home. I can't even think of that time, even now, without crying.

It was exactly three weeks after Dana gave me her "I hope you dance" message that my beautiful ballerina slipped away to the other side, after ovarian cancer ravished her body, but never her spirit. I had

not cried again until just before Dana died and I felt her starting to grow cold, then with a last gasp it was over. It was 3:00 a.m. I held her in my arms and cried, Patrick soon came in the bedroom and laid down next to me. He put his arm around me and his mother and sobbed as well. I don't remember how long we grieved there, but finally came the time when we knew we had to get up and face the reality of what had just happened.

I had gone with my Dana to that curtain that leads to the other side and held her in my arms as she slipped off our life's stage onto the next. The love of my life had died and a deep darkness was setting into my soul. Andrew walked around to the others in the house expressing concern for the welfare of his father. He was wondering how I would survive this great loss. I was wondering the same thing.

I don't know what I would have done without the help of my sister, Marcy, who came to help the week before Dana died and the boys who were there to give support at that most difficult time. Dana's family had been to see Dana a few days earlier to tell her they loved her and tell her goodbye. As soon as she passed Marcy called Bob and Ann and they immediately came to Jacksonville to give their support. When Ann got there, she and I went in the bedroom, washed Dana, dressed her and brushed her hair. She looked so beautiful and peaceful I just didn't want to let her go.

It was ten o'clock that morning when the mortuary people showed up. Before they took her, we gathered around the bed and Marcy led us in a prayer and a reading of scripture that was on a card Dana was sent by my mom's best friend, Joan Mattingly. The bible passage was Philippians 4:6&7. It wasn't until weeks later that I found Dana's Bible. I had not remembered Dana even had a Bible. The Bible had been given by her dear friend, Vicki Lynn back in 1977. Vicki Lynn had noted Philippians 4:6&7 in her note to Dana in the front of the Bible.

"Don't worry about anything; instead, pray about everything; tell God your needs and don't forget to thank Him for his answers. If you do you will experience God's peace, which is far more wonderful

Chapter Eight

than the human mind can understand. His peace will keep your thoughts and your hearts quiet and at rest as you trust in Jesus Christ."

Vicki Lynn did not know when Dana died but called the morning of her death to say she awoke to an incredible vision of Dana in a brilliant light and with joy like she had never seen before. The time she awoke, 3 am.

There were many wonderful family members and friends who gave us constant love and support through the difficult three-year ordeal. I can never thank Dana's family, my family, our friends Chuck and her best friend, Maria (the last person Dana talked to), Jeannie Edwards, Darin and Betty Rogers, Lou and Sarah Libby, our Jacksonville neighbors who brought daily meals to me for a month and gave constant loving support, and so many others who were there to carry us through those most difficult times. Andrew as always was hovering over me too.

ANDREW

HE KNEW HOW MUCH I LOVED HER
FOR HE SO LOVED HER TOO
HE GRIEVED UPON HER PASSING
BUT HAD SOMETHING HE MUST DO
MUST TELL THEM HE DIDN'T KNOW
IF HIS DAD COULD MAKE IT THROUGH
HE BEGGED THEM HELP HIS FATHER
THIS WAS HIS SON ... ANDREW
TO HELP HIM WITH HIS FEAR
HE KNEW HE COULDN'T LEAVE HIM
FOR HE HAD SEEN HIS FATHER
IN A PLACE WHERE NO LIGHT SHINED
IN A STATE OF DESPERATE SORROW
HE WATCHED HIM LOSE HIS MIND
HE HAD TO HELP HIS FATHER GRIEVE
TO STAY AS LONG AS NEEDED
AND WHEN THE OTHERS HAD TO LEAVE
HE KNEW THAT HE COULD NOT...

 *Journey to Life's Dance Ranch*

….and so, this beautiful boy stayed with his dad and they grieved together for what was such a major love and force in their lives… now gone. Andrew had been the little helper who shadowed his mother. He learned to cook, sew, rug latch, water color paint, write and sing from his mother. She gave him dance, color, movement and an appreciation of music and the arts. Andrew's reflection of his mother in what he did and what he became - an incredibly good, talented, intelligent, considerate man - helped his father immensely through his darkest hours. The gratitude and love of a father for a son who has stayed with him through periods of insanity and lifted him up at a time when no one else could have can't be put in words. Suffice it to say, in many ways, I owe him my life.

Marcy stayed on for another month and helped me more than I can ever thank her for. I'll always be thankful to her husband Kelly and their children who so graciously and lovingly encouraged her to be with me. Patrick, Lizzie and Tessa had gone back to Ohio, and Andrew back to school in Tallahassee. When Marcy left, I finally felt the intense darkness and loneliness of being without my soul mate. I believe those who experience such a great love are then destined to experience a great loss and grief. I was in the darkest period of my life. It took hold of me for several months.

MARCY

BORN TO BE TOGETHER, OR IN CLOSE PROXIMITY
A BROTHER AND A SISTER WITH A COMMON DESTINY
BORN TO DO SOME GOODNESS, TOGETHER OR APART
BORN WITH SEPARATE BODIES,
JOINED WITH THE SAME HEART

Chapter Eight

HE'LL WANT HER THERE

WHEN DEATH BROUGHT BLINDNESS TO HIS LIFE
AND STABBED HIS SOUL, AND TOOK HIS WIFE
HE KNEW SHE'D COME AND HELP HIM THROUGH
HE KNEW SHE'D KNOW JUST WHAT TO DO
HE KNEW SHE'D BEEN THERE OFT BEFORE
AND NOW HE NEEDED HER ONCE MORE
AND SO HE CALLED AND ASKED HER FOR
WHAT ONLY SHE COULD GIVE
AND IN AN INSTANT, SHE WAS THERE
HIS SISTER BROUGHT HER LOVE AND CARE
AND WITH A STRENGTH BEYOND COMPARE
SHE HELPED ALLAY HIS DESPERATE FEAR
AS ONLY SHE COULD DO
AND STILL IT'S SHE, HIS PARTNER NOW
WHO KEEPS HIM GOING ON SOME HOW
SHE IS HIS ANGEL, HE HAS NO DOUBT
HE'S KNOWN IT ALL HIS YEARS
SHE'S ALWAYS BEEN THERE FOR HIM
WITH LAUGHTER AND IN TEARS
AND WHEN HE'S LYING ON THE BED
PREPARING FOR DEATH'S RIDE
HE'LL WANT HER BY HIS SIDE

Everyone left and I was alone in the darkness and oh so lonely for my wife.

LONELINESS

SOMETIMES YOU FIND THAT LONELINESS
WHEN NOTHING ELSE IS THERE
AND YOU FEEL YOUR HEART IS SAYING
...THAT YOU DON'T REALLY CARE
IF YOU SHOULD STAY OR MOVE ALONG
WHEN EVEN RIGHT, SEEMS LIKE IT'S WRONG

Journey to Life's Dance Ranch

HER SEPTEMBER SONG

They met in the winter
And she left in the fall
He had spring and summer
And he captured it all
She didn't like the winter
With its wind and its cold
The winter was death
It's when you grow old
He didn't see the wrinkles
As they came to her face
He saw only beauty
And goodness and grace
Still, she left in the autumn
And as the winter drew near
She lay bravely dying
And conquered her fear
She had watched how the winter
Took the life from the old
And she hated the winter
With its wind and its cold
And she didn't want them seeing
The rose in the snow
So she left them in autumn
It was her time to go
And what we remember
Are her summer and spring
And the beauty of life
These seasons bring...
He'll remember her beauty
As he heads for the cold
As life brings him winter
As he starts to grow old
And he'll go through that winter
For he's much to do yet

Chapter Eight

> He has to keep dancing
> Not let them forget
> Her beauty in springtime
> Summer and fall
> The life of great goodness
> She shared with them all
> Then winter will bring
> His life to an end
> But he'll come back in springtime
> And she'll find him again
> She'll never stay in winter's vase
> And watch herself grow old
> She'll always leave in autumn
> Before the winter cold
> She'll never stay
> With life too long
> Instead, she'll sing
> September's song

This was one of the early poems I wrote. In some ways, it troubled me. I knew Dana didn't really like getting older though she always seemed young and beautiful to me. It was almost as if she had chosen her time to go.

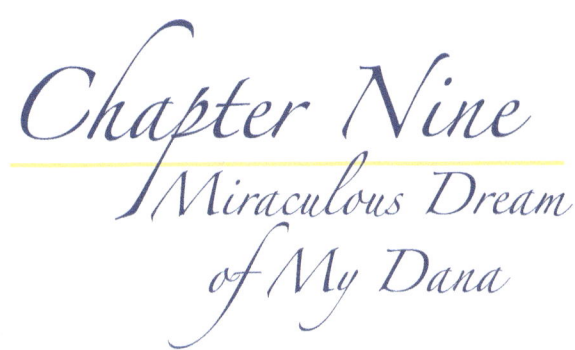

Chapter Nine
Miraculous Dream of My Dana

After four months of deep depression, a miraculous dream changed my life and brought me back to the light in a way I could never have imagined. Dana's sister, Belinda, her husband, Tom, and their daughter, Kelsey, were coming the next day to see me and stay the night. Dana's sister, Belinda, is a potter and teaches her clay arts at the Crealdi School of the Arts in Winter Park, Florida. When Dana died and was cremated, Belinda made a beautiful urn for her ashes. The urn proved to be just a bit small to house all the ashes. Belinda said she would make a base for the urn to sit on which would hold the remainder. Months went by and I had forgotten all about it.

They planned to leave their two dogs with me while they took Kelsey to the University of North Carolina to audition for a ballet scholarship. I spent the day getting ready for their arrival the following evening. When I finally went to bed, I found I was unable to sleep. I tossed and turned until the clock showed 5 am and had decided I might as well get up when I laid back one more time and fell asleep. Thirty minutes later, I awoke from an incredibly vivid dream. I had dreamt of a sky with iridescent green stars and across the sky, my Danalee was a dancing starry figure doing a grand jete. I knew it was real...I had to go outside to see. When I opened the front door and went out on the stoop, there was a beautiful sky, but no iridescent green and no dancer.

NIGHT VISION DREAM

OH MY DARLING, I SAW YOU TONIGHT IN A DREAM
OR WAS IT A DREAM? I DON'T KNOW
FOR I SAW YOU SO CLEARLY AND HELD YOU SO NEAR ME
AND I BEGGED YOU, OH PLEASE, PLEASE DON'T GO
AND I SAW IN YOUR SMILE, AS I HELD YOU... A WHILE
IT WAS REAL, I CAN SWEAR THAT IT WAS
I KNOW YOU WERE HERE, TO HELP WITH MY FEAR
AND I KNOW YOU WILL ALWAYS BE NEAR
AND I HOPE YOU CAN HELP STOP MY TEARS
THIS LIFE OWES NOTHING TO ME
FOR GOD GAVE ME MUCH MORE THAN I EVER DESERVED
WHEN YOU SAID THAT YOU'D MARRY ME
WHEN MY LIFE BECAME MY DANALEE
OH THANK YOU FOR COMING AND HELPING MY HEART
I NEEDED TO SEE YOU TONIGHT
NOW I CAN GO ON WITH THIS LIFE, AS I MUST
AND I KNOW YOU ARE STILL BY MY SIDE
WAS IT A DREAM? IT DIDN'T SEEM SO
...I DON'T THINK SO

Tom, Belinda, Kelsey and their two dogs arrived. We had dinner, a nice visit and shortly thereafter Belinda said, "Mike I have something for you." She handed me a plastic bag. I reached in and pulled out the base for Dana's urn. As I looked at the inscription on the base of the urn, chills went up and down my spine. There was written, "I'm waiting

Chapter Nine

for you, dancing among the stars." Belinda knew nothing of my dream, and I had known nothing about what she would bring. I knew Dana was watching over us and sending her love.

DANA'S URN

BELINDA...A SISTER'S SONG

AND THE HANDS THAT WORK THE MUD WITH LOVE
HID A HEART THAT HAD TO CRY
AND USED THAT HEART FROM KNOWING THAT
SHE'D HAVE TO SAY GOOD-BYE
TO THE ONE SHE LOVED AND WHO LOVED HER
THAT THROUGH HER GOODNESS
WHO THAT EVER-LOVING SISTER
AND WHEN HER SISTER WENT AWAY
LOVE BROKE HER HEART
BROKEN WITH THE REST
FOR SHE USED HER HANDS TO MOVE THE CLAY
SHE FOUND RELIEF...WAS BEST
WHEN THERE, SHE COULD BE...NEARER
HER BELOVED SISTER, BY USING HER CREATIVITY
FOR DURING THOSE TIMES
WHEN YOU USE THAT ART
YOU CAN GO THOSE PLACES
IN THE HEART
THE PLACES WHERE
YOU'LL GO AND FIND
GOD IS THERE...
AND, PEACE OF MIND
SO WORK THE MAGIC WITH YOUR CLAY
FOR YOU WILL SEE HER SOON, ONE DAY
YOU'LL BE TOGETHER...IT WON'T BE LONG
AND THEN YOU'LL SING...YOUR SISTER'S SONG

From that day on, more magical and miraculous things started to happen. I went from the state of darkness to a state of euphoric energy and light. I started to write frantically, first a song with words

Chapter Nine

coming then a melody; the second, a melody, then words. These were the first and last songs I've ever written. My mind was a symphony of rhyme, rhythm and dance. I was unable to sleep for more than a few hours a night, often awaking with an overpowering need to write. My first poem was, "It's Only God You See" then more poems kept flowing through me day and night. I had to stop and write no matter where I was. I wrote of my "Nothing Beliefs," of "Love," of "Joy," of "Sorrow," of "Life," of "Death," of "Time and Space," of "Free Will," of "Darkness," of "Ego," of "Nature," of "Life's Truths," of my life of "Magic and Miracles," of how life owes me nothing for I am given so much, yet continues to bless me with everything.

CRAZY ENERGY

THEY SAY THAT HE'S NOT CRAZY
THERE'S NOTHING THEY CAN FIND
BUT, HE, REALLY ISN'T CERTAIN
HE HASN'T LOST HIS MIND
AT TIMES WHAT DANCES IN HIS HEAD
AND THE MUSIC THAT HE HEARS
THE WORDS COMING IN RHYTHM
AND RHYME RING IN HIS EARS
HE CANNOT SHUT IT OFF AT TIMES
IT WAKES HIM IN THE NIGHT
ITS ENERGY POSSESSES HIM
HIS PEN IS FORCED TO WRITE
IT ISN'T THAT HE WILLS IT
OR TRIES TO MAKE IT HAPPEN
IT'S SOMETHING THAT COMES THROUGH HIM
IT'S SOMETHING THAT CAN SAP HIM
OF ENERGY, YET ODDLY, IT'S ENERGY IT BRINGS
BUT A SPECIAL TYPE OF ENERGY
THE TYPE THAT MAKES ONE SING

 *Journey to Life's Dance Ranch*

Three wonderful men, David Milam, Jamie DeFrates and Dana's brother, Dan, helped me record a CD with my songs and many beautiful songs of David's. I really believe the CD helped my sister, Marcy, and me get through some of the early dark times and helped others get through some of their sad times as well. The lyrics to the songs follow:

My Danalee

She was born to be a dancer
She was born to make things grow
She was born to give life's beauty
To everyone she'd know

She was born of love and goodness
She was born to give and care
She was born to bring her love to us
It was always hers to share

Refrain:
And she made the world better
For she showed us how to be
God gave the gift of goodness
When God gave us Danalee

And nature was her nature
And she loved her nature so
She loved to see the Butterflies
She loved to watch things grow

She reveled in the beauty
Of a dewdrop on a rose

Chapter Nine

In the plethora of miracles
Her Mother Nature sows

And with her Mother's nature
She gave to us her love
She gave us grace and goodness
The things her life was of

Refrain:
And she made the world better
For she showed us how to be
God gave the gift of goodness
When God gave us Danalee

She is not gone, she's still right here
Her goodness she imparts
As she waits for us amongst the stars
And dances in our hearts

Oh, she made the world much better
And especially for me
She truly was pure goodness
My wife, my Danalee

STILL IN HIS HEART

Oh, he sensed the first moment he saw her
She was different from others before
It was clear in that moment he saw her
It was she, he was meant to adore

So, he asked her, her name, she said Dana
And he knew she'd been sent from above
It was right from the start, she'd stolen his heart
God had sent him an angel to love

They were friends first and then they were lovers
Then they married and knew it would be
A lifetime of love and devotion
A dance that would set them both free

Then she left in the Fall when she had to
Which left him alone once more
But she's still in his heart, as she was from the start
And he still has his love to adore

Yes, she's still in his heart, as she was from the start
Her memory is his evermore

No Illusions

I have no great illusions
My songs will never be called art
They're merely simple musings
Coming from my heart

Chapter Nine

DAVID & PAMELA MILAM

Perhaps one of the stranger things that happened at the same time I started writing spontaneously, was that Patrick and Andrew started composing songs. Beautiful love songs, fun beach songs and even some thoughtful social commentary songs. I remember the day Patrick visited his Uncle Dan and asked if he could record a few songs in Dan's studio. I was driving to Montana at the time and got a phone call from Dan. He said he had just witnessed one of the most amazing things he had ever seen in his musical career. He told me Patrick had sat down, no practice runs, just played nine songs, then went back over the recordings and added his own percussion and accompaniment.

Several months later Patrick and Andrew got together with their Uncle Dan to record their first and only music CD. Patrick still enjoys playing his guitar and writing songs. Andrew has moved on to other endeavors. I will always remember that as a time of magical creativity in our lives.

Chapter Ten
Dana's Butterfly Awakens and Slowly Begins to Dance

Shortly after Belinda's visit, I found the "Butterfly" necklace. I believe Dana wanted me to find it and sent me suggestions throughout my lonely nights. When I saw it again, I thought perhaps it could be used to raise some money for Ovarian Cancer Research and awareness and to foster her love of dance. A new passion was being created for me. I took the pendant to the director of the Ovarian Cancer Alliance of Florida, a truly wonderful lady named Bonni Donnihi. She said the organization could not help financially but was excited at the idea and strongly encouraged me to pursue this venture.

MY DANA DANCER

GOD LET HER BE A DANCER
AND GOD WAS NOT DISAPPOINTED
FOR SHE ALWAYS KEPT THE PASSION
FOR WHAT GOD HAD ANOINTED
AND SHE DANCED WITH JOY
AND LOVE AND PASSION
AND IF THE WORLD
COULD ONLY FASHION
MORE LIVES TO BE
LIKE HERS

Journey to Life's Dance Ranch

With the help of my dear sister, Marcy and a good friend jeweler, Steve Gus, in Boone, Iowa, we began searching for a producer who might want to produce the Butterfly Ballet pendant. Almost miraculously, we were able to talk with James Louviere who was director of a department for the world's largest jewelry producer, Stuller, Inc. James' mother had been a ballerina and he instantly fell in love with the design. A new company, Butterfly Ballet, LLC was born.

Marcy, Steve, Gus, another good friend, Barb Pucci, and I created a company that would last for almost ten years. It would take us up and down the east coast, to Washington, D.C. mid-America and states out west. However, just like my father before me, I'm not a businessman. We did make some money all of which we gave away for the cause. I actually ended up spending over half a million dollars of my own money mainly paying lawyers and promoters as well as giving away jewelry and money.

Little did I know that I was going broke. I was enjoying the work so much, meeting others and sharing the story of Dana and educating on the symptoms of Ovarian Cancer. I had a purpose. I'd found a new passion, a new Life's Dance and my sister Marcy shared this with me as we made plans to share the story with as many as we could reach. Marcy almost single handedly had the whole town of Boone, Iowa outfitted in butterfly necklaces, their support of our cause was tremendous and I will always be grateful.

PROMOTION POSTER WITH BUTTERFLY BALLET PENDANT

Chapter Ten

Unexplained events can happen after losing a loved one like I lost Dana. We experienced many things which seemed to come from the other side. They would always send chills up and down my spine. One in particular happened during a fundraising event my sister, Marcy and I were doing at a Jacksonville Nutcracker performance. We always set up a display with our jewelry and with Peterbrook Chocolate Company who made chocolate Butterfly Ballets for us to help with our cause.

JEWELRY LINE

CHOCOLATES

Marcy and I got there early to set up and waited for Peterbrook to show and set their station up next to ours. All proceeds from the sales would go to the Ballet. As show-time neared and patrons started coming in, we were concerned that Peterbrook was not going to show. I called Peter and asked if they were going to set up that night. He said he felt sure they were and he would call the lady responsible. Shortly, he called back and apologized saying she was unable to get a person to staff it and had decided to cancel.

Marcy and I thought maybe we should just pack up and go home, but our good friend Mark Spivak came by and in his wonderful enthusiastic Russian accent said, "No you stay, you sell jewelry and whatever little bit of chocolate you have on hand." Marcy and I stayed (though we were only dressed in our most casual clothes) and actually did very well that night. As we were closing everything down after the show, we commented how Dana must have wanted us there. Then we saw a mother and her little girl standing over in the corner and they slowly approached our table.

The little girl's mother said her daughter was a miracle baby and had survived a rare ovarian cancer several years prior. The little girl could not have been older than 5 years and had the familiar look of one of Dana's childhood pictures. I asked her if she would like a Butterfly Ballet chocolate and she said yes. I then asked her mother if it would be OK and her mother agreed. As I was handing her the chocolate I asked, "What's your name?" She said, "Dana." Unbelieving, I asked again, "What did you say your name was?" She replied, "Dana." Still not believing, I asked her mother, "What is your little girls name?" "It's Dana," she said. As they left Marcy and I were both crying. I still believe Dana had come to tell us thank you for our efforts that night.

Even while working the company, I continued to miss my Dana desperately. I was overjoyed with what I was doing but still experiencing great sorrow and depression.

Chapter Ten

Let My Dana Come Dancing to Me

Oh my love, how I miss you
How my lips long to kiss you
How my arms want to hold you again
Though I feel you are near me
And I know you can hear me
Since you've gone my heart can't seem to mend

Now here it's your birthday
And I wish there were some way
I could hold you and tell you once more
No love can compare
To the love that we share
And you still are the love I adore

When the music starts playing
I remember us swaying
Holding tight as we danced 'cross the floor
And we found in each other
A joy like no other
And a love that will last ever more

Though these tears fill my eyes
I do realize
I'm the luckiest man to have been
For God gave me a lover
Unlike any other
My Dana, my dancer, my friend

Oh Sweetheart, Oh Sweetheart
I know I must wait
And be patient 'til we meet again

But with each tomorrow
I find, that my sorrow
With you gone
Just won't seem to end
And my heart
Just won't start to mend

I know they say time, it will help with this fear
But my love, it has now been almost a year
I'm so hopelessly lost, until when?
Yes, I feel you are near me
And I know you can hear me
How my arms want to hold you again

How I miss the romance
When life gave us the chance, to embrace
And to dance cross the floor
I am sure, that you know
I could never let go
If only I held you once more

Oh God, thank you God, for giving me life
And giving, something much more
My Dana, my dancer, my prayer that you answered
You sent me my love to adore

Though I shouldn't ask again
I've been given so much
And you know life owes nothing to me
Still I ask in your kindness
When I die, what I find is
Let my Dana come dancing to me

Chapter Ten

TRUE LOVE

So what is true love made of?
A feeling of amore?
A feeling of the heart?
Perhaps that is a part of love
But only just the start of love
And both can take you where
You find...your love is not quite there
For true love then to happen
First, one thing is a must
For love can't be eternal
Without eternal trust

WAITING

For we need time if we must wait
Or waiting makes no sense
It's time that gives us waiting
From time we get suspense
With nothing, time does not exist
Nor does itself, existence
And yet from nothing time does come
And existence that it gives us
So with its lover time goes space
Together they must dance
And wrap their arms around us
To give us...existence
But when embrace comes to an end
Our lessons learned from our two friends
We are set free to be as one
With nothing, where we first begun

So perhaps... it is not waiting
As you are on the other side
Where you told me you would wait for me
With your love, where you'd reside
Til once again our energies formed
With nothing then to be
At peace in non-existence for all eternity

Bow to the Audience

Her life ended with a dance of goodness
Her audience in tears
But God wouldn't let them stay that way
That didn't allay their fears
So her husband gets a chance to dance
Now in his later years
His dance will raise them up
He'll take his bow to joy and cheers

Eternity's Dance

Dana brought me everything
That set my heart on fire
Her passion and her beauty
Were all my heart's desire
And still her love resides in me
For we became as one
And it will always be there
Until my life is done
Now she's gone back to nothing
Where I know she waits for me
She's waiting for her partner
And our dance...eternally

Chapter Ten

DANA...

How we laughed and we touched
And I loved her so much
And tried to show her each day
How the depth of my love had grown even more
Yet mere words, they just couldn't say
What I felt at the end of each day
So I told her I loved her
Said, you are the best
Thanked God for her love
And how greatly I'm blessed

GOD, I MISS HER

I thought it would be easier
This season she loved so
A year after she left me
But, God, you have to know

Each day that we get closer
To, your most holy day
My heart becomes more lonely
And I'm not sure I, can stay...

Think going to Montana
Might help to ease this pain
I know she will embrace me
As I come home again

And bring some comfort
To my soul

> EASE THE PAIN
> HELP FILL THE HOLE
> BUT THEN, I'LL LEAVE
> I'VE MUCH TO DO
> 'TIL I AM HOME FOR GOOD
> 'TIL I AM THROUGH
>
> WITH A MISSION SHE HAS GIVEN ME
> I KNOW IT SAVED MY LIFE
> IT IS A JOYFUL MISSION
> BUT, GOD I MISS MY WIFE
> OH, GOD, I MISS MY WIFE

AM I CRAZY?

For almost two years, I continued to have unlimited energy. I was not sleeping more than three hours a night. Exhausted but full of energy and thrilled with our work on the company, I became concerned about my mind and my health and made an appointment with my physician to see if I was going crazy. I read her a few of the things I had written, they made her cry, then I asked her, "Am I nuts?" She wiped her eyes and said, "No, you are not going crazy, but something very strange is going on with you." She then ordered a plethora of blood tests; thirteen tubes were drawn that day. All tests came back normal. She referred me to a psychologist.

Again, I was told everything I was experiencing was normal, but the psychologist referred me to a psychiatrist for evaluation. Again, I was told everything I was experiencing was normal, but the psychiatrist referred me to a grief counselor. She told me I was doing exactly what I needed to. Sleep still would not come, even with prescribed sleeping pills. Finally, the physicians ordered CAT scans, MRIs and even a brain

Chapter Ten

scan. They found nothing. And so went my life for over a year and a half. I was working on the company with Marcy, spontaneously writing at all hours of the night and day, and still wondering about my sanity.

JOYFUL SORROW

I checked with the doctor
And asked her to see
What causes, this
Mirthful energy
She said she'd run tests
And tell me tomorrow
Perhaps it could be
A part of my sorrow

Part II:

*Life After Loss
Comes Love Again?*

Chapter Eleven
There Are No Coincidences Only Miracles for Me

A most serendipitous meeting would occur between my sister Marcy, her husband, Kelly and a lady named BB Webb who they met on the plane. They were all flying home from a Christmas visiting relatives in Montana. They just happened to get seats next to one another. They struck up a conversation and told BB Webb about their rescue cat named BB. She was named for the fact she was shot by a bb gun and still had bb's lodged in her head. They then told BB about their brother who had started a "BB" company, <u>B</u>utterfly <u>B</u>allet. BB was intrigued with the story and the cause. She asked Marcy if she thought her brother might be able to do a segment on her TV show in Atlanta. Marcy was sure I would and promised to help make connections. They all left friends, with Marcy and Kelly back to Boone, Iowa, and BB back to her special event businesses, book writing, television and radio shows and speaking appearances in Atlanta, Georgia.

Soon I received word from Marcy about the meeting and she gave me BB's email so I could contact her. I thought "Why not?" a trip to Atlanta to meet a nice lady and a great way to promote ButterflyBallet. BB and I started corresponding via email and soon decided on a future time to meet for dinner and to discuss the TV spot. Sometime during those communications, BB mentioned she had a friend, an ovarian cancer survivor who was fund raising for the same cause and that I might want to meet her and maybe do some fund raising at BB's event facility. I actually forgot all about her mention of this friend.

The time neared for the meeting with BB, so I gave her a call to

confirm our dinner meeting on the coming Friday. When she answered the phone and I asked her if we were still on for Friday night, she said, "Oh my gosh, I thought we were meeting Saturday and I am booked to speak downtown on Friday," I said, "No problem we can meet another time." Then I remembered her saying something about a friend. I said, 'Well, since I will be in Atlanta anyway, do you think your ovarian cancer friend might want to meet for dinner and talk fund raising?" BB said she couldn't say for sure but would contact her and give her my email. Little did I suspect that my Dana was beginning to orchestrate new miracles from beyond.

BB called Annie and told her about me and my Butterfly Ballet mission. Annie told BB she would be happy to talk with anyone about ovarian cancer and raising funds and awareness. BB emailed me that Annie was open to meeting for dinner and gave me Annie's phone number. Little did I know that Annie had just moved into her new condo the day I called her. I later learned that the Realtor had given Annie a welcome home gift when she turned over the keys. She asked, "Is there anything else I can do for you?" Annie, who had been divorced for a year and a half and was content with her single life, jokingly replied, "How about finding a nice widower who really knows how to love a woman and sell him one of these condos." They both had a good laugh.

So, I called Annie, and we had a nice talk. She later told me she thought I was a much older man because I talked funny and said "gals", and seemed to have some antiquated ideas… so she thought she was "being called" to meet with this nice old man and help him anyway she could. She agreed to meet for dinner. I made it to Atlanta and my hotel thanks to my Garmin GPS. After settling into my room, I gave Annie a call to confirm our dinner engagement. She said she would be in my hotel lobby at 6:30 and she had made reservations for one of her favorite restaurants, Cabernet, which was only a short distance from the hotel. I told her I'd be waiting in the lobby wearing khaki pants and a yellow shirt.

She said I would not have trouble recognizing her as she would

Chapter Eleven

be wearing a pink coat but then added a quirky comment about me not bringing any scales. Hmm, strange comment, I thought and so I expected to meet a rather large woman. When I got to the lobby, I was the only person there. No trouble for her identifying me, and I figured Annie would be the first rather large woman to walk through the door at 6:30. What a surprise when in walked this beautiful trim lady wearing a cute pink jacket. I stood, walked over to her and said, "Annie?" She said "Yes" and then, without thinking, I looked at her and exclaimed, "You have my wife's eyes!"

I immediately started to apologize thinking she may think this was a come-on line but she gratefully just smiled and said she felt it was an honor. She also later told me that she was shocked not to find an old man waiting for her in the lobby. After our first phone conversation she had imagined me to be a little white haired 80 year plus man and instead she found, as she described to me, a handsome, well dressed, trim, middle aged man! We drove to the restaurant and I turned down a one-way street the wrong way. When Annie pointed this out to me, I told her not to worry because that is how we drive in Montana. She laughed and the evening was off to a good start.

MEETING

SHE WAS SMILING AS THEY MET IN THE HOTEL
JUST FOR DINNER AND TO TALK A BIT
NEITHER LOOKING FOR LOVE, ON THAT EVENING
OR SUSPECT THAT THIS COULD BE IT
A NEW LOVE MIGHT FILL WHAT WAS MISSING
HAD BEEN LOST OR HAD NOT BEEN BEFORE
THOUGH THEIR GOOD HEARTS, HAD LATELY BEEN WISHING
LOVE WOULD SHOW UP AND KNOCK ON THEIR DOOR

WHEN MIDDLE AGED AND FALLING IN LOVE AGAIN
WHERE LOVE ONCE WAS, OR MAYBE HASN'T BEEN
NOTHING'S SURE, EXCEPT YOU'RE SURE YOU KNOW
LIFE IS SHORT, CAN'T LET LOVE'S CHANCE, COME AND GO

Journey to Life's Dance Ranch

ON THE WAY... TO LOVE?

A SUNNY DAY IN WINTER
TOWARD ATLANTA, ON THE ROAD
MOVING CLOSER TO THIS WOMAN
NEVER MET AND DID NOT KNOW

WHAT HE'D FIND THERE IN THE LOBBY
OF THE HOTEL WHERE HE STAYED
THIS WAS STILL A MYSTERY WOMAN
AN ACQUAINTANCE TO BE MADE

MYSTERY WOMAN, HE DIDN'T REALIZE
WHEN HE SAW YOUR EYES OF BLUE
THAT BEFORE THE EVENING ENDED
HE WOULD FALL IN LOVE WITH YOU

IN THE LIGHT OF EARLY EVENING
HE LOOKED INTO YOUR EYES
AND SAW THE BLUE/GREEN FIRE
THAT HE SOON WOULD REALIZE
BROUGHT LOVE AND LIGHT TO ALL
WHO WERE BLESSED THOSE EYES TO SEE
AND WHO FELT THE JOY OF LIFE
BEAMING FORTH FROM ANNIE Z

A JOY BORN OUT OF SORROW
A JOY BORN OUT OF PAIN
A JOY BORN OF A WOMAN
WHO WAS LOVING LIFE, AGAIN
WHO WAS SHARING, WHAT WAS GIVEN HER
IN HER TIMES OF DESPERATION
GIVING COMFORT TO THOSE OTHER SOULS
HELD IN LIFE'S INCARCERATION

Chapter Eleven

FIRST EVENING

In a restaurant, where the light was dim
Her blue eyes lit the night
They let him see inside her heart
And what a lovely sight!

Not what he had expected
But nothing ever is
He had found this magic in her
He hoped forever his
Those eyes would only show so much
Then...closed their window pane
And left him with a mystery
But he'll look there again
And if he doesn't frighten her
Her trust he'll gently gain
She'll share her scars and sorrows
That have given her much pain.

Oh, he must not push too quickly
For some things just take time
Like healing and revealing
What now must stay the mime
If he's been sent to know her
He must not rush this dance
Lest in impatient carelessness
He'll lose his only chance

That evening he spent with her
Is one he won't forget
It was a magic evening
With this woman called, Annette
...In her eyes of blue
He knew, he knew
He'd seen these eyes before
Was this a different person?
Or, had she come back for more?

 *Journey to Life's Dance Ranch*

SO MUCH WAS DIFFERENT
YET MUCH THE SAME
SHE CAME BY WAY
...OF DIFFERENT NAME
WHAT WOULD HE FIND
DEEP IN THESE EYES?
ASIDE FROM THAT...
THEY MESMERIZE

A FRIEND

HE ONLY MET HER YESTERDAY
BUT HE'S KNOWN HER FOR ALL TIME
HE KNOWS THAT YOU CAN'T MAKE A FRIEND
IT'S SOMETHING THAT YOU FIND
YOU SEE IT IN THEIR EYES
AS YOU LOOK INTO THEIR HEART
BEATING WITH A RHYTHM
THAT CAN'T TELL YOURS APART!

That evening, we ended up talking about everything but ovarian cancer fund raising. I learned much about Annie, formerly known as Annette, her birth name. However, I did not find out the name changing stories that night. I found a warm, sensitive woman with a wonderful sense of humor. I learned about her daughter, Meghan, and Meghan's husband, Trent, grandchildren, Emma, Zack and Libby, her brothers and sisters, her career, her friends, her recent divorce, her new townhouse, her love of horses and how she credited a horse named Steppes for helping cure her cancer. She told me of her love for her current horse, Sonnet. She told me of an upcoming trip to France with her pregnant daughter.

Chapter Eleven

ANNIE'S PASSION FOR HORSES AND HEALING

Early in our relationship, I learned one of Annie's gifts is that she talks to horses and swears they talk to her. She told me that prior to being diagnosed with ovarian cancer back in 2002, she had been craving riding a horse. She explained she'd had a bad fall from a horse some 20 years earlier, was traumatized and wanted to heal this fear of riding. She explained that she'd been in love with horses most of her life, but being a city girl there was little chance of having one. So instead she watched Bonanza, Alias Smith and Jones, and any other horse show where she could watch these majestic animals move.

A friend of hers, Pam, had some horses, and told Annie she could come ride her horse named Steppes. When Annie went out to ride Steppes, she got on but the mare would not move. Annie heard Steppes say, in the way that only those who hear horses can understand, "I won't move for you until you start taking better care of yourself." Annie thought about it and agreed that her career with the Georgia Department of Corrections while successful had always been highly stressful. Even though she was admittingly a proudly recovering workaholic and over achiever, she still spent too much time with the job and not enough on her health and home life.

Steppes prophetic words came true as one week later, Annie received the unexpected diagnosis of late stage ovarian cancer. She would not see Steppes again for almost three years. The time in between was filled with surgery, radiation, a reoccurrence, chemotherapy and medical retirement. She also made weeklong horseback riding trips to several European countries, in between rounds of chemo. These were two items on her bucket list, to learn to ride horses and see Europe. She was not going to leave this world without these experiences and it was with great joy she experienced the magic and beauty of the horses and the lands they traveled together.

Then one day she got a call from her friend Pam, who said Steppes needed her and wanted to talk with her. Annie went out to the

Journey to Life's Dance Ranch

farm thinking she was going there to help Steppes. Annie walked into Steppes' stall and the mare turned to her and said, "I am going to do for you what a loving mother would do for her child. I know you did not have that kind of mother. So, I am going to take your cancer from you and leave this earth with it so you will never have to worry about it coming back again." Annie began sobbing, Steppes continued, "But daughter, you can hear us (meaning equines) and so you must promise me you will help us evolve in your world."

Annie called to her friend Pam and said the vet needed to come right away. Pam told her the vet had already been there and Steppes was covered with "female area cancer" and was to be put down the next day! Annie was there the next morning and thanked and kissed Steppes before they administered the lethal dosage. To this day Annie has never had a recurrence which is rare indeed for Stage IV ovarian cancer. To this day Annie still feels the love of Steppes following her from the other side, just like my Dana. Perhaps Steppes and Dana had met and started a new dance involving all of us.

ANNIE SAYING GOODBYE TO STEPPES

During her chemo time, Annie took some of her first horse lessons and fell in love with dressage. Dressage is often referred to as dancing on horseback and well, you know the history of my Dana. Two very different kinds of dancers but could they both be mine? I really felt Dana's approval and encouragement. Maybe Annie and I were also meant to be dancing through life together? Time would tell.

Heaven's Steppes

She stepped back into life again
Through the mare who stepped aside
And when she steps through heaven's door
She'll find Steppes at her side
And dancing Steppes now awaiting
Will spin her across the up above
With Steppes of selfless giving love
The Steppes, so strong, so sure
The Steppes who'd stepped away from life
Who gave Steppes' life, of Annie's cure
The Steppes of mother's sacrifice
The Steppes of love and care
The Steppes that rose to heaven
For Annie, will be there

Annie's Sonnet

Her Sonnet was her true love
And Sonnet loved her too
Always sure they knew of
Their lover's retinue
And together
They would take life's ride
The Belgian maid
Her Georgian bride
And move as one
Upon the earth
Part then with…
Touch of sorrow
But love would always linger there
And there, they'd ride…tomorrow

A SCENT

THE PRICE WAS VERY MINIMAL
SHE ONLY ASKED A SCENT
WITH ARMS AROUND HER SONNET'S NECK
TO HER, IS HOW LIFE'S MEANT
TO BE, WHEN WE NEED GOODNESS
TO FEEL THE JOY OF YOUTH
TO BE, WHEN WE NEED HONESTY
AND FIND A PERFECT TRUTH

ANNIE WITH HER TRUE LOVE, SONNET

I knew I was infatuated with Annie at our first dinner meeting. In fact, after we returned to the hotel, we sat in the lobby where I read her some of my poems for the first time. She exclaimed that some of my poems reminded her of one of her favorite poets, Rumi, a 13th century Persian poet. She even nick named me the "Rumi man" and agreed many of my poems were coming from the other side. She had no problem understanding and embracing my "Nothing Theory." As I took her back to her car at the hotel, I told her if she ever came through Jacksonville, she should stop by and visit. I never dreamed she would really do it. I will admit that after she left, I did phone her to make sure

Chapter Eleven

she had gotten home safely. A miraculous thing then happened. For the first time in almost two years I was able to sleep through the night. The date was February 23rd, 2008.

And once I got home to Florida, the next day, I emailed her again... she responded... and we began a courtship dance via the internet. From the first, Annie had struck me as a bit nutty, not in a crazy way but in a fun and funny way. Our playful banter via the web only reinforced my original diagnosis! My Navy life with Dana and the boys had been so structured and the last years so hard, that now I found in myself a silliness and playfulness I didn't know I had, and I was not sure I trusted.

My Annie

She danced among the loonies
In her madness, she fit in...
No, she starred amongst the loonies
And it sure delighted him
For he always felt the most alive
When he was on the edge
And she knew just how to dance with him
Upon life's loony ledge
And sometimes step, where most wouldn't dare
She'd take the chance, to dance on air
Knowing nothing, might be hiding there
Among the stars she loved
And if she found her nothing waiting
...Her angel there, anticipating
She needed nothing's space
She might just dance away from him
As he would watch this loony's whim
And wonder, at her requiem
'Til she returned...to life again

Journey to Life's Dance Ranch

When Annie eventually left with her daughter for their Paris trip, I felt this relationship could become more. Perhaps it would be only a wonderful friendship; maybe much more. I still couldn't imagine another love in my life after my Dana. And I knew Annie had only been divorced from her second husband, for a couple years so I was uncertain. But Annie certainly did have a magic about her and not just the way she affected me but everyone she was around. Life was changing very fast for me...perhaps too fast.

PARIS

She was off to Paris
The city of amore
Not sure, of what
She was looking for
Perhaps just beauty
A different place
Perhaps the need
For a different space
Relationship ended
He's still her friend?
But something's gone
The heart won't mend
No matter what
She tries to say
Those years and tears
Won't go away
And can true lovers
Grow apart?
Or, was it, true love
From the start?

For what's true love
Can one outgrow?
The warmth that comes
With true loves glow
Can true love be just momentary?
A fantasy that can leave?
An interest that now wanes
A heart that now must grieve
Then search for something other
That something deep within
No, true love didn't happen
And now she feels the sin
And longs for what she longed for
And longs still now again
To find true love, to be as one
She won't have peace 'til then
She won't be free 'til then

Chapter Eleven

FIRST VISIT TO JACKSONVILLE, YIKES!

Weeks later after her return, Annie called and said she would take me up on my offer to listen to the recording of the music Dana's brother Dan was making in Jacksonville. I'd forgotten I had made the offer. I thought I had just made a generic stop by and say hi kind of offer, but I must have hinted at more. She was coming down and I was terrified. I had never been alone with a woman in our house since Dana died. I called Andrew who was living in an apartment nearby where he was attending school at the University of North Florida. Andrew knew his mother's final unselfish wish for his dad. She wanted him to find someone and love again. Andrew did not necessarily think this was it but he did step up and was there for me again.

I asked him if he would come over and stay in the house with me while Annie was there at least to begin with. We all had a nice visit and dinner and ended up chatting away in the living room. In fact, Annie and I were doing all the chatting and Andrew was obviously getting bored. He eventually asked me if he could go home. I felt reassured that Annie and I were just managing a nice friendship and sent him on his way. At the end of the evening, Annie went upstairs to the guest bedroom and I retired to my bedroom. Phew, I had made it safely through the first night!

With Dana, whenever we had company come for a visit, especially if they were not from Florida, we would show them around Jacksonville and usually take them down to historic St. Augustine. I felt this might be the best way to entertain Annie while she was there for her visit. Our trip to St. Augustine the next morning was more magical and miraculous than anything I could have imagined. Prior to Annie coming for her visit I had felt she was different in a funny fun kind of way and she found me different and funny in a crazy kind of way. Now I was with this delightful crazy sensitive lady totally enjoying her company.

The first place we visited was the old St. Augustine Fort and its prison. Annie had talked with me about her energy and spiritual connection with animals and even human souls which were stuck in this world that she would help release from their darkness into the light. As we were walking through the old Fort prison, Annie sensed two young soldiers' souls who were still stuck in the prison. She immediately found a couple of small stones and went to the place where she felt their trapped energy. As she stood there, she invited/retrieved their souls and then blew the souls into the stones, so she could carry them out and release them to the light. She then asked me if I would help her.

She explained, the souls had requested to be thrown into the ocean, towards their home shores away from America. Again, like the horses, Annie heard their request, in an inexplicable way that only those who know it can understand it. I took the stones and we walked together to the waterfront outside the Fort. I threw the stones as far into the ocean as I could. I must admit when she first began her procedure, I was a bit skeptical and thought perhaps she was a bit strange and crazy. But afterward, I felt Annie had allowed me to help her with something real and sacred.

I later learned that in addition to her traditional academic education with a Bachelor in Social Work and Masters in Adult Education /Organizational Development, Annie also had extensive training in non-traditional energy healing. Her passion, while working in the field of Corrections for over 23 years, had always been trying to provide "programs" to rehabilitate offenders and stop the cycle of violence. She felt called to always search for the light in the midst of darkness and to help the light expand. Her career managing the rehabilitative programs in Georgia's large prison and probation system, provided her with many opportunities to pursue this passion. It was her Life's Dance.

Post medical retirement her passion shifted and her new Life's Dance became focused on finding alternative forms of healing both for herself in managing her M.S. and the ovarian cancer and to help others who were stuck in some way in their healing journey, be it in this world or another. She was trained in Reiki, Shamanism, soul retrievals, and

Chapter Eleven

other forms of energy healing. And she now followed the energy of the equines as a guiding light for her life's choices. I found her to be an incredibly spiritual person embracing much of Eastern spirituality, Native American spirituality, as well as that of her Christian faith.

After releasing the two soldiers to the light, we walked in the light of a beautiful day through downtown St. Augustine. We stopped at an outdoor Art Festival where Annie purchased a painting of a Dove flying from the darkness into the light. We walked on through the city and heard music coming from a beautiful old rock church. As we walked in to look at the church, we found ourselves in the middle of a wedding ceremony. We quietly backed out of the church and I believe both of us felt this a possible omen, although of course we did not dare to put these thoughts into words so soon into our relationship. We walked to a very nice Deli and had a delicious dinner and as we were eating who was to walk into the Deli but the father of the bride we had seen at the wedding. Annie was quick to say hello and congratulate him.

ANNIE'S CHALICE

SHE WAS A LOVELY CHALICE
ON THE ALTAR OF EXISTENCE
AND THE WINE OF LIFE
THAT FILLED THIS CUP
FLOWED FREE WITHOUT RESISTANCE
NOT JUST TO LIFE THAT WAS LIKE HERS
BUT OTHER LIFE SHE KNEW SO WELL
THOSE LIVES WITH COATS AND FURS
AND WHAT POURED THEN, FROM THIS CHALICE
FROM THIS CREATURE WITH THE GIFT
TO SEE INSIDE OF OTHER LIFE
AND WITH HER LOVE TO LIFT
THE SOUL AND SPIRIT LOST WITHIN
A CELL ADRIFT FROM ONE
AND FREE THEM FROM THEIR DARKNESS
RELEASE THEM TO THE SUN
HELP THEM BACK INTO THE DAYLIGHT
WITH HER LOVING ENERGY
BRING THEM NECTAR FROM HER CHALICE
THAT WOULD FINALLY SET THEM FREE

We headed back to Jacksonville and when we got home, I set some candles on the table on my screened porch. I put on some soft easy listening music. We poured a glass of wine and went out to the patio to enjoy the warm soft Florida evening. After a while I went to get us another glass of wine and when I returned, I found Annie dancing on the patio floor: slowly moving to a romantic instrumental. It took me by surprise, delighted me and I leaned against a pillar and watched as she moved. Annie later told me she noticed me watching her from the pillar and it was the first time she felt me see her as a woman, perhaps more than friend? The evening ended with some joyful conversation and recounting of the wonderful time we had in St. Augustine.

Chapter Eleven

Annie said good-night and went upstairs to the guest room, while I retired to the master bedroom. I was quite overwhelmed by this woman, her goodness, spontaneity and at times her funny insanity. The next morning, we spent visiting until it was time for us to go to see my friend Jamie DeFrates. We were going to meet Dana's brother, Dan, at Jamie's recording studio where Dan would record a version of Jamie's song "A Woman's Dance. Annie and I had listened to another song of Jamie's "It's a Miracle" as we drove to the studio and it moved us both deeply. Watching and listening to Dan play his violin with an incredibly beautiful version of Jamie's song was an equally if not more moving moment for us. I looked over at Annie and she was crying throughout the recording and later told me she was crying for my loss. I eventually used Dan's rendition as an accompaniment to a beautiful porcelain twirling ballerina on my Butterfly Ballet web page, *Butterflyballet.com*.

After we finished at Jamie's we headed downtown to the "River Landing" where we walked along the St. John's River for a while then dipped into a river front café for a wonderful seafood lunch/dinner, before it was time to take Annie to the airport. As we came out of the restaurant, we witnessed something neither of us had ever seen. It was mid afternoon and to the West was the full sun over the river, to the East was a full beautiful big moon sitting on the Eastern horizon. I know we both felt it was a sign. What a beautiful memory as an ending to a wonder visit from Annie. I can still see Annie's walking through security and waving goodbye. She later told me she was thinking *God, maybe I was just here to help a man through his grief or maybe I will see him again, I don't know.* But I trust you do.

I knew then that it was more hello than goodbye. However, little could I ever imagine this visit would set the stage for what would become the beginning of our journey to "Life's Dance Ranch." I'm sure Dana and Steppes were once again orchestrating our dance from their sacred space.

First Visit

She came to see him
Hoping she would find
A friend to bring her magic
And ease her troubled mind
To share her joy
To share her sorrow
To share today
Perhaps tomorrow
To be a friend
Perhaps a lover
She came to him
Would she discover?
Who was this man
She'd only met?
What would she find
She didn't know yet
But felt her visit
Was a must
She thought she'd find
A friend to trust

Chapter Eleven

First Visit Challenge

He would not call her nutty
At least not use that name
For then she would rejoice in it
And think she'd won the game
And want the prize he'd promised
For whomever proved the best
And he did not want her gloating
Thinking she had won the test
For she was a little cocky
And in fact, she was quite good
Her nuttiness came naturally
And though, he always thought, he would
Win out in any contest
Where "insanity" won the prize
Well, there she was, this nut case
With those magic gray-green eyes
He knew she'd had more practice
But he knew his state of mind
This contest was a Super Bowl
And much was on the line
So when the weekend ended
There'd have to be a vote
But can there be a winner?
They're sailing the same boat!

Annette

She'd only showed him Annie
He still didn't know Annette
Perhaps one day he'd meet her
But she wouldn't let him yet
For Annie was her cover
Her safest place to be
Annette must not be introduced
'Til she feels a certainty
She must be sure she trusts him
And she must understand
She must answer her question
And know…"who is this man?"

Revelation

Annie spoke to him tonight
And told him how she'd found the light
And crawled out of the darkness
The courage that he found in her
To share her painful past
Would meld a new born friendship
And it would now hold fast
The trust had been established
The bond had now been made
She knew she now could trust him
And no longer was afraid

Chapter Eleven

~ ### The Visit

The day he spent with Annie
Went long into the night
Until night, became the morning
And it gave him such delight
For she had shared a gift of hers
And so then, too, had he
She'd opened up her heart to him
Showed her ...vulnerability
Then, this day came to a close
A day he'd hoped wouldn't end
For he had found a miracle
In this wondrous, new friend

~ ### End of Visit

She stepped back on the airplane
As he walked in reverie
Not sure of what had happened
On this three-day magic spree
He knew he'd shared another's soul
She gave her trust, she gave herself
She gave his heart a lift
And though there was a dark past
She knew she had to share
She also sensed instinctively
She did not have to fear
For she saw it in the eyes
That peered within her being
This was a man whom she could trust
Her own goodness, she was seeing

Chapter Twelve
The Courtship Begins

Now the ball was in my court and I began planning a visit to Atlanta to see Annie again. I don't believe it was more than two or three weeks before I was in my little Nissan Sentra, the company car, headed up Interstate 295 to catch Interstate 10 across the Florida panhandle to Interstate 75 North to Atlanta. Annie and I had communicated often by phone and email since her visit. I was becoming more and more infatuated and still I had my fears. These fears would haunt me for it had been less than 2 years since I lost my Dana. Was I ready to commit to a relationship this soon? I really wasn't sure, yet something about Annie was very uniquely special and felt right in so many ways. I was headed down the highway excited about what could be, afraid of what might be. I still knew so little about this woman, Annie. There was so much to learn, so much to know.

When I reached Annie's housing development, Vickery Village in Cumming, Georgia, I found a beautifully planned, family oriented upscale community. There was a central square with multiple stores, restaurants, a courtyard with outdoor tables, an ice cream parlor and many more amenities. As I drove up to Annie's 2nd floor flat, she was standing on her balcony waving. I was overwhelmed with joy to see her again. As she walked down the stairs from her balcony to meet me, she brought what would become another love of my life, her little Shih Tzu, Dudley. I followed Annie and Dudley up the stairs to her flat and she showed me to my room.

Journey to Life's Dance Ranch

ANNIE'S GRANDDAUGHTER EMMA & DUDLEY

    We had dinner and then decided to watch one of her favorite movies "The Sound of Music." With Dudley on the couch between us, for my safety and hers, we watched that delightful movie. Then it was time to go to bed. Annie said goodnight and went down the hallway to her bedroom. I went into her guest room, also her spiritual energy/meditation room. It was an incredibly unusual room complete with drums, bells, gongs, wondrous paintings, a fountain which flowed continuously and softly rang a little bell and a fabric day bed/couch which she had explained was her goddess healing couch from the cancer years. What was I getting into? This was all somewhat unsettling to me, but not unusual for this woman "Annie." I must say I slept very little that night. I was up early the next morning, at least an hour or more before Annie, so I brought one of my journals out and did some writing before she finally came smiling down the hall in her pajamas and housecoat.

    Her hair looked crazy messed up and yet there was a beauty about it that I enjoy to this day. We had coffee and some breakfast and then it was time to go to her stables and meet Annie's Sonnet. Sonnet

Chapter Twelve

was a beautiful Belgium warm blood mare, whose name fit her perfectly. Annie said watching Sonnet was like watching "poetry in motion." She was a gentle creature with soft loving eyes. When she first saw me, she tipped her head back a bit and opened her mouth and appeared to give me a big smile. I gave Sonnet some peppermints as these were some of her favorite treats. Then we headed back to Vickery and grabbed a bite of lunch. Now it was Dudley's turn for some attention. We took him for a long walk through Vickery enjoying the parks, trails, ponds and beauty of the day.

Back at Annie's flat we visited, rested and got ready for dinner at the Vickery Italian restaurant. The weather had changed from delightful to clouds building for a thunderstorm. We just made it to the restaurant as it began to rain, then pour. We were seated at an outside table with hanging heavy clear plastic sheets protecting us from the rain. The rain certainly didn't dampen our spirits. We had a wonderful time enjoying each other's company, laughing, delighting in good wine and fine food and becoming more and more comfortable with each other. As we were getting up to leave an older lady came to our table, chuckled and said, "If you two are not married, you should be." We both laughed yet I think we both felt this could be another omen of possible things to come, or maybe not?

The next morning it was time for me to head to Jacksonville but I knew it wouldn't be long before we would see each other again. And it wasn't, perhaps only a couple weeks, before Annie was driving her car down to see me. She arrived mid-afternoon and much to my delight she was wearing an Italian outfit with hints of a gondolier. Annie has always dressed with a flair of brightness and joy. She loves clothes that sparkle as brightly as her eyes, her smile and her personality. She is a beautiful woman and can certainly turn heads when she dresses up. We continued our courtship dancing via emails and when we could we would visit each other, either in Florida or Atlanta.

I believe it may have been on one of these visits that she asked me if I would like to make a trip to Italy with her and her travel friends

in October. Although we had not known each other all that long, something told me to say yes and I did. I had no idea who her friends were except she had worked with them at the Georgia Department of Corrections. They were all retired or close to it and had been making travel plans for the years ahead. A hint of more adventures to come?

TROUBLED PAST

During all this time as we shared stories of our lives, Annie never mentioned her parents. After a few months I got up enough nerve to ask her about them. She slowly began to open up to one of her darkest truths. I came to learn that Annie had endured one of the most difficult evil childhoods any person could imagine and yet, miraculously, she and her siblings survived with each other's help and love. For her this healing journey brought her through a lot of years of intense healing work. Ever since Meghan was born, trying to be a good mother was her primary motivation for healing from her past. And her healing journey is what led her to the many different types of alternative healings and the equines. She learned there was so much more needed beyond traditional therapy in order for her to release her demons. And she is certain that her childhood traumas contributed to both her M.S. and the Ovarian Cancer, the fall-out from which she is still is challenged today.

Chapter Twelve

Annie...

Wouldn't it be nice to have someone who
Wouldn't look to be in control of you
For that is what you've had before
And if you tell me true
It may be something that you chose
Or something that chose you
Regardless...now, the choice IS yours
To make here once again
This time the choice is critical
Your final chance...to win

Phone Call

He...
Called her later than he should
Hoped to talk, but wasn't good
Time to make, this night connection
Or touch, just now, his friend's affection
Her life was where it had to be
And he must wait for her, you see
For things must happen patiently
...or happen, not at all
Their meeting, it will soon take place
And again, he'll see her face to face
And see her blue/green eyes
Will see within her mystery
And understand her openly
Until he knows her well
Then as he sees what she reveals
And finds what magic there he feels
He'll know their true direction
If goodness there, resides in her
Then something else, it might occur
And bring their resurrection

Journey to Life's Dance Ranch

Hidden in Her Eyes

She listens, oh so patiently
As now, he calls more frequently
To pass his life to her
And she listens to his nonsense
Then he captures her, with suspense
And holds her there a while
'Til he tells her of her magic
Or of things he sees as tragic
All those things, he sees in her
And she knows, though he seems strange
When around him, she does change
And finds more freedom, for her soul
What he brings, she isn't certain
For though open, he has this curtain
And she cannot see, just what is there...behind
If she can draw the curtain back
Is it nothing...she will find?
No, but it's something of great value
If it's dropped it turns to dust
It's his most precious gift to give
Made of truth and love...his trust
When they're there once again
Will he see in those eyes...
Her gray/green life reflectors
Will she let him visualize
Still deeper, where her soul resides
And see, from most, what Annie hides?

Chapter Twelve

EARLY FEAR

What is it he fears, as he goes to her lair?
She's only shown goodness, is that all that's there?
We are all just the products of what we have been
Things in our lives of goodness and sin
We are given the options, and then we must choose
And some have it tougher...destined to lose?
Born amidst evil, escape can be hard
When evil's your parent, when evil's your bard
Embracing an aegis of goodness and truth
And choosing a life, not there in your youth
Takes courage beyond what most, then can glean
To pull off their bard, and strip their soul clean
Discard, their evil, refuse to inherit
Turn against evil, so they won't have to share it
To break evil's chains, and dare to be free
Is an act of great courage, we so rarely see

...if she's truly one that did escape
Who wouldn't pass on her evil's rape
Then she is more than goodness
An awesome strength is here
God has sent this miracle
A friend he must keep near
For life has destined them to laugh
And destined them to cry
Together for a while
...perhaps, until they die

Journey to Life's Dance Ranch

ON THE ROAD AGAIN

As time went on, I made many long trips to Atlanta (6 hours no matter how fast you try to drive) and Annie made the drive to Jacksonville just as many times. Always stopping at the Chick-Fil-A at the Valdosta, Ga exit for chicken salad and an ice dream. During these visits I met many of Annie's family and friends. It was a wonderful courtship. Yes, I was falling in love with Annie Z but still felt some fear and reservation. I met her wonderful quirky neighbor Emily who was a very young 80-year old. She whispered to me one night when we had all gone out that Annie was one "kick ass lady" and encouraged me to continue our relationship.

One day in May we were watching the Kentucky Derby at Annie's, and a terrible accident happened to "Eight Belles," the filly who had just finished as runner up. Tragically, she broke her front ankles and they euthanized her on the track. Annie was so upset by this she swore she would not watch horse racing again, as they pushed young horses to run fast, despite the damage it does to their young bones. Later, to cheer her up I played one of her favorite songs by Dan Fogelberg, "Run for the Roses," and I asked her to dance. It was our first waltz together. I twirled her gently around her living room floor with little Dudley watching over us.

Run for the Roses

As they sat upon the couch
And talked into the night
Drank some wine and laughed and cried
And shared what others might
Not find a comfort in
For this was revelation
Their love, their soul, their sin
And this comfort with each other

Chapter Twelve

> Was growing with each word
> And as he looked into her eyes
> It was her heart he heard
> So finally, he came closer
> As the night came to an end
> He touched her hand, he hugged her
> And waltzed with her again
> And they ran for the roses
> There was love upon the floor
> For they were both quite certain
> Their friendship would endure
> This love they felt was pure
> And sometimes, he's uncomfortable
> With how comfortable he is
> Whenever he's around her

Annie had laughed as she told me about her early attempts at cooking. Annie had divorced Meghan's father when Meghan was 10. Annie became a single parent juggling a successful but stressful career, while processing a lot of her personal healing work, and trying to be a good mother. Let's just say she was a better employee and was rather lacking in the maternal instinct category. And certainly, cooking was not her strong suit. She thought a good dinner for Meghan could be a bowl of cereal and if there was no milk in the refrigerator then water would do. Or better yet, throw a tortilla with a processed slice of cheese in the microwave and you had an instant dinner.

When Meghan was 12, she came home one day and said, "If you don't put a dead animal on my plate tonight, I am out of here!" Annie quickly went to the freezer pulled out a frozen chicken breast, thawed and then nuked it in the microwave, and triumphantly placed it before her daughter. Meghan rejected this pitiful offering because there was not even any sauce on the meat. Annie assured her the next day she would do better. Annie remembered to pull the meat out to thaw at 5:30 a.m. the next morning as she left for work. She stopped by the grocery

store on the way home and bought a package of gravy mix.

At home she followed the instructions and began stirring the gravy. She became a little concerned when tears started to flow down her cheeks, but she persevered thinking it was probably just her guilty conscience for not having gone down this culinary path previously. She then nuked the chicken and poured the sauce on top and set it in front of Meghan. Meghan took one sniff and her eyes teared up as well. "Something is wrong with this!" she shouted, and pushed the offensive meal out of her way. Annie looked around for an explanation and saw that instead of using vinegar she had accidentally grabbed the bottle of ammonia from under the sink!

I must say, I was very wary of Annie's cooking for a long time. I even wrote a poem about this but mistakenly used dish soap as I had blocked the horrifying ammonia story from my mind. I do remember her making tiramisu in my kitchen in Florida. I started to talk with her as she was blending her recipe. She turned to listen better and held the mixer up in the air with the mixer still going. Tiramisu went everywhere. I swear I was still finding it in cracks and crevices in the kitchen months later. Yes, she was different indeed.

Chapter Twelve

Cooking History

New emotions are now his
Things she's shared with so few others
Yet now, she lets him see
Lets him look into her life
And her cooking history
Tells him things about her family
How she always gave them hope
She'd start cooking with the olive oil
Instead of using soap!

FINAL LOVE?

Oh yes, she was an angel
With a devil of a past
For she had been to hell and back
With loves that did not last
And they would always take their toll
They'd break her heart
They'd rape her soul
Until she let them take no more
Then she'd depart
But still not sure
Of what she needed, what's the cure?
Her spirit needed to be free
Who was her final love to be?

Soul's Safety

The first time, he spoke to her
Her energy flowed through him
Came to him through the phone
And what he sensed within the voice
Was something he had known
He couldn't recall just what it was
He couldn't remember yet
Perhaps it was another life
Where he had known Annette
But the comfort, there, between them
Existed from the start
Perhaps another time or place
They'd shared a common heart
And soon, he'd look into her eyes
Those mirrors of green and blue
And what he'd sensed upon the phone
He'd see... was really true
Still, he couldn't quite remember
The place or time or name
Was this... once an ember?
Or had it been a flame?
And what now would this be?
As once again these two souls touch
Though apart they've been
They <u>now</u>, bring much
That they can share

But is there safety waiting there?
Safe from harm, is not their goal
They both want, safety, for their soul

Chapter Twelve

One of the funnier phone calls we received was from Annie's daughter the night after we attended a Cinco de mayo party in the Vickery Square at Annie's housing complex. There were tables, a Mexican band and Mexican food out in the square. Annie and I were sitting outside at a table and unbeknownst to us one of her daughter's friends was sitting in a restaurant on the square looking out the window at us. As Annie and I were talking, the topic of teeth came up. As I had been a dentist, I asked Annie if I could look at her teeth. She opened wide and I observed her beautiful teeth and mouth. After all you don't buy a mare without checking her teeth. We joked and thought that was that.

We went on to have a great evening of dancing and celebrating. I remember going up to one of the band members and asking him to write some things for me in Spanish on some napkins I had. I told him to write, "You are a beautiful woman, I am happy I am with you and I love you." I took the napkins back to Annie and told her these were my Cinco messages for her. Her response, "I don't read Spanish." I told her she would have to go ask the band member to translate for her. She was very moved when he read them to her. The next day Meghan called and said, "Mom, Marilyn was in a restaurant at Vickery and saw a man looking in your mouth, what's going on?" After Annie explained, we all had a good laugh over it. Just goes to show that when you are dating there is no place to hide!

One evening when I was back in Jacksonville, I had gone for a long run. I witnessed one of the most beautiful sunsets I had ever seen. I kept wishing Annie could be there to share it with me. As soon as I got home, I had to sit down and write what I had seen and was feeling.

Journey to Life's Dance Ranch

IF SHE HAD BEEN WITH HIM

AND IF SHE HAD BEEN WITH HIM
HE WOULD HAVE SHOWN HER THIS
FOR THE CLOUDS HAD COME TOGETHER
AS A GIANT ANGEL FISH
AND IT SWAM WITH GENTLE GRACEFULNESS
UPON THE AZURE SKY
AS GOD WOULD PAINT THIS MAGIC
FOR THOSE WHO'D LIFT THEIR EYE
AND THE BREEZE WOULD GIVE THE CURRENT
TO HELP THIS ANGEL SWIM
AND HE WOULD HAVE SHOWN THIS TO HER
IF SHE'D ONLY BEEN WITH HIM
THEN A SCHOOL OF SMALLER FISH ARRIVED
AND THE ANGEL DISAPPEARED
TO LEAVE A LOVELY MACKEREL SKY
AS THE EVENING SUNSET NEARED
OUT OF NOWHERE CAME A GIANT WAVE
FROM AN OCEAN THAT WAS SKY
AND CRASHED UPON THE SETTING SUN
TO SEND IT INTO NIGHT
AND THE WAVE WOULD TAKE THE SUN AND FISH
TO ANOTHER TIME AND PLACE
WHERE ONCE AGAIN IT WOULD APPEAR
AS GOD'S ETERNAL FACE
AND IF SHE HAD BEEN WITH HIM
HE WOULD HAVE SHOWN HER THIS
AND TOLD HER THAT HE LOVED HER
WITH A GENTLE EVENING KISS

Chapter Twelve

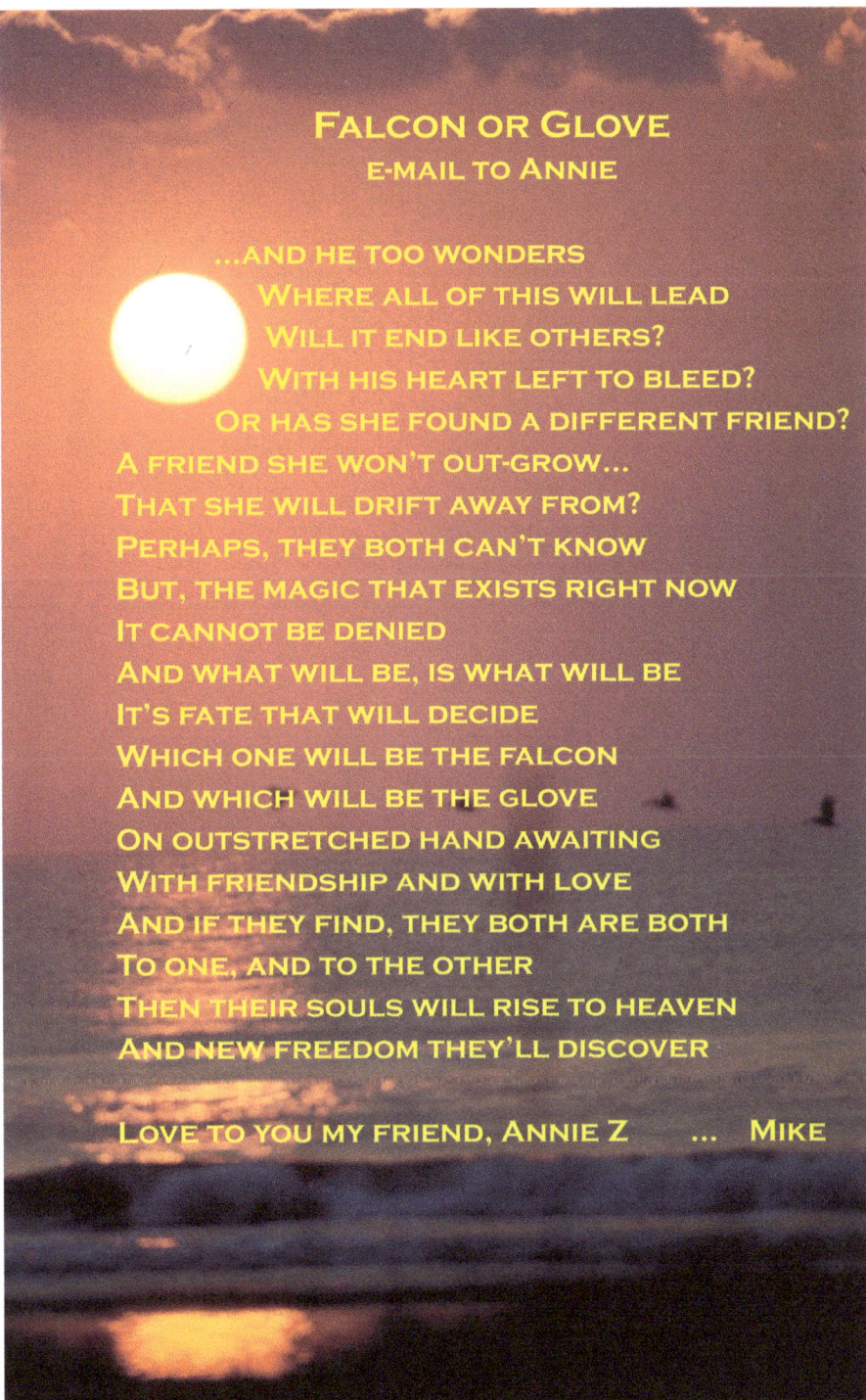

Falcon or Glove
e-mail to Annie

...And he too wonders
 Where all of this will lead
 Will it end like others?
 With his heart left to bleed?
  Or has she found a different friend?
A friend she won't out-grow...
That she will drift away from?
Perhaps, they both can't know
But, the magic that exists right now
It cannot be denied
And what will be, is what will be
It's fate that will decide
Which one will be the falcon
And which will be the glove
On outstretched hand awaiting
With friendship and with love
And if they find, they both are both
To one, and to the other
Then their souls will rise to heaven
And new freedom they'll discover

Love to you my friend, Annie Z   ...   Mike

Ego's Permission

And if his ego'd let him
Perhaps then he would see
A love between the two of them
Would help to set him free
In ways he hadn't known before
A new and different vision
Fear held him in its grasp
Could he make this decision?
Was he now...to take the chance
And step back in the stream
Would she be his new love?
With whom he now could dream

    As I mentioned, Annie swears that Pam's beloved horse Steppes and her Sonnet helped cure her of ovarian cancer, and so much more, mentally, physically, emotionally and spiritually. I have seen what being around horses does for Annie and I absolutely believe they are medicine for her body, mind and soul. I think this is true for many others too. I have come to love riding horses as well, especially with my Annie.

Chapter Twelve

Sonnet Ecstasy

Annie looked for magic there
And Sonnet would reveal it
As their hearts would touch with energy
And both of them would feel it
Then they'd transcend the difference
Between man and horse, and see
As their spirits blended, one to one
...in blessed ecstasy

Ready to Swim?

What happened last night
Had happened before
It happened the first time
She walked through the door
The first time he saw her
The first time they met
The first time they spoke
He knew this Annette
He's spoken to her so many times
Since Dana went over
Annie was different
He thought he might love her
Or maybe he had
In some distant past
Emotions felt right now
This couldn't be bad
But was he now ready
To get back in love's stream
With this lovely creature
To start, a new dream?
He still had fear
Was he ready to swim...
now?

Deep Waters

And she let him touch her gently
Feel her feet in sweet embrace
As his hands caressed her soul
The tears ran down her face
He felt her heart and it felt right
This blessed day, now blessed night
What brings them now together?
What is it they will share?
Yes, this is still as friendship
But something more is here
How soon will he be ready?
To step yet further, still?
Into the waters of her being
And find eternal thrill…

Her Face

He brought laughter to them
But she, brought this to him
And too, she brought a woman's touch
A feel, a warmth he'd missed so much
He felt his hand caress her face
And found there was another place
Where once again, his heart was safe

Chapter Twelve

Visit to Annie's

For three days, he felt again
A woman's touch upon his skin
Her gentle hands, between his own
A soft caress, he had not known
Since life took that away

Visit to Mike's

She arrived Italiano
With her usual style and flair
Her shih tzu, Dudley, with her
Her magic in the air
Her eyes, that steely blue / gray / green
An energy, strong, and yet, unseen

MAGIC EVENING

AN EVENING OF PURE MAGIC
MOST CAN'T EVEN DREAM OF
AND WHEN THE NIGHT WAS OVER
HE KNEW HE'D FELT A NEW LOVE
OF GENTLE, TENDER, CAREFUL TOUCH
A TOUCH THAT HE HAD MISSED SO MUCH
A KISS, INTENSE, WITH PASSION THERE
A KISS THAT HE HAD LONGED TO SHARE
AND, SHE KNEW WHEN THE TIME WAS RIGHT
TO GO UPSTAIRS AND SAY GOOD NIGHT
...LEAVE HIM WITH DESIRE
ANOTHER DAY WOULD SOON ARRIVE
AND RE-IGNITE THE FIRE

Chapter Thirteen
Bumps in the Road

Annie and I were spending much more time together. We were fund raising for Butterfly Ballet all up and down the east coast, Washington D.C. and Atlanta. Before she flew to Denver to do a fund raiser with me, she had called to say she would see me soon and had just had lunch with her ex-husband at their favorite sandwich shop. She was returning from a medical appointment and happened to see his car there. She said they had a great talk and she enjoyed the time with him. She said not to worry ... there was nothing to it, just friendship. Needless to say, I was a bit concerned but then thought maybe I was just being over-sensitive.

I was really looking forward to seeing her again and had even had a special Tlingit drum made for her by an artist in Ketchikan, Alaska. It was a beautiful deer skin lover's drum with Eagle and Raven painted upon the skin and deer skin/branch drum stick. So, I went to the Denver Airport later that day to pick her up. To my surprise, when she got off the plane she was with another man. She was aglow after they had arranged seating together, so they could talk about old times. She introduced me to a former lover she had told me about. I was shocked. Again, she said there was nothing to it; they were just good friends now, wanting to catch up on things. Still, I was very uncomfortable that she was so happy to have made contact with two former lovers on the same day she was coming to see me. We went to my sister, Mary Lou and her husband Gene's beautiful house in Parker, Colorado and used it as a base for attending our convention fundraiser. Marcy had also come in to work the big event in Denver with us and she stayed at Gene and Mary Lou's as well.

 *Journey to Life's Dance Ranch*

That first evening in Colorado, down in a guest bedroom, I gave Annie my gift. She loved it.

LOVER'S DRUM

SO, HE GAVE HER A DRUM
WITH A WISH THAT SHE HEAR
THE BEAT OF LOVE'S HEART
AS BRANCH TOUCHES DEER
AND THE BIRDS ON HER SKIN
AS THEY TAKE FLIGHT IN SOUND
IS A PLACE WHERE HIS LOVE
WILL ALWAYS BE FOUND

AT THE DENVER BUTTERFLY BALLET BOOTH

It was fun doing the event with Annie and Marcy and getting to visit with Mary Lou, Gene, and some of their children, and seeing her get to know some of my family. Later that evening Annie felt as if she could trust my family like she had trusted me. She shared some of her heinous background which involved familial and ritual abuse, governmental mind control programs such as MK Ultra, where multiple personalities were forcefully created in children via torture, etc. She told them of various successful therapies she had been through to help rid her of these demons. She felt that if she could trust me with her history, she could trust my family. She later came to realize her mistake. Since she had lived with these truths for so long it was not a big deal to her, but to my family it was a very big deal and one they were afraid of.

After we completed our fund-raising in Denver, I took Annie back to the airport, kissed her goodbye and said I would see her in Atlanta in two days. I had driven to Denver and the plan was for me drive to Atlanta and pick her up and take her for a visit to Jacksonville with me.

Chapter Thirteen

After Annie was gone and I returned to Mary Lou and Gene's place, I found my sisters and an older niece in a panic. Who was I dating? What was I doing? Things she told them sounded impossible, crazy, unbelievable and scary. I told them she was different, but she was a wonderful woman and I really enjoyed her and loved her. That did nothing to allay their concerns. The next day I headed for Atlanta in a state of confusion and emotional turmoil. After all, Annie had come to Denver excited to introduce me to her old lover. Was I the one who was crazy? I wanted so much to trust Annie. I was now wondering…could I? Should I? Was she really what she said she was, or should I be concerned? I was scared and confused.

The trip back to Atlanta was one of the most difficult times of my life. By the time I reached Atlanta, I wasn't sure what I was doing or what I was thinking. I finally decided to tell Annie I needed to cool our relationship and think about it for a while. When I arrived at Annie's, her place was all set up for a wonderful evening together before our trip to Jacksonville the next day. When I told Annie what I had decided, I could feel her anger at first, but then in her wonderful way she kindly let me go. That was one of the worst nights of my life.

A Frightened Man

He told her good bye
Saw the tears in her eyes
Felt the pain start to pulse
Through his heart
Then, he, drove away
Knowing he couldn't stay
From her magic
For more than a day
And his heart, broken now
From his weakness, somehow
Would come back
To love her once more
And they would be one
Something never undone
A love that would last evermore

DESPERATION

I CAN'T BELIEVE I HURT HER
AS I LEFT HER WITH THE NIGHT
GOING OFF TO DESPERATE DARKNESS
LEFT MY LOVE, TO FIGHT THIS FIGHT
WITH THE DEMONS THAT CONTROLLED ME...

GRIEF

I CAN'T BELIEVE I HURT HER
AND LEFT HER WITH THE PAIN
SIX HOURS ON THE ROAD
'TIL I'D BE HOME AGAIN
BUT THE NIGHT BECAME SURREAL
AS I LOST REALITY
AND SLIPPED INTO DEPRESSION
AND THE PAIN SURROUNDED ME
THE PAIN I FELT, THE PAIN I'D CAUSED
THE LOVE THAT I HAD MISSED
THE TIME I COULD HAVE SPENT WITH HER
THE LIPS I COULD HAVE KISSED

My trip back to Jacksonville that night was one of the most desperate, surreal falls into depression I've ever been through. Once home, sleep was impossible. I couldn't wait to call Annie, tell her I was sorry, that I had made a mistake and I hoped she would forgive me and give me another chance. I couldn't wait until morning when I could call her. Time seemed to stand still. Would morning never come? Would she answer? Could she forgive me? Finally, after what seemed an eternity, the new morning arrived. Frantically I dialed Annie's number.

Chapter Thirteen

No answer. I dialed once more, again no answer. I dialed once more and left a message that I was so sorry and hoped she could find a way to forgive me.

I was sinking deeper and deeper into depression. And I knew what depression was, for I had been there before. It was a lonely place of desperate darkness where you felt you couldn't escape, where nothing mattered, where the world went away, where all joy was lost. Yes, I had been there before and now I was falling again, losing my mind. I am not ashamed to admit I have suffered with situational depression throughout my life. It has made me more compassionate towards those who suffer with any kind of mental health issue. Like many of those kindred souls who have experienced such darkness, I understand the overwhelming relief and gratitude one feels when finding one's way back to the light. I could not see any light from where I was now.

Then miraculously that afternoon, the phone rang. It was Annie. She was very kind. I told her I was suffering from severe depression and needed to get professional help. I said I would do that, but I really would like to see her again when I got through this. I apologized over and over and asked for forgiveness. She was so kind and agreed to keep in touch and to meet again sometime. That day I made arrangements to be seen and get help. And it took some time, but I did. We continued to correspond, and she even sent me a get well note with a small bottle of Sonnet's manure in it, for healing purposes and to bring a little laughter in my life. After several weeks, she finally suggested that she drive to Jacksonville to visit me. I was overjoyed yet filled with apprehension as to what the reunion would bring.

 *Journey to Life's Dance Ranch*

OUT OF DARKNESS

IT WAS FROM THE DARKEST MIDNIGHT THAT
HER LIGHT BROUGHT BACK THE DAWN
AND LET HIS HEART BELIEVE ONCE MORE
THAT HE COULD NOW GO ON
TAKE FLIGHT WITH HER INTO A LIFE
OF NEW LOVE AND ROMANCE
THE TIME WAS NOW FOR BOTH OF THEM
AND SO, THEY TOOK THE CHANCE
AND THOUGH THEY BOTH HAD QUESTIONS
OF THE PAST, AND FUTURE'S FATE
IT WAS ONLY HE, REGRETTABLY
WHO WAS…TO HESITATE
BUT LOVE AND LIGHT WOULD URGE HIM ON
THEIR LOVE WAS MEANT TO GO BEYOND
TO WHERE, THEY'D BOTH BE FREE
AND MELT INTO A ONENESS
FOR ALL ETERNITY

THE WAIT

ONCE MORE THEY'D FOUND EACH OTHER
THOUGH THEY'D HAD TO WAIT THIS TIME
AND THE GIFTS THEY BROUGHT EACH OTHER
THOUGH, NOT, THINGS OF THEIR PRIME
WERE SOMETHING MORE SIGNIFICANT
OF DEEPER VALUE TOO
THEY GAVE THE BEST OF LIFE THEY'D LEARNED
AND WHAT THEY'D BOTH BEEN THROUGH
THE CHALLENGES WERE GIVEN
AND THEY'D BOTH PASSED THE TEST
WHAT THEY NOW WERE, AND HAD TO GIVE
WAS CERTAINLY, THEIR BEST
THE WAIT AND STRUGGLE, NOT IN VAIN
THEIR LOVE, ONCE MORE TO BE
TOGETHER NOW, YET ONCE AGAIN
IT IS THEIR DESTINY

Chapter Thirteen

VALENTINE FORGIVENESS

GOODNESS LIGHT ARRIVED IN TIME
AND BROUGHT WITH HER, A VALENTINE
A CARD OF LOVE THAT OPENED WIDE
AND GAVE THE SAFETY THERE INSIDE
EMBRACED A SOUL, WAS SOON TO DROWN
UNLESS HE FOUND SOME SOLID GROUND
SHE CAME AND PULLED HIM FROM THE STREAM
AND RESCUED FROM THIS DESPERATE DREAM
WHAT HAD FALLEN IN THE WATER
AND THOUGH, HE USUALLY…COULD SWIM
YES, USUALLY WITH THE BEST OF THEM
TODAY THIS SKILL ELUDED HIM
BUT SHE WAS THERE TO HELP
AND WITH HER LOVE AND LIGHT AND DRUM
SHE CAME WITH WHAT SO FEW CAN COME
A SPIRIT SHE WOULD BRING HIS WAY
THE LIGHT TO CHASE, HIS DARK AWAY
HIS LOVE FOR HER GREW BOUNDLESS
WHEN HE FOUND SHE WOULD NOT LEAVE
THOUGH HE'D STUCK A KNIFE INTO HER HEART
AND LEFT HER THERE, TO GRIEVE
WHEN HE ASKED HER THEN TO RESCUE HIM
THERE WAS NO HESITATION
SHE CAME WITH LOVE AND LIGHT AND STRENGTH
FORGAVE HIS EXTRICATION

 *Journey to Life's Dance Ranch*

The reunion in Jacksonville was everything good I could have imagined. Annie was her wonderful self and I fell deeper and deeper in love with her. I found Annie to be a wonderfully passionate and joyful lover and the best snuggler and cuddler I could have ever imagined. I am blessed to still enjoy a wonderful love life with this beautiful loving woman. She brought back a special part of my life I had so missed since I lost Dana.

Before

She touched him with her eyes
She touched him with her smile
She touched him in so many ways
And, it had been a while
For he had known her long before
But not yet, in this life
She'd borne his children, long ago
When she was then his wife

Beautiful woman, beautiful eyes
Beautiful face, beautiful hands
Beautiful scent, beautiful soul
Beautiful touch, beautiful voice
Beautiful touch, beautiful kiss
Beautiful walk, beautiful warmth
Beautiful mind, beautiful woman

Chapter Thirteen

NEW LOVE

In morning light
He thanks the night
For bringing her his way
And loves this sight
Which gives delight
As at his side she lays
And with each breath
He sees her take
In quiet peace
Before she wakes
He finds he loves her more
And can't believe his passion
For this new love, he adores

Those days I'd spent without Annie, waiting to see her again, wanting to hold her again and tell her how much I'd missed her seemed like a lifetime. And, perhaps then it was.

Lifetime Wait

He'd had to wait a lifetime
For Annie to arrive
But waiting had been worth it
For now he was alive
In ways he'd never been before
In things that he could do
And say and feel and celebrate
Those things he always knew
Were locked within his fearful soul
Awaiting her brave heart
To come and make his spirit whole
And free it from the dark
With love and light, she took his hand
And walked with him 'til dawn
Brought sunlight, of this new love
Enjoined…forever one

Her Eyes' Reflection

Those eyes, those eyes
And oh...the face
From which those eyes reflect
In morning light, his favorite sight
She's still not woken, yet
And so in dawn's first gentle glow
He feels the love, within him grow
His eyes, awaiting hers, a while
The open eyes will bring her smile
Embrace, and love's caress
He'll hold her and give thanks to God
His life, she now does bless

What He Knew

Though he knew, it would never happen again
What he knew, he knew...was wrong
And she came, in spite of what he knew
And brought him, her new song
Then his heart began to sing again
As he danced with this new lover
In her special eyes and gentle face
He knew he would discover
A part of him, he'd kept
And from the world, he'd hid
But now, he gave his love to her
And one day they'd be wed

Chapter Thirteen

Our courtship continued. Many trips made between Atlanta and Jacksonville. Magic and miracles with Annie that have never gone away. Annie also loved to write and she has her own stories and poems. We often enjoyed writing poems back and forth whenever we are sitting at a café or a restaurant. Sometimes we made a competition out of it. One evening, I had a feeling I needed to write but didn't have any idea what I wanted to write about. I asked Annie if she would pick a random word and I would see what happened. She said, "Love." I said, "No that isn't random enough, please try and give me a different word." She said, "OK, how about *hearth*." This is what flowed from that word:

HEARTH

THE HEARTH THAT HELD THE FIRE
IN THAT MAGIC HOLY PLACE
WHERE THE FIRE ROSE OUT OF THE WOOD
AND BLOSSOMED THERE WITH GRACE
WARMED THE NIGHT AND WARMED THEIR SKIN
AND WARMED THEIR WEARY SOULS, WITHIN
MOVED THE DARKNESS, HERE AND THERE
PUT ITS SCENT UPON THE AIR
THEN FIRE, TURNED TO EMBER
WHICH HELD A RICHNESS LUST
'TIL LOVE AND LUST, ESCAPED IT
AND EMBER, TURNED TO DUST

More Love

If he could love her more
Then it would be tomorrow
For she had brought him joy
When he was lost in sorrow
He loved her more and still somehow
He loves her, still more, yet
With every waking sunrise
And every day's ... sunset

My penny poem was inspired by a penny I found in Annie's parking lot and memories of finding those lucky pennies all my life. I took it back to Annie's flat and wrote the poem then told Annie what I wanted to do that evening. We collected a bunch of loose change, pennies, nickels, dimes and even some quarters. We headed for the square and its stores and parking lots. We scattered the coins around. It was a joyful time for us and hopefully for those who found the lucky coins we had left for them.

The Penny

As he bent to grab the penny
Where it glistened at his feet
He knew this was his lucky day
For it smiled from the street
And he put it in his pocket
This great treasure he had found
There, awaiting his arrival
With its magic, on the ground
Should he keep it in his pocket?

Chapter Thirteen

Or give this gift away?
If he gives it to another
It will brighten both their days
What he'd learned about a penny
In the wonder of his youth
Would always bring good fortune
Would always be his truth
What so many, would not bend for
For the effort makes no sense
They forget these cents of magic
Are not just...common cents

Annie's Birthday Eve

As this evening now grows late
And I anticipate
The day my love chose life
And came to be, for me

Chapter Fourteen
And Away We Go, Go, Go

I decided I wanted to train for a marathon. With my past heart condition and diabetes, I wanted to consult with a cardiologist first. I had raced in many 5K, 10K and 15K runs and one half-marathon. My new cardiologist ran a bevy of new tests and reviewed my history. He told me he didn't think I should be running without someone with me in case I had a heart attack. He confirmed I had the "widow-maker lesion." Whoa, running was an important part of my life! He said he thought I could keep running but when I asked how much, he said he really couldn't say. So, I asked what can be done to resolve the problem. His answer, you need a by-pass surgery.

I said, "let's do it." His answer, you are not a candidate for surgery because all your tests were absolutely normal. Wait, this put me in a catch 22 position; I needed surgery but wasn't a candidate for it until I had a heart attack while running. I said, "Wait a minute, the last time I had an angiogram they determined I really didn't need surgery. Do you think it might be a good idea to perform another angiogram and see if there have been significant changes and revaluate"?

Thankfully he agreed and said there was a new procedure, a "flow wire angiogram", that may give a more accurate picture. When the new test results came back, he said it was good we ran the new test. The lesion they diagnosed the first time as an 85% blockage, with the new test, showed only a sixty percent blockage. He said no cardiologist in the country would perform a bypass with that amount of blockage. He said I could go ahead and run all I wanted and live a normal life. He

did say that down the road I might need a surgery but that would probably be many years down the road. Whew, another bullet dodged.

THE GANG

One of the great blessings of our relationship was eventually meeting Annie's traveling "gang" from her career in Georgia Corrections. This special group of people are Annie's sacred inner circle of most trusted friends, as they have been with her through her life of ups and downs. They know her well the good, the bad and the ugly and they love her anyway and have had her back as long as she has known them. There was JoAnne (Jo Jo), Linda and Denny, and Elaine and Annabeth. Their first trip was being planned for Italy and Annie had asked the group if they would be willing to let me join them on this trip. Without even meeting me, but just learning about me through Annie, they all happily agreed. And so, we became the "Five Wise Women and Two Wise Guys!"

THE GANG

The trip was in October and I was on a plane with JoJo, Denny and Linda. Annie had made her reservations before she knew I was coming so she was on another flight, although we were both on the runway at the same time. Elaine and Annabeth had gone on to France

Chapter Fourteen

first and were going to meet with us in Switzerland. As magic and miracles happen, there was a man on Annie's plane who was being very disruptive. So much so that the pilot decided to abort the take off and return to the terminal to remove the man from the plane. This took a while and Annie was able to rebook on our flight during this commotion. I was so happy to see her walking down the aisle where they had arranged a seat right next to me. What a joyful beginning. Annie introduced me to the rest of the "gang" sitting elsewhere on the plane.

When we arrived in Europe, we picked up our van and Denny drove it (bless you Denny) to our first VRBO (Vacation Rental by Owner) in Lake Como. Gorgeous! And what fun it was getting to know this amazing group of people, intelligent, funny, spiritual, etc., just good people and I felt right at home right away. We then moved onto Venice where Annie and I celebrated my birthday at a quaint restaurant along the canal. Next stop was Florence and then on to Rome. Those who have been can understand the awesomeness of this beautiful country. Those who have not been there please go if you can! After Rome we hired a tour guide to take us to Pompeii and then headed down the Amalfi Coast with our next stop being in Sorrento.

With this group magic and craziness occurred on a regular basis. JoJo and Annie made a spectacle of themselves as they plunged fully clothed into the very cold waters of Lake Como, to the astonishment of the locals. Later Annie took a dip in the cold pool in Sorrento, not sure she had any clothes on this time! The owner of this home, Maria Laura, actually cooked for us a homemade eggplant parmigiana dinner. She did have a crush on me and I was kidded about it often. She told Annie emphatically that I was for her, Maria Laura, not for Annie.

Although very sweetly she gave Annie a horse figurine Annie was admiring, Maria Laura said she had bought this when she was on her honeymoon with her deceased husband many years ago. Of course, we were not on our honeymoon! However, the gang had drawn straws to see who would use the "honeymoon cottage" behind the main house. As luck would have it, Annie and I drew the straw and off we went for the

night. I guess it was just another one of our omens which seemed to always be popping up.

Annie and I had taken a special hike up a mountain to reach a sacred place where there was a beautiful old cross at the top. It touched both of us very deeply Afterwards we walked back towards our house but were very hungry. It was mid-afternoon in a small Italian town so not much was open. However, one kind owner told us to come on in. He opened the whole restaurant and prepared a beautiful meal for us. The hospitality of the locals was wonderful. And obviously the "gang" ate and drank amazing food and wines throughout the regions. During the course of our trip we consumed a considerable amount of fine wine. Someone suggested we save the corks. I volunteered to be the "Keeper of the Corks." When Annie and I got home and I retrieved the corks from my suitcase, I thought it might be nice to save them in a fun little memorial to our trip. Thus, the "photo cork jar" was born.

ONE SIDE OF THE "PHOTO CORK JAR"

Chapter Fourteen

Journey to the Cross

If he should die tomorrow
He would not feel a loss
For he had made the journey
Up the mountain to the cross
And on the way, found love and life
Joined spirit with her there
And kissed her in this holy place
As wind, blew through their hair
They held…each other's souls
In the mist, they did embrace
Gave thanks, unto their God
And reveled in this, grace

Dad with Them

And his father would have walked with them
If he had been alive
But they knew that they would find him
At the cross when they arrived
And they were not disappointed
When the mist did disappear
The cross rose up unto the sky
And he was standing there
Then the mist came back
And hid the cross
An illusion, took its place
And as we looked into the cloud
'Twas God…we saw God's face

HEAVEN'S TOUCH

AND THEY REJOICED IN TUSCANY
AND THEIR LOVE FOR ONE ANOTHER
THEY FOUND, THAT THIS WAS JUST TO BE
WHAT TOGETHER, THEY'D DISCOVER
WAS MORE THAN, TUCSON LANDSCAPE
ARCHITECTURE OR FINE WINE
THEY'D TOUCHED TOGETHER...HEAVEN
IN THEIR HEARTS NOW, SO ENTWINED
AND WHAT THEY SHARED IN LOVE
WAS NOW LOCKED IN SPIRIT
A GIFT, FROM UP ABOVE

CERTAINTY

THIS WAS SO VERY DIFFERENT
AS HE KNEW, IT HAD TO BE
IT DIDN'T ALWAYS FEEL RIGHT
SO MUCH, UNCERTAINTY
BUT HE PRAYED
THEY COULD WORK THROUGH IT
'TIL CERTAINTY WAS THERE...
OR WAS, TOO MUCH EXPECTED
TO LET THEM BE A PAIR?
I GUESS, HE'D HAVE TO WAIT AND SEE
IF HE WAS MEANT...FOR ANNIE Z

Chapter Fourteen

We finished this trip back in Rome. Annie and I had another spiritual experience as we climbed the stairs above St. Peters at the Vatican. We stood behind all those beautiful statues of Jesus and the saints and we felt the peace and beauty of this sacred place. Then it was time to go home. Annie was again on another flight home, as we dropped her off at the airport, I shouted out to her "ti amo," I love you in Italian. Her smiling reply was my reward.

ANNIE'S GREATEST BLESSINGS

From the first, Annie always let me know her greatest accomplishment in life was her daughter Meghan. Despite Annie's challenge of balancing single parenting with a career, and processing active healing work from her past, she is awed and so grateful for how her daughter turned out to be such an amazing person. Annie gives a lot of credit to her siblings for helping raise Meghan. When Annie needed to travel for work or had health issues, her siblings were always there to help out with Meghan.

TRENT & MEGHAN

One of the greatest privileges and blessings I had was given to me by Annie's daughter, Meghan, and her husband, Trent. Meghan was 9 months pregnant with Trent's and Meghan's second baby. They invited me to be with them at the hospital for their baby's birth. Meghan had been taken away to the delivery room. Annie and I were in Meghan's hospital room with Trent, his mom and Annie's granddaughter, Emma (3). Emma and "Ami" were eating a Chick-Fil-A Ice Dream. When they brought Meghan back, she held a beautiful baby boy in her arms, Carter James. He was a strong healthy baby with good lungs and good color. We were all thankful and thrilled to have healthy new baby boy.

ANNIE SINGING TO CARTER JAMES

My most poignant memory of that day was seeing Annie take Carter James into her arms and singing "Baby Mine" to her new grandson. I captured it on my phone and it is a treasure I enjoy watching. I am sure that one day Carter James will enjoy it as well and perhaps show his own children, his grandma, "Ami," singing him this lullaby. Her grandchildren call her "Ami" because Emma first used that name to identify Annie and it stuck. She was probably trying to say Annie but it came out Ami instead! The recordings and all the photos we made that day are now family treasures and I am gifted to now be "Grandpa Mike" to Emma and Carter, as well as to Meghan's two older step children Zach and Libby.

Even though my love for Annie was growing deeper, I, unfortunately, still had my fears.

Albedo Knight

She knew her alcheringa (dreamtime)
Would always be of him
And not just be an alba
But poem without an end
A journey from the night
Finding dawn, albescent there
And her albedo knight
Would not be leaving her

Chapter Fourteen

Enigma Test

She was a true conundrum
An enigma, test for sure
And, all that he felt sure of
Was, he had a love for her
But there was fear
Of what the mirror
Would show him of himself
And doubts of his ability...
To figure, Annie, out

The Web of Love

Her concupiscence allured him
Was this something he could trust
Or just a sensuous longing
Perhaps an ardent lust
Was he to be, the victim
Of a widow's sensuous web?
Must he step upon her silk?
Then venture further still?
Would he find his love esurient?
Could, he be, her next kill?
Or would sweet love be waiting?
Make his move, then move away
And live to feel the magic silk
Of ...love, another day

Journey to Life's Dance Ranch

TRAVELING AGAIN

Annie and I would make another trip to Italy the next October to again celebrate our birthdays. First, we stayed at a beautiful chateau in Tuscany. A stunning place with olive groves and scenery which brought joy to one's heart. They also had stables and an opportunity to ride horses through the Tuscan county side. Annie was in heaven. Next, we went back to Sorrento. Sorrento is known for its inlaid wood creations. We were interested in finding a company that could produce inlaid wood music boxes with Dana's Butterfly on it. We were lucky to find a nice lady who agreed to have her artists make a prototype box for us. While she did design the prototype, we sadly never ended up having boxes produced. The owner explained the Chinese would steal the design and make another cheaper version of Dana's Butterfly. I did not want this to happen. We also managed to visit the beautiful island of Capri on this trip.

PROTOTYPE MUSIC BOX

Chapter Fourteen

ANNIE'S TUSCAN BIRTHDAY

Her day arrived with clear blue sky
And chill upon the air
She sensed this day was different
The magic now was there
So they walked down, and mounted up
To ride a spirit's gift
And with the spirit's nature
On gentle mares to lift
Them up, then into heaven
As chill would fade away
Exposing all God's glory
On a perfect Tuscan day
He marveled at her being
As he watched from just behind
He felt her spirit rejoicing
And knew that she was high
On autumn leaves, autumn trees
And autumn…butterflies
On chestnuts falling to the earth
With bright brown gentle eyes

Simple Man

Just a simple man, you see
But I love my simplicity
For complication troubles me
And I don't function well there
So, love that's simple
Love that's pure
A love of which, I can be sure
Will be a place for us to share
A place of joy, a place to care

We enjoyed other fun trips together including going to New York City where I had never been. We saw the Broadway musical Billy Elliot, all about dancing the story of our lives. It was wonderful and the trip was very romantic.

Chapter Fourteen

We also went on a trip to Albuquerque New Mexico to see the Balloon Festival with the gang, along with other adventures along the way.

We continued our life together for several more months before I finally did the right thing and asked Annie to marry me. It was a beautiful Easter Sunday, 2010 in Atlanta. We had just been egg hunting with Meghan, Trent and the kids. We came back to her flat and were sitting on the porch when I asked Annie to marry me. Dudley was wagging his tail in approval. We talked about getting married in June in a simple ceremony behind my house, on the golf course. Although Annie cared less for Florida than even I did, because of the flatness and humidity, we never even dreamed about another option at that time. Sonnet had already been moved to a stable down there, and although she was miserable in the muggy heat, we never questioned that this was our future. Little did we know that Dana and Steppes were already orchestrating another dream which would later become a reality.

Chapter Fifteen
My First Love & New Love Meet

Annie had not yet met my mother, or sister Marg and her husband Vern, who all lived together in Butte, Montana. We flew to Butte in May and had a great visit with Mom, Marg and Vern. Mom and Vern immediately loved Annie and welcomed her into the family. Margaret, after talking to our other sisters, was a bit cautious, but kind. Marcy and Kelly ended up joining us since it was our mom's birthday. And I had a radio spot to promote Butterfly Ballet in Butte.

Annie had been helping me with the company once we were officially dating. Her background in managing large budgets was badly needed to get our books straightened out. She came to me shortly before our trip and told me I had a lot of money going out over the years but I had nothing coming back in. My losses at this point were very great and it was during this time I decided running the company as planned was just not realistic. Thus, began the dissolution of the company but not my passion for sharing ovarian cancer awareness or the love of dance. Our company web page, with the story of Dana and our family, still exists at butterflyballet.com. But we eventually stopped having the jewelry or chocolates made.

I must say I don't regret a single penny spent honoring my wonderful Danalee and the thousands of pendants, earrings, bracelets, pins which made a difference in the lives of those to whom we gifted them, and in our lives as well. It was something I had to do to honor Dana and our life story, and to promote ovarian cancer awareness which I knew robbed too many women of their "life's dance" way too early.

Journey to Life's Dance Ranch

ANNIE'S RELATIONSHIP DISCLAIMER

Annie did mention to me, shortly after we were engaged, that she absolutely believed me when I said my marriage with Dana was beautiful and perfect. And she would always honor Dana and the role she played in my life. She did caution me that she herself was not perfect, and she certainly could assure me she was not meticulous in her housework. This proved to be true which has been a learning experience for me! She felt I had Dana up on a pedestal, which I did, but that she Annie never intended or desired to be put up on a pedestal. "Too far to fall from grace," was her explanation. Her life experience had taught her the truth of the saying, "after the ecstasy, comes the laundry."

She was not afraid to admit that she, like most people was a work in progress. Actively committed to trying to improve as a human being but keenly aware that perfection was an unrealistic and exhausting goal. I do believe that Annie and Dana would have gotten along and enjoyed each other's company. However, they were two very different kinds of woman and my adventures with Annie would be completely unique and at times very unfamiliar to what I had been used to with Dana.

While we were in Montana, Annie and I wanted to see the new house Mary Lou and Gene were building in Helena. We borrowed one of Marg and Vern's cars and headed north. Mary Lou and Gene had purchased forty-five beautiful acres west of Helena on Ten Mile Creek. They planned to build their retirement home and then move to Helena when it was finished. They had a guest house on the property and offered to let us stay there while in Helena. We had barely settled in when Annie said, "Let's go write our wedding vows up the hill on that beautiful massive rock formation." We grabbed a bottle of wine and a couple of glasses and were on the rocks writing words of love we would say at our wedding. When we finished, Annie said, "If we are going to be visiting Montana occasionally, I need to know where we can go to ride horses. Because you know for me riding is as necessary as oxygen!" We looked in the yellow pages and found a place in Wolf Creek not too far north of Helena.

Chapter Fifteen

And we were off to take Annie for her first horse ride in Montana. It was a glorious ride, just Annie, me and our guide. We started into the mountains with a gentle shower kissing us. The shower soon gave way to sunshine, rainbow and spectacular mountain meadows and peaks. It was without a doubt one of the most magical times of our lives. On the way back to Helena, Annie, marveling at the ride, said, "Mike I've ridden all over Europe and never had a ride that wonderful or beautiful!" And then she said words which were magic to my ears. She said, "I wonder what a little piece of horse property out here would cost?"

I had never dreamed that I could possibly come home to my first love, Montana. And Annie had never dreamed that she could look for property where she could have her beloved horse live with her. Back at the guest house we quickly looked up realtors on line. The next morning, we made an appointment and started looking at properties. The first stop left us underwhelmed but then the realtor said he knew of a place that had just been put on the market. So, we headed off to Clausen Rd., to a little valley right below the Continental Divide at MacDonald Pass. We turned onto a dirt road, drove for a mile, and then turned into the ¼ mile driveway. Immediately we were in awe and in love with this land. We felt as if we had come home to a place we never could have imagined.

Annie saw the 1880's rock/log barn first and hardly had eyes for anything else. We both knew we had to have this.

Journey to Life's Dance Ranch

EARLY PHOTO OF OUR BARN AND PREVIOUS OWNERS

It was way more than we had expected to buy, and we were not sure we could afford it, but I knew we would have to find a way. The owner, Peggy even agreed to redraw the property in a way that gave us 40 acres of "the heart" of the 160 acres she was selling. It was forty beautiful historic acres with Helena's original 1860's stagecoach tollhouse, a large log cabin, many historical outbuildings like a cowboy bunkhouse, old horse breaking round pen and cattle corrals, an old milk house and a grainery, creeks, pastures, hay fields, pine/fir forests, a beautiful aspen grove, all nestled in a very private valley beneath the mountains at the Continental Divide. And so, in less than twenty-four hours, an offer was made, money was put down, and the purchase agreement was signed. We had bought the ranch. We were ecstatic, in total joy as we headed down the driveway to head back to Butte.

Then as life can turn on a dime, we went from the highest high to the lowest low. We received a phone call from Linda telling us that JoJo's only child, her 29-year old son, Derek, (D-Rock) had died of heart failure while on the golf course with his buddies in Jacksonville. He was there for a groom's party and a wedding. He himself had just gotten engaged and was planning his wedding. We cried all the way back to Butte. We made emergency arrangements to fly back to Jacksonville, so we could be with Jo Jo and attend his beautiful celebration of life. To this day we feel there is a part of Derek's spirit out here at the ranch and every time we see a rainbow, we know it is a sign from Derek. Now, in addition to Dana and Steppes we also had Derek watching out for us from beyond.

DEREK "D-ROCK" CHANCE

D-Rock... always watching over us.

OUR WEDDING

Only two weeks after Derek's celebration of life, Annie and I were married on June 19th, on the golf course behind my house. Her daughter Meghan was her maid of honor and her horse Sonnet with roses braided in her mane was her flower horse/girl, and my boys, Patrick and Andrew, were best men. It was a small wedding. All our travel friends, including JoJo, were there along with Meghan's and Patrick's families and a few neighborhood friends.

Journey to Life's Dance Ranch

Mike's wedding vows to Annie

So with the spirit of our spirit

From which our spirits come

Today we'll join the spirits

And make them, then as one

With those we love most, near us here

I pledge my trust to you

It is my life's most precious gift

What makes a true love...true

And I promise now true love

As I take you for my wife

And give thanks for this miracle

Of you, and me, and life

Chapter Fifteen

ANNIE'S WEDDING VOWS TO MIKE

Today I make this lifelong pledge
to my Montana man,
Born from the prairies, wind and sky,
I promise to be open, every day
to all the magic and miracles
Our bodies, minds and spirit can create together,
AND
I willingly choose to join in sacred union with you,
As we in turn share this loving energy
with our beloved children,
Grandchildren, families, and our marvelous
2 legged and 4 legged friends,
...as well as with those in need.
I promise to always honor those in your past
who have loved you into being the man you are today,
and it is with great joy I choose to enter into
holy matrimony with you,
to begin our journey together,
towards who we will become tomorrow.
I give you my trust, loyalty, love and friendship
and I will cherish whatever time God allows us
to be together on this earth.
"Oh Captain my Captain"
in closing I must borrow a line
from a Rascal Flats song and simply say,
"God bless the broken roads that
led me straight to you."
Yours forever, Annie Z.

Journey to Life's Dance Ranch

    The "The Hills Are Alive," from the "Sound of Music" played when Annie came through the garden with Meghan. I wore my dress whites as Annie had always dreamed of marrying a Navy Captain with a sword just like Christopher Plummer's character in the movie. We waltzed to "Run for the Roses" during the ceremony and as we walked out of the ceremony we got on my motorcycle to the sound of "Up Where You Belong" from "Officer and a Gentleman." I had always wanted a motorcycle and with Annie and my new found life I splurged and bought one, took lessons and was semi qualified to have my new bride ride with me after the ceremony towards our new life. At least we made it safely to the end of the driveway before it was time for pictures! We had a reception dinner at one of our favorite restaurants, Clark's Fish Camp. Then we were off to begin our honeymoon adventure!

Chapter Fifteen

Journey to Life's Dance Ranch

HONEYMOON

The next day we were off; first to Prague, Czech Republic (where we had never been and I am Czech!); then Salzburg, Austria, (home of what else? Sound of Music and birthplace of Mozart); and Vienna (to see the Lipizzaner's perform at the Spanish Riding Academy.) We wrote poems back and forth to each other all the way through the marvelous journey.

Vltava River
(Prague…River Vltava…our honeymoon)

Upon the river…Vltava
In prayer and love we are
Where my ancestors, begat me
Where they had loved before
Where my father's father
Met his wife
And where we now
Begin our life
Together, as man and wife

Chapter Fifteen

An unexpected blessing occurred on our trip home from Prague. We were handed a complimentary upgrade to first class. We had just sworn off all good food and drinks, yet we could not resist the delicious complementary food, beverages and wonderful beds to sleep on. It was an amazing trip home and now we were ready to head towards the Ranch.

We arrived back in Atlanta, then headed back to Florida to pack up my house and put it on the market. Then it was back up to Georgia to pack up Annie's household goods, rent her flat and drive our new Nissan Armada out west to Montana. Annie was very sad to leave her daughter, family and friends, as Atlanta had been her home for the past 35 years. However, Atlanta had become too overgrown for her and as she meditated on the decision, "follow the horses," was the insight she received. The horses nodded west. We had no clue what to expect but we trusted we were following a path set by the Divine.

And so, it came to pass that I made it back to my first love, Montana, with this wonderful new love, Annie Z. Just as the first poem I wrote after Dana died had prophesized, I would be going home to live in my Montana, perhaps my final resting place would be here in the arms of my Montana. We arrived at the Ranch with great gratitude, never suspecting all the magic and miracles we would begin to experience here. From the first day we arrived at our new home on the Ranch and the first night we spent in an empty house anticipating our household goods arriving the next morning, we were blessed. We have experienced this every single day and continue to give thanks for this incredible blessing and all the miracles since we arrived.

Journey to Life's Dance Ranch

ANGELS CALLING

And so, the three, came to them
To show them where they'd been
To show them how they got there
To show them where they'd sinned
To give a clearer vision
Of what now lay beyond
To show them their new mission
Before their time was gone
They both believed in angels
For they had seen them 'oft
And accepted their existence
While others, merely scoffed
One angel came with nothing
One angel...had it all
The last, explained the others
The grand and then the small
And clarified our focus
Why they...had come to call

Angel 4 My Love

They came to me this morning
Both on the other side
Of the middle in between them
On their celestial ride
I put them in my pocket
And held them for my love
Two angels...shining brightly
God sent from up above

Part III:

Life's Dance Ranch

Chapter Sixteen
Coming Home

We were feeling so blessed for the chance to start a new life's dance together. Instantaneously we looked at each other and exclaimed, this is our "Life's Dance Ranch." And so, it began and the name stuck and we soon created Life's Dance Ranch, LLC. We were already eagerly anticipating bringing family, friends, and others to share in the peaceful and joyful sacredness of this land. It was a "Field of Dreams," moment where we too felt, "If we build it, they will come." Of course, we have always felt you can't really own land. Rather we see ourselves called to be good stewards of the land and help it flourish under our care for as long as we are gifted with the ability to do so.

Once we began to unpack, we realized we needed a washer and a dryer. So, we headed to an appliance store which was having a going out of business sale. The owner Tom told us to look around, we didn't see anything plain and simple which we were looking for. However, we actually bought an old antique Maytag washer with wringer. We thought it could be an interesting historical talking piece in our laundry room. We have ended up using it to hold water bottles and drinks during our barn parties.

While talking to Tom, I noticed a picture of a mule on his computer. I said, "Hey, that's a nice-looking mule." Tom said, "Her name is Paula. She is my wife's and we are selling her." We had shipped Sonnet out and she was the first animal we had on our land. We knew she needed another buddy to socialize with, and so, I bought my first equine, Paula the mule. She arrived the next day complete with her

saddle and other tack. She has been the most gentle, wonderful animal we could have ever imagined and a great pal for Sonnet and eventually our other equines as well. Only in my Montana could I go looking for a washer and dryer and come back with a mule instead!

THANKS

For I've been given
More than most
In this my earthly
Now…a heaven
Where every day's
A miracle
Awaiting 'morrow's
Yet, ungiven
Thankful for
What's now my, life
My mountain days
My, Annie wife
Amen

THREE YEARS

Three years ago tonight
I looked into her eyes
They told me she was joyful
They told me she was wise
I knew that she was special
Something, I've never known
Something I couldn't, be without
Or I would live alone
But now, she is my love
My angel and my life
A gift from up above
My Annie…my new wife

Chapter Sixteen

New Love

The incredible goodness
Which came to his soul
And the freedom of nothing
Which made her feel whole

Walking with Annie

If you think you'd like to walk with me
On this pathway to eternity
I think I'd probably like that too
It's what I think I'd like to do

Reflection

No more with bated breath
Did she await his eyes
Her breathing, deep and joyful
For now she realized
That what he promised
From the start
To show, from deep
Within his heart
A pure reflection
...of her soul
The goodness that he...
Found there,
Was now
To make her whole

Since arriving at our new home, at the end of a beautiful day, we enjoyed walking up the hill to a big wooden swing behind our house to watch the sunset. Here we have a magnificent view of the mountains in this special valley. One evening, Annie mentioned she would need to find an arena in town to ride Sonnet during the winters. As we were talking, she gazed across the road and kept staring at one of the buildings on the Zinn Ranch. She suddenly grabbed my arm and said, "Mike, I think that's an indoor arena on the Zinn's property!" She added, "Oh my God, if it is, that is another sign that we are indeed in the right and perfect place." Annie couldn't believe it. A place to ride horses outside and maybe inside as well, wow, her heaven on earth for sure!

ANNIE ON OUR SWING

NEIGHBOR BLESSINGS

And as blessings happen, it was shortly after that evening, we met our neighbors, Ray and Delona Zinn. It was the beginning of a beautiful friendship. They have been such amazing neighbors and friends. The Zinn's graciously offered for us to not only use their indoor arena but also allow us to ride the "Z Trail." The Zinn's have 500 acres of beautiful Montana mountains which has access to primitive Forest Service land. They built a well-maintained trail throughout this property which they named the "Z Trail." The Zinn's are very devout Mormons and their goodness and kindness reflect their spiritual values. Delona once told Annie that she too felt as Annie did, that they were led to this

Chapter Sixteen

valley. It was almost as if there were a sacred spiritual vortex calling us to be here to live and honor this land. The Zinn's even have a beautiful monument which Ray and his son built at the top of their mountains honoring their sacred place.

As soon as we met the Zinn's we also met their foreman, Jordan Alexander. He was a friend when you were in need. With Ray's support, Jordan would often snow plow many of our driveways or help fill the pot holes for the neighbors on Clausen Rd. He saved me when I got my tractor or truck stuck or needed some other help on our ranch. Between Jordan and first Peggy then Cassie, our log cabin occupants, I received some great education over the years about ranching. I was a dentist and a dentist's son, but I always wanted to be a rancher. Here I am fulfilling my dream, although my body is not always operating at the same youthful enthusiasm as my mind desires. Despite the body signals of discomfort, I am able to forge ahead and get on the tractor or snow-blower and spend days working on our ranch. I do love it so.

Over the years we have adopted the Zinn's as family. Annie even kiddingly refers to Ray as her "Pops," as he was happy to step in as a late in life adoptive father, after learning she had not had a positive relationship with her biological father. It was only a matter of days, after we first arrived, before Ray asked Annie to go on a " Z Trail" ride with him and his son-in-law Brian. Even though Annie loves horses and riding, she is not a strong rider. She first learned when she was undergoing intense chemo and with her multiple sclerosis, she has frozen hips and legs which don't always move when asked resulting in poor balance. So, riding for her is also a therapeutic exercise which helps her improve her balance. Annie and her Sonnet were arena riders and not used to trail riding. Ray was an expert rider having grown up with horses and a former gymnast who was in incredible shape. Annie did not let Ray know of her limitations.

Annie told me later it was an amazingly beautiful ride and even thought it started raining and began to thunder, they sang along the way up the mountain and even as they were coming down. However, near

the bottom of the mountain, Ray suddenly took off at a full gallop towards the barn. Sonnet was so shocked at the change in pace and terrain that she tripped and then crow hopped over some rocks. Sonnet then threw a shoe and next came Annie over Sonnet's head, landing on her tail bone right on some rocks.

She did get back on her horse and arrived back at the ranch, I could see she was in considerable pain. We took her down to Urgent Care where they took one x-ray, saw nothing and had their chiropractor do some manipulation on her. Trying to ignore the pain and continuing to see a chiropractor, Annie persevered in decorating the house. Shortly after we moved to the ranch, we were invited to a neighborhood barbeque where we were meeting many of our other Clausen Road neighbors. A guest there happened to be involved with the Montana Historic Society. She knew the historic significance of our home and property. She asked us if we would be willing to decorate and have a Christmas open house, one of five historic houses done each year for Helena. We were delighted to be asked and agreed, but we had a lot of work ahead of us to get the house ready.

Perhaps one of the first persons we met on arriving at the ranch was Allison Bell. Her husband Shannon has a construction company and they live just a few miles from us up toward the top of the pass. One day we looked out and saw a couple of kids petting our horse and mule. It wasn't long before we got to know the whole wonderful family. They had six beautiful children and have had two more since we met them. They have become more like our children and grandchildren. They all ride our horses and Paula. We have had the joy of watching the children grow into beautiful adults, two now in college.

Chapter Sixteen

OUR 1860'S HISTORICAL PROPERTY

Our historical property dates back to the American Indians who often encamped along our creek long before the white man came in the mid 1800's with the gold rush. Our home, built in the 1860's, is the original stage coach toll house for Helena. There was a log toll road starting at the toll house and then over the Continental Divide onto Elliston and the French Woman's place, another stage coach tollhouse. A man named Dunphy built the tollhouse and hired a man named MacDonald to help him run a work crew to build and maintain the log road.

We have several sources of history about our property, many of them contradictory in dates and ownership of the toll road, toll house, barn and out buildings. The first Territorial Legislature authorized the construction of toll roads in 1864. A man named Constant Guyot was the owner at that time. E.M. "Lige" Dunphy eventually bought out Guyot and completed construction on the toll road. Dunphy hired Alexander MacDonald to maintain the road and manage the toll road business.

Half of our home is still the old toll house with original hand hewn logs, beams and pine floors. MacDonald eventually bought out Dunphy in 1879. Our beautiful rock/log barn was built in 1887. Once the railroad and the automobile arrived in the Helena area, the need for a toll road or stage coach stop became less and less. A new highway 12 over the pass had construction started in 1936 and built about a mile and half north of us. This pass was named after MacDonald. MacDonald Pass is known to have one of the prettiest vista's in Montana. The historical overlook is right above us and passing tourists often look down on our beautiful valley which we gratefully now call home.

Journey to Life's Dance Ranch

The MacDonald Pass Toll Road

The road between Elliston and Helena originated as a toll road built by Constant Guyot in 1866. Travelers christened it the Frenchwoman's Road for Guyot's wife, who collected the tolls and provided hot meals and a place to sleep for weary sojourners at their cabin near Elliston. In 1868, the Frenchwoman was found murdered in her cabin. Fearing the vigilantes, her husband fled the area. Operation of the toll road then fell to Elijah Dunphy, who hired Alexander MacDonald to maintain the road and collect tolls. You can see portions of the old toll road on the mountainside below this overlook.

Motorists on the MacDonald Pass road around 1920.

SIGN AT MACDONALD PASS LOOKOUT

VIEW OF LIFE'S DANCE RANCH FROM HWY 12 GOING UP TO MACDONALD PASS

WINTER AND SUMMER VISTA FROM MACDONALD PASS LOOKOUT

Chapter Sixteen

FROM THE HORSE'S MOUTH OR NEAR ENOUGH!

I don't remember all the people we have talked with who gave us historic information about the property. We have been able to visit with several whose families lived here in years past. We have made copies of some early deeds and property sales. I do wish I had written down all their names and had them all back to the ranch to go over their historic family connections. As far as we have been able to ascertain, after Dunphy and MacDonald owned it, a family named May bought it and ran a dairy farm on the property. The acreage of the property was much greater than we have now but we are unsure of the exact amount.

We believe the next owners were Albert and Bertha Clausen, and they put the stucco over the house. The Clausen's were German ranchers who ran a dairy supplying Helena with butter, milk and cream for many years. The dirt road to our ranch still bears their name. Prior to his death we were fortunate to know Howard Clausen, one of their sons, and he told us many historical stories about the property from his early years. After Albert died, Bertha split out some of the acreage to their children. After Bertha gave each of her children their acreage, Bertha sold the remaining acreage with the house, barn and other properties on it to a Helena pediatrician, Dr. Bob Keckley. Bob and his wife, Darlene, raised their eight children in our home. There are some Clausens who still live in the area, and if I have misrepresented their homestead property history I sincerely apologize.

It was the Keckleys who built out the garage and added a mudroom and 2 bedrooms upstairs. The Keckleys eventually bought the beautiful acreage across from us, now the Zinn Ranch. Bob then sold some of this property and began to build a huge Canadian Cypress timber Lodge. Unfortunately, Dr. Keckley went to Hawaii with his sons and passed away in a scuba diving accident. His wife, Darlene was left to finish out this lodge which is now the home of some of our dearest friends, Dr. Steve and Renee Liston.

Dr. Keckley had sold the stagecoach property to another man named McDonald who was a dealer in historic documents. He had a huge fear of fires so he added metal roofing to many of the old buildings to make them as fire safe as possible. He also added a 24,000 sq foot log cabin to the property right in front of the old barn which he used as his office and a mother-in-law suite. He eventually sold the property to Ambrose and Peggy Phalen and moved to California where unfortunately, he had a huge fire which destroyed much of his work.

Peggy and Ambrose were ranchers from White Sulfer Springs, MT and Peggy was also an amazing gardener. Her Irish ancestors would be very proud of her ability to create a little Ireland in Montana. Ambrose passed away, and Peggy did not feel she could run the ranch on her own, so she decided to sell the place. And that is when we were divinely led to find and buy our "Life's Dance Ranch." We must admit no Irish blood runs through our veins so Peggy's beautiful gardens have suffered a little over the years. We have tried to make up for this in many ways as you will see.

Peggy told us much about the early history of the property. She had compiled a binder with early photos and newspaper clippings of the toll house and stories of previous owners. We have enjoyed sharing the binder with interested visitors. Peggy was a wealth of good information. I had been so excited about the chance to own this property I had excitedly asked Peggy to move into the Log Cabin and help us learn how to take care of the ranch the right way. I told her she could stay there free of charge for life! This was one of my occasional spontaneous generous offers I tend to make without consulting my new life partner. Oops.

Peggy did stay with us for a little over a year and showed us the ropes but eventually she felt the need to move closer into town in her own place. I am grateful for Peggy teaching me so much about caring for the land. I know we kept her amused or perhaps even a little scared as she watched us fumble our way around this new ranch life, which neither of us had a clue about. When she met our next renters, Cassie and Dorothy, she told them "good luck now you can have them!"

Chapter Sixteen

Cassie and Dorothy were old family friends from my Harlowton days. They had just sold their ranch and were not sure where they were going next. Once again, being the generous guy I am, I told them to come stay at our cabin and to bring all their ranch stuff to Life's Dance Ranch until they could figure out what they wanted to do. Once again, I made this generous offer to old friends, without consulting my new life partner. Big oops!! Dorothy did pass away several years later and Cassie found a new home last year.

HISTORICAL HAPPENINGS

Early on we learned of many purported historic happenings on our property. It may have been Peggy or perhaps others with historic ties to the property who told us the homestead papers were signed by President Abraham Lincoln. We were also told that after the Civil War ended, General Sherman, was sent West to fight Indians and stayed overnight in the Toll House. Howard Clausen told us of finding arrowheads and spearheads up behind the milk house along Little Porcupine Creek where 250 Flathead Indians encamped yearly on their way to hunt buffalo.

Tyler Keckley, Dr. Bob and Darlene's son, told us of growing up in the house. He remembered going downstairs with his brothers and sisters to look at the floor with a bullet still imbedded where a cowboy had been shot and killed in a poker game back when the Toll House had a saloon. Several also told stories of the upstairs bedrooms being called "haunted."

One of the most delightful persons Annie and I have encountered is also a person most connected to the early history of the ranch. His name, Mario Cervelli.

"Raised in the small agricultural community of Temu in the Italian Alps, Mario Cervelli grew up a typical Italian child of that era— going to school, helping with farming, playing marbles ... and joining the fascist youth organization.

"When tensions arose in Europe in the early 1930's with Benito Mussolini in power in Italy, Mario's father, an American citizen, fled Italy before he could be drafted into the Italian army. Leaving his family behind, he made his way to Helena, Montana, where he worked on a ranch.

"Just ten years old when he arrived in the United States, Mario enjoyed his life in his new home – hunting, helping around the ranch, golfing, caddying, and killing gophers. When his father became ill and died, Mario, at fifteen years of age, left school to help support his family. Mario later returned to Italy and his hometown as a member of the United States Army."

From <u>Rising Above, The Early Years of Mario Cervelli</u> *by Keith Johnson*

When we heard about Mario, we called and invited him to come for dinner. When he arrived, he came with a wonderful Italian dessert/bread and a plethora of stories about his work at the Clausen dairy farm. The Clausen family had hired Mario after his father died, and Mario was trying to help support his mother, sisters and brothers. He was given a bed and small space on a north porch. He talked about no heat in the winter, waking up with frozen socks which he would put on then walk to the barn in his icy socks and boots to milk the cows. Some days the snow was so deep he could not drive the dairy truck over the entryway. So, the truck would be left on the county road and Mario would harness a team of horses and large sled and take the dairy products across pastures to the dairy truck waiting on the county road.

Mario had nothing but kind words for the Clausen family and it was a joy listening to him reminisce about his times in their home and on their ranch. When I told him some of the things we were working on in the barn, he just laughed and said, "Oh Albert, look what they are doing to your barn now!" Mario is now well over ninety, still very sharp minded and physically sound. We are always tickled when we meet someone who grew up or worked in this valley or on the property or had

Chapter Sixteen

great or great-great ancestors who did. So, if you happen to know of anyone, please send them our way!

PAS DE DEUX: DANA & ANNIE'S SPECIAL BOND

We began decorating our old/new 4,200 square foot house. We had a ton of stuff, some treasures, some not so much. Most of the furniture, art, books and household goods were from all my years with Dana. The remaining were Annie's furniture, works of art, books, etc. It was an eclectic assortment of furnishings. We both wanted the house to reflect the Montana history contained within its walls. A lot of Dana and my furnishings fit the bill. So, my things furnished our dining room, living room, Montana room, our Master bedroom, another guest room, and we both filled the library room and the little craft/writing room in the back corner of the house. However, most of Annie's furnishings were more reflective of her travels through Europe with paintings, dishware, and drapery reflecting this tone, along with her equine art. Besides creating one bedroom and an office upstairs, most everything from her condo fit in the large den. There we have the European flavor which she loves and which overflows a little into the hallway and kitchen.

I will say that from the beginning of our relationship Annie has always respected Dana, and even prays to her when she needs help with me! She has made it clear to my sons that Dana will always be a part of this family and she encourages them to share memories, especially with the grandchildren. Our library has beautiful pictures of Dana dancing at Disney along with my military retirement memorabilia. Annie strategically decorated our living room to honor both her and Dana's passion, DANCING! We have Dana's ballerina curio in one corner, which contains all the ballerina sculptures I gave her over the years as well as Dana's Urn. The walls and shelves are covered with some of Dana's beautiful pieces of ballet art in various forms. Annie blended this love of Dana's dancing passion with her own passion for dancing with horses. So sprinkled throughout are crystal, jade, copper and glass horses I have given Annie, as well as other pictures and statues of horses in various dressage movements.

Journey to Life's Dance Ranch

Dressage is often described as horse and rider dancing as one and actually dates back to 430 BC. It was the original military training for horses preparing for battle. The levade and capriole and other movements are "school jumps" or "airs above the ground." These horse moves were used to scare the enemies in battle and now are movements dedicated to peace and beauty. If you ever get to see the Lipizzaner's perform these amazing movements, it's well worth the effort. Common ballet terminology such as pas de deux, and pas de trois come from the original military training where horses mirrored each other's movements in pairs, threes and more. Some claim it is these delicate and powerful dressage movements which inspired humans to emulate and ballet was born! Annie in particular loves to spend time in this living room and reflect on all these beautiful items and feels honored to share something so unique and special with just her and Dana.

ARTIST KIM MCELROY'S PICTURE ENTITLED "PAS DE DEUX" HANGS IN OUR LIVING ROOM

"At times, the horse and rider are one being. The horse's body and attitude mirrors the rider's requests. Thus, they embody the elegance, discipline, and contained passion of the ballet dancer."

~ Kim McElroy, Spirit of the Horse Gallery

Chapter Sixteen

Much to Annie's dismay my love of thrift shopping began. I would come home with "antique" items I had found for a deal which I was sure would improve the feel of our home. Some were accepted several others declined. I soon learned Annie and I had different tastes in what we considered to be an "antique treasure." I did leave most of the indoor decorating to Annie because I was starting to have a vision for our barn. I turned my attention to this massive project.

Every now and then I would find a real antique treasure in our barn which we would later find a space for usually in our outdoor solarium. This is where the front of the old stagecoach tollhouse is and visitors were dropped off to enter into the old saloon, have a bite to eat or something to drink, and then go upstairs to sleep before their next stagecoach ride. The original hand hewn beams are still in place and are now covered with interesting antique ranch equipment I found on our property from days long ago. This is where we were interviewed by the local newspaper about our upcoming Holiday Tour of Homes.

Journey to Life's Dance Ranch

Couple shares 'blessing' of historic home

From left, Mike and Annie Maixner sit in the solarium of their home that was built onto the MacDonald toll house, used from 1878 to 1885 to collect tolls from those using the road across the Continental Divide. The home is part of the 2010 Original Governor's Mansion Holiday Home Tour.
Eliza Wiley Independent Record

Holiday tour opens doors of former MacDonald toll house

By SANJAY TALWANI
Independent Record

Back in the 1860s, Alexander MacDonald had some ranchland and a road heading up toward the pass that would bear his name, and he charged tolls for passage: $2 for two horses and a wagon, on down to 3 cents for loose sheep.

A century and a half later, his toll house — and the various additions and improvements to it — is part of one couple's Montana dream home, a return to the Big Sky for a native son after a long military career, and the ultimate equine paradise for his bride.

It features rough-hewn wooden beams, historic outbuildings, modern conveniences, a bathtub that once belonged to celebrated Helena madam Big Dorothy, and possibly even some ghosts.

The house, along with four others, and the Original Governor's Mansion and the Montana Club, will open their doors Sunday from noon to 5 p.m. as part of this year's Original Governor's Mansion Holiday Home Tour.

Mike and Annie Maixner call their arrival in their home a blessing, and marvel at the turn of events that led them there.

Alexander MacDonald's toll house dating back to the 1860s, still stands off Route 12 near MacDonald Pass.
Photo provided

The Maixner house now has a solarium where the front entrance to the MacDonald toll house once was. The old road, partially their driveway, is still visible on the hillside.
Eliza Wiley Independent Record

Mike and Annie dreamed of a Montana life. He's from Harlowton, attended Carroll College and served as a naval dentist for 27 years, retiring in 2005 only when his then-wife, Danalee, a ballerina, fell ill with ovarian cancer. She died in September 2006.

Annie worked for more than two decades in the Georgia Department of Corrections and its rehabilitative programs. She retired when she contracted ovarian cancer for the second time and spent a few years working on healing herself. That included getting a horse, Sonnet

More **HOME**, *page 10A*

"TRAVELING GANG" TIME AGAIN!

Around early October, we were also getting ready to go on another amazing overseas adventure with the "gang." Annie's pelvis pain continued to intensify, especially during and after the manipulations. She carried on the decorating and sewing new drapes despite the pain. She still could not ride or, at times, could barely move. Getting nervous about flying to Europe and going on the trip, Annie confided to Linda that she was not sure she could make it. Linda replied, "Have you consulted a real doctor – like an orthopedist?" Well we hadn't, so that was our next step. Dr. Steele, a Helena orthopedist, took a round of x-rays and was amazed that Annie had been able to move at all with three broken pelvis bones! He put her on crutches and wanted her to confine activities to minimal movement. Despite the discomfort, she was not going to miss our next travel trip with the "gang." She progressed from crutches to two canes, so off we flew a few weeks later to meet the group for more adventures in Scotland, Wales, and England.

On arriving in Scotland our first visit was to the place where golf began, St. Andrew's Golf Course. Our next order of business was to head for the "Whiskey Trail," the Scottish road that took us to many distilleries where single malt Irish Scotch Whiskey was made. We had

great fun sampling the various scotches along the Trail. Annie and JoJo did not disappoint in their crazy antics as they danced into all hours of the night at a local pub with Annie bouncing around on her canes. She paid for that mistake for the rest of the trip as she missed many of our side trips due to the pain. But like one of her favorite songs by Garth Brooks, a motto she adopted for her life, "I might have missed the pain, but I'd a had to miss the dance."

We were then off to Wales. We had a harrowing ride to our next VRBO on an extremely narrow dirt road with bushes lining each side. When a car would come from the opposite direction, we were literally brushing against the bushes and the rock walls to keep from side swiping the oncoming vehicles. Wales is a beautiful country with many verdant small farms with sheep and cattle and occasional horses. We stayed on a sport horse ranch so we could all enjoy watching these magnificent creatures.

Next were many stops throughout the English countryside. We visited Stonehenge, the homes of Beatrix Potter and then William Shakespeare, royal palaces and cathedrals, and rode London's giant Ferris wheel. Of course, we drank our share of Scotch and wine and ate plenty of good food including plum pudding and our favorite, "sticky toffee pudding." Our waiters tried to push "blood pudding" on us but we all declined.

BIG DOROTHY'S INFLUENCE ON OUR RANCH

After this delightful October trip to the UK, it was back to our best place, the USA, Montana and our Life's Dance Ranch. Annie would spend the rest of the year healing from her fractured pelvis and to continue decorating our home, getting ready for being on the Christmas tour of homes. We had an enormous task ahead of us. The house was full of unpacked boxes in every room. The Christmas decorations were somewhere, but we had many boxes to unpack and put away before we were to find them. Annie decided we needed to fix up our upstairs bathroom to honor "Big Dorothy" who was the madam who ran the oldest operating brothel in Montana. We were blessed to have an original piece of her property in our master bathroom.

"Big Dorothy's Rooms" were functioning well into the early 1970's. Police finally raided her and shut her down in 1973. Rumor has it she kept a little black book with names of very powerful men in the legislature and businesses around town. The story goes "someone" got worried about being found out and pressured law enforcement to finally

Chapter Sixteen

shut her down. She was sent to prison where she died soon after under mysterious circumstances.

BIG DOROTHY BAKER

BIG DOROTHY BOUDOIR DOOR IN OUR BARN

BIG DOROTHY'S PERSONAL CLAWFOOT BATHTUB IN OUR MASTER BATH

Annie developed an interest in Big Dorothy as she saw her as a strong business woman, who was known for taking very good care of her girls and was a big philanthropist in the community. Back in the early western days there were not many options for women to work. Some women came out west with their husbands who died along the way. Widows were left with children to raise and very few employment options. Others turned to this life to get away from the cruel treatment they were receiving from their husbands or families. Annie even has a book about how prostitution helped shape the west. It was and is an impactful and controversial institution in our country.

"Big Dorothy's Rooms" now houses the Wind Bag restaurant in downtown Helena, which has gone through various changes over the years. When "Big Dorothy" passed away there was an estate sale held for all her personal property. Dr. Keckley, who owned our house at the time, only wanted one thing. His wife Darlene told us he paid an enormous amount for "Big Dorothy's" personal clawfoot bathtub. He moved it into the master bathroom. Annie decided to decorate the bathroom in a brothel style in honor of Big Dorothy and this beautiful historic gift left to us. For the Christmas open house Annie dressed up as "Big Dorothy" and shared with our guests a little history of this most beloved Helena benefactor. Our bathroom later became the inspiration for Annie's "Big Dorothy's Boudoir" in our barn.

MORE FRIENDS AND FAMILY GATHER ROUND

Perhaps one of the most magical meetings was with a couple named Tom and Tana Dearborn. They came through the open house like all the other visitors, and frankly we had so many (over 600) we couldn't remember half of them. A week or so later, we received a note from Tom and Tana in the mail. They had both recently retired and moved to Helena to be near some family. They had arrived almost the same day we had in August 2010. They said they were new to Helena and didn't know many people. They had enjoyed our open house and said we seemed like their kind of people, and wondered if we might get together for coffee, dessert and a visit sometime. The first thing Annie said, "Gosh, this is the nicest, sweetest note I have ever received, but you don't think they're swingers, do you? Cause I am not into that kind of thing!" I said, "No I don't think they are swingers and rather than meeting for coffee, let's have them up for dinner." Such was the beginning of one of the most wonderful magical friendships of our lives. Life does send you great blessings and Tom and Tana and their family are certainly one of ours.

My sister, Mary Lou, and her husband Gene finished their beautiful home in 2013 and permanently moved to Helena. Having them here has been absolutely wonderful. They have introduced us to many friends of theirs and they love the friends we have brought into their lives. Gene is on the Carroll College Board of Directors and we are involved with a lot of all things Carroll. We jokingly refer to their mansion as the upper crust of the family and we are the down home and dirty ranch. Gene always says, that between us, we have the best of both worlds and we could not agree more.

 *Journey to Life's Dance Ranch*

It was great having them here as our mother declined in health and finally passed away. Unfortunately, my dear sister, Margaret, who had taken care of my mother in Butte, Montana with her husband, Vern, was to experience the loss of the love of her life. Vern was diagnosed with esophageal cancer. Trips to Salt Lake for surgery and chemo gave Vern and Marg a short but beautiful time of remission, but the cancer came back and finally took Vern's life. We were all devastated. Marg couldn't stay in Butte as there were too many difficult memories. She sold her house and came to Helena where she lives in a beautiful log A-frame on Mary Lou and Gene's property. It has been such a blessing having her here with us.

MARGARET

MARGARET DORENE, YOUR NAME BELIES

WHAT ALL YOUR SIBLINGS REALIZE

THE GIFT TO US, GOD SENT IN YOU

YOUR MOTHER'S KEEPER, AND WE KNEW

YOU HAD THE HEART AND STRENGTH SHE NEEDS

AND WHAT YOU GAVE US, SO EXCEEDS

WHAT WE GAVE YOU IN RETURN

WITH YOUR MAN OF GOODNESS

FRIEND, LOVER...VERN

YOU CARED FOR THIS DEAR WOMAN

OF WHOM WE ALL CAME FORTH

WE THANK YOU, SISTER MARGARET

FOR YOUR GOODNESS, BEYOND WORTH

Chapter Sixteen

Margaret's and Vern's loving care of our dear mother, Dorene, gave the rest of us kids the opportunity to live our lives in different places, raise our kids and go through our careers never worrying that Mom was not getting the best of care. We owe Marg and Vern more than we can ever say.

Wish for Mom

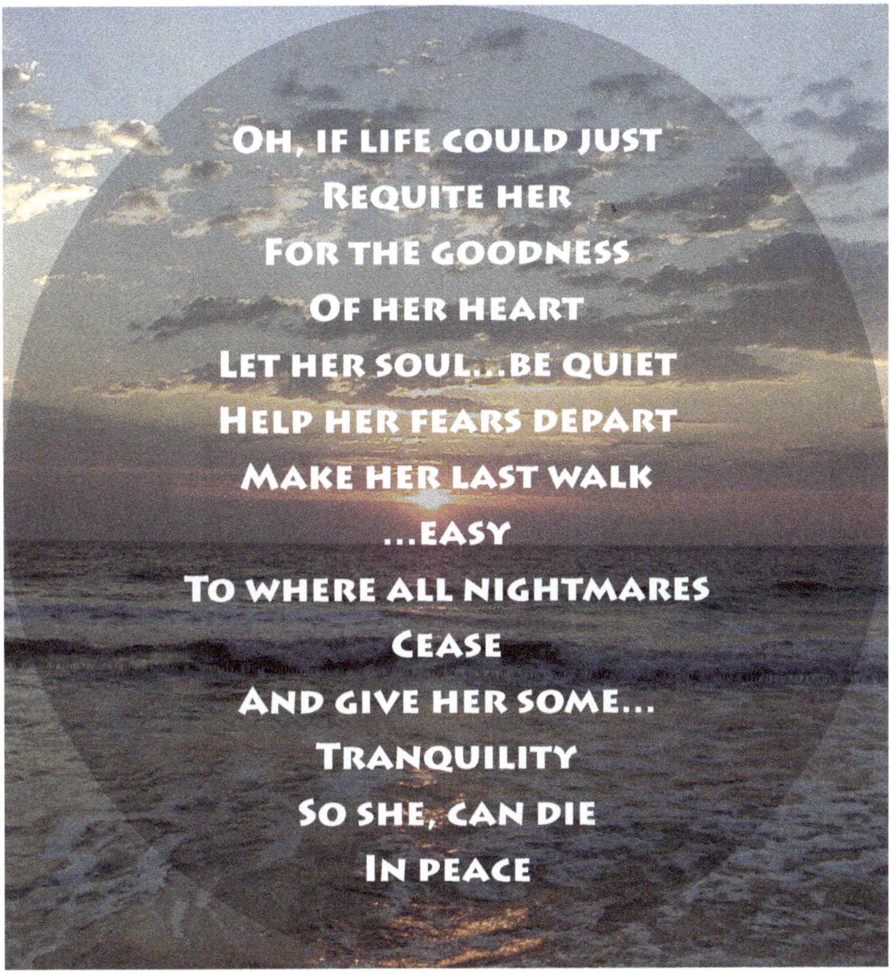

Oh, if life could just
Requite her
For the goodness
Of her heart
Let her soul...be quiet
Help her fears depart
Make her last walk
...easy
To where all nightmares
Cease
And give her some...
Tranquility
So she, can die
In peace

Chapter Seventeen
Life on the Ranch

HEALTH ISSUES

It was around this time my heart problems started to manifest in the form of atrial fibrillation. When first diagnosed, the fibrillation was controlled to some extent with medication and of course blood thinners to reduce the high chances of stroke. It didn't take long, however, before we were going to the emergency room at least once a week. Every visit was the same; ECG, IV medication and an alteration of my medications. The medications were becoming ineffective and our visits to the ER much more frequent. I think Annie would take me to the VA's ER over thirty times with chest pain, high BP and racing heart. God bless her, she was so strong and wonderful for me, and she felt like we should be getting frequent flyer points for all our efforts. Finally, there was a trip to the ER where they were unable to stop the fibrillation. They put me out with general anesthesia and then put the paddles to me and electro shocked my heart to get it back to a normal rhythm. Then it was back home with more medication changes.

The next week after three more visits to the ER, Annie had had enough. She told the VA doctors she wasn't taking me home again until they could get me under control. Through her persistence and strength, the VA doctor who was treating me that day was able to get special permission to go outside the VA system and they med-evac flighted me to Billings Clinic where an ablation procedure would be performed to hopefully stabilize the rhythm. I was loaded on a small jet and was off. Annie was in her car for the four-hour drive to Billings. I knew I would be OK if Annie was with me. I really needed her unwavering strength.

I arrived at the clinic first and was settled into a very nice room. The Billings Clinic's rooms are equipped with a couch/bed so a family member can be with you. Annie soon arrived. It was so comforting to see her. I was sure everything would be alright. The next morning the cardiologist came to see us and they performed the ablation, a burning of small spots on your heart that are misfiring and causing the fibrillation. Later that day he said the ablation had gone well but before he sent me home, he would like to have another angiogram performed just to check the blood vessels of the heart.

I was pleased and thought it was a good idea to get a new base-line. It had been about four years since my last one when I was told I did not need by-pass surgery. I was confident they would come back and tell me I still did not need by-pass surgery and the ablation should solve my atrial fibrillation problem. I was sure they would tell us everything looked fine and we could head back to Helena.

By this time my sister Mary Lou had arrived and was keeping Annie company as they waited for the doctor to come out and tell the family the angiogram results. The doctor told them the results were right on the cusp, 50% indicating a problem, 50% possibly not indicating a problem. They suggested we go home and see how I do. Annie who had enough of this kind of treatment at the VA said, "Can't you do another procedure to see what the risk is? I hate to take him home and then end up right back here again! His tests have traditionally never indicated there is a problem when indeed there is." The Dr. did say there was another procedure which could give them a better read on the risk. So back I went for yet another procedure, gratefully so.

Soon after this procedure, the cardiologist came into my hospital room and with him was a cardiac surgeon. The surgeon told us my left anterior descending artery was 95% blocked and calcified. He said they usually didn't work on Labor Day, but his team was coming in and I was going on the operating table early the next morning for by-pass surgery. Wow, in only 12 hours they would be opening my chest and performing major surgery on my heart. Annie and I were both grateful the problem

had finally been identified, yet we were fearful of what lay ahead.

When I came out of open-heart surgery Annie was there for me and my sisters Margaret and Mary Lou were there as well. There were three tubes coming out my chest, one down my throat, an IV, of course, a catheter bag to collect urine and multiple electronic monitors. I had never felt so physically helpless in all my life. I had hit "rock bottom" and knew I had a long hard climb ahead of me. In a couple of days, I had gone from lifting relatively heavy weights and running at a quick pace, to barely being able to walk and not being able to lift two pounds. For me it was a challenging time I really was not prepared for. If Annie had not been there with her smile, her positive attitude, love and encouragement, I am sure I would have descended into greater depression and despair. She kept me as sane and upbeat as possible under the circumstances.

Gene Prison

Within the confines of my genes
I am, imprisoned
Or so it seems
'Til death comes round
And sets me free
From life that now...
Imprisons me

Over the next 6 months I began to recover, thanks to the wonderful care I received at the Billings Clinic, equally great care from physicians, nurses, physical therapists and friends at our VA Hospital in Helena, I was alive again. I eventually could lift light weights, walk or jog on a treadmill and enjoy working out with Annie again. Life was getting back to normal. A year later it was back to Billings for an atrial fibrillation specific ablation procedure. Fortunately, we had worked through the system once and this procedure went well and only reinforced my recovery.

Annie has her health challenges too and as a result is not able to always help me out on the ranch. She has been on medical disability since 2003, as the ovarian cancer with the two plus years of chemo, radiation, etc. left her with some severe on-going side effects and combined with her MS, she is challenged in maintaining a healthy balance. I can always tell when she gets stressed because she starts limping and cramping with the MS and gets rather emotional. Her outwardly emotional expressions at times has been a learning curve for me, as Dana rarely cried and kept her emotions in check.

The land and the horses in particular are Annie's best medicine and they are always who she reaches for when needed. Her beloved book club and prayer group friends are also a very necessary balancer for her. Plus, we are so filled with gratitude for the blessings we have been given we do not focus on what is not working but rather on what we are given every day. Thus, making everyday a good day on "Life's Dance Ranch."

HAUNTINGS OR HELPFUL ENERGIES?

I mentioned earlier that the previous owners described spiritual energies in our home particularly in the back, upstairs bedrooms. On top of that Helena is known as one of the most "haunted" cities in America. Ellen Baumler is a local historian who has written many books on the subject both about the Helena area and Montana. Our ranch is located in one of the exact areas where Ellen has documented several "sightings" all within 15 miles of our ranch. So, it did not surprise us when our first visitors began to experience "sightings" when they stayed at our house. Let me quickly add never have we ever felt there were any evil or hurtful dark energies in our home. In fact, the opposite is true as we have experienced some very helpful energies.

One of Annie's brothers, his wife and their three beautiful daugh-

Chapter Seventeen

ters came to our first Thanksgiving. The morning after they arrived their youngest daughter, who was about 6 at the time, came down the stairs to breakfast. She casually asked us if we had seen the beautiful lady in gold with a small child in the bathroom upstairs. We all looked at her with shocked expressions which she matter-of-factly ignored as if what she said was perfectly normal.

The next incident occurred the following summer when Annie's son-in-law was upstairs in one of the older bedrooms and he said there was a point during the night when he could not get up from the bed. He was experiencing weird sensations almost electrifying, not frightening, but energetically tangible. After an extended period of time these vibrations left him and he was able to move again.

The next experience was when we hired a cleaning service to clean our house. Annie was out riding horses and I was downtown. When Annie came back into the house the cleaning lady asked her what she was singing when she was downstairs in the cellar. Annie assured her that she had been out riding her horse and had not done any singing. The cleaning lady insisted because the cellar light had also been turned on and off several times. Annie explained that we have had certain "sightings" in our house and it was probably these energies who were responsible.

Remember, Annie at times purposefully communicates with those "on the other side" so it does not bother her at all that we have some "energies" in our home. In fact, she believes they are some of the former owners who are happy about how we are using the Ranch. However, the cleaning lady left quickly and Annie received a call shortly after from the owner of the cleaning service. "Is your house haunted?" she asked. Annie replied that we do not feel it is haunted but there does appear to be some inexplainable activities at times. The owner quickly replied she would no longer be able to have anyone service our house!

Our friend Tom Dearborn's sisters all felt they were touched by a spirit coming down our main stairs one day. They whispered to Tom,

"They do know this house is haunted, don't they?" Tom just smiled. Another event occurred during the time I was going through my heart issues. Annie's nephew, Collin was visiting and staying in the back bedroom upstairs. Everyone was worried about my health and Collin was upstairs looking at Dana's old Disney book. He felt someone reach down and touch his shoulder and when he turned around, he saw a beautiful lady with red hair. He just felt her assuring him that everything with my health would be okay. When he told us about this incident, Annie asked me if I knew anyone with red hair. My immediate answer was "Dana, (who was blond) always wore a red wig when she danced for Disney!" We all felt Dana was reassuring us from the other side. Collin did move his mattress in with our other visitors as this was a very new experience for him.

Perhaps the most interesting and fortuitous sighting was made by our daughter-in-law, Lizzie. We had all gone to bed after a joyful Christmas day with the kids. Patrick, Lizzie, Kailyn and Tessa were visiting from Florida. Unbeknownst to us we had left a candle burning on the wooden fireplace mantle downstairs in the living room. In the middle of the night, Lizzy was awakened by a vision of the lady in white standing in their bedroom doorway. And then she smelled what she thought might be smoke. She awoke Patrick and he ran downstairs to find the mantle and floor below on fire. He grabbed the burning boxes and Christmas stockings and quickly got them out of the house and into the snow outside. He then ran back in and put the rest of the fire out. By now everyone was awake, downstairs and thankful for Lizzie's vision and Patrick's quick action. Had Lizzie not been awakened the fire could have been disastrous. We do feel thankful for the visit from the lady in white that night.

One night, Annie had a sleep over with Tana's sisters, Tiffany and Kim and a neighbor Terry. They all slept in one of the back bedrooms upstairs and were particularly interested in seeing if there was any communication going on in the house. They giggled themselves through the night and some left early in the morning. It was not until several days later that Kim shared that something woke her in the night

Chapter Seventeen

and when she sat up in bed, something started pulling on her pony tail! I personally have never seen or heard anything out of the normal, but Annie has. However, as I have said I am indeed grateful for any help in watching over our Ranch and keeping my family safe.

Annie absolutely believes some of their beautiful energies surround us and help and encourage us to grow the Ranch in a different way from previous owners but one that always honors the sacredness of this beautiful valley. Neither Annie nor I feel that what may inhabit our home is anything but kind, good energies. They can be seen as guardian angels as well as spirits of the past. They are one in the same to us. It delights us to think we may have some gentle helpful spirits lovingly and helpfully residing with us. Because honestly, we need help, since we sometimes don't know what we are doing!

OVERWHELMING AT TIMES!

The second summer we were here we had a houseful of guests all summer. Even our wonderful "gang" came out to visit over the fourth of July. I of course was running around the ranch and house happily announcing all the work projects that needed to be done. Little did I know that Annie was becoming increasingly overwhelmed. I love work and the prospect of endless projects is a joy to me. Annie on the other hand felt her energy drain at all the work needed and saw it as precious time away for her horses and her own mental and physical health! We even had my oldest granddaughter Tessa visit for a few weeks. I had both Annie and Tessa helping me with the ranch work and ordering them around to lift this rock or move that log. I even told Tessa to go weed the garden, which was a four-tiered huge garden in our back yard.

Eventually, Tessa looked at Annie with tears in her eyes in exhaustion and Annie finally spoke up. "You do realize we are not Patrick and Andrew? Tessa and I just can't do this kind of work!" And off they went. I guess I was so used to my boys following my work orders over the years, I must admit I did not notice the strain it was putting on both Annie and Tessa. I have gotten a little better over the

years. But I still love to talk about all the work that needs to be done. It's endless. Every now and then, even I can get a little overwhelmed.

OVERWHELMED

THE RUSH AT ONCE SUBSIDED
BUT THE ENERGY WOULDN'T GO
IT LINGERED AND IT PUSHED ME
TO WHERE, I DID NOT KNOW
I SHOULD HAVE FELT THE QUIET
BUT THE QUIET, WASN'T THERE
THE PRESENCE OF THEIR VISIT
STILL LINGERED…EVERYWHERE
THE MOON WAS NOW THREE QUARTERS
ABOVE DUSK'S COMING NIGHT
THE SKY HAD PEACE AND CALM
BUT I WAS STILL WOUND TIGHT
SO, I SAT WITH THE MOON AND THE SKY
KNEW PEACE WOULD COME AGAIN
BUT MY NATURE WOULDN'T TAKE IT NOW
AND I, JUST DON'T KNOW WHEN

MY BARN VISION MANIFESTS

Perhaps one of the most joyful projects on "Life's Dance Ranch" happened with a vision I had after first being upstairs in the old hayloft in the barn. It was an utter mess, pigeon poop, rat and mouse droppings, spider webs and all sorts of junk and trash. I knew it could be something much more. I got to work cleaning, tossing out junk and trash and closing the openings where pigeons were getting in. Then, I told my friend Tom of my dream. Tom's a great dreamer and he immediately wanted to help me with this giant endeavor. Our first project was building the bar. We made many trips to Mark's Lumber, south of Helena. We found a beautiful ten-foot-long blue pine slab, the

Chapter Seventeen

perfect top for our bar. We also saw a big pile of old barn wood and we envisioned these boards as the backdrop for the bar and to build a big hood over the bar. We actually found the original toll house bar at a local antique dealer. So, we used this material to make a back drop and cabinets. The bar turned out just beautiful, thanks to Tom's help and imagination. We call our bar the Mike & Tom Bar, known by all of our family and friends as the "MT Bar."

Our next project was to put in a twenty-four by twenty-four-foot dance floor. We then solicited our friend Shannon Bell and his kids to help us put big sliding doors out the back of the barn and a beautiful deck with handicap ramp. The view off the ramp is spectacular! You look out on our pasture and up into pine forested mountains. The view to the left is our glorious aspen grove with creeks, meadows and more giant pines, firs and junipers. From the deck we also have a fabulous view of Annie's outdoor riding arena. We weren't finished with the barn. Next came electric wiring, ceiling fans and lights. We put in a shuffle-board table, two pool tables, ping pong, darts, a poker room and a magnificent "Big Dorothy's" ladies' boudoir. Andrew built the boudoir while Annie decorated the unique sitting room. A fitting tribute to this

historic Helena philanthropist. We eventually plan to move her clawfoot bathtub from our house to the Barn and set up an indoor bathroom in a complimentary style as the boudoir.

The barn loft has become a place of good will and good times for family, friends and neighbors. I could not have built or even imagined it without the help of Tom and Tana, Andrew, Annie and Shannon Bell. We have had numerous requests to have weddings and special events, but until recently we have kept it for family and friends. We have done a few fundraisers and had a couple of memorial services for dear friends. Everyone loves coming to the barn, the "MT" Bar for a drink, to shoot pool or to have a book club in the ladies' boudoir. Without a doubt it has been and continues to be a uniquely special experience for anyone who is here. Between our Barn and Annie's Book club we have attracted such wonderful people and experiences into our lives!

BOOK CLUB BRINGS JOY, FRIENDSHIP, AND LAUGHTER

Annie, an avid reader, felt she needed to have a book club. She had been a member of one in Atlanta for twenty years and loved the camaraderie she found in her book club friends. So, Annie started a book club and through that club we have been given many more wonderful friends. The women became part of the book club and their spouses, if they had one, became part of the fun club as we did many social outings together. Tana was the first member. Then Cassie, our renter. The book club expanded to include Sandra who Annie met in a French class, also thereby including her husband Kim. As luck would have it another amazing couple retired on Clausen Rd. Bill and Terry Mede. Bill's father had lived here for a long time and Bill grew up coming to Montana to hunt over the years. Terry soon joined the book club. And again, as luck, fate, or blessings would have it another couple retired from California to Clausen Road, Steve and Renee Liston. Renee also

Chapter Seventeen

joined the club and was thrilled as she too had been in a book club many years in California. Annie's theory about a beautiful energy vortex in our little valley certainly bore fruit for us with these fantastic neighbors and friends.

Annie also asked Dr. Marie Suthers, who runs the Anthrozoology Program at Carroll College, to be a part of the book club. When we had first arrived in Helena, Annie had no friends here. The first thing she did was find a horse group to join, the Tri-Arabian endurance club. Never mind that she did not have an Arab or do endurance riding. She claimed she just needed to be around people who loved horses and the rest would take care of itself. Truer words were never spoken. Marie was one of those friends she met through that first group. We have been very supportive of Carroll's Anthrozoology program particularly the equine students. We have been blessed over the years to attract several "ranch daughters" who often come out to our ranch to work with Annie and our horses. It's a win-win situation because Annie needs the help and the students just want to be around horses. Annie feels God keeps providing us with gifted students to help us grow in our knowledge and ability to care for our beautiful equines.

Finally, Tana's good friend MC, a very active and beloved community member in Helena, became the 8th member of the book club. They called their group the G-8 book club, later they would switch at times to calling themselves the Swans after a book they read called, "The Swans of 5th Ave." It was this special group of women, who Annie felt deserved a special book club meeting spot, plus Annie's admiration for Big Dorothy, which inspired Annie to create our "Big Dorothy's Boudoir" in our event barn. This group is serious about their book reading and discussions, so no gossiping is allowed! They often have dinner themes which match the book they are discussing. However, they did add an occasional "Wise Woman Wednesdays" to their routine so they could spend time catching up on each other's lives.

Sometimes the husbands are invited to these dinners. We all have great fun together. As life does change quickly, we unfortunately lost MC last year. She is greatly missed but her husband Leroy still stays in touch. Cassie moved on as well. I'm sure this group will continue to expand and contract as life calls the shots. They are a determined group of women who embrace life with joy and believe and celebrate their "get 'er done years," as Terry Mede refers to this time in their lives.

THE ORIGINAL G8 "SWANS" BOOK CLUB

OFF TO DONEGAL

One of the most enjoyable albeit most stressful trips Annie and I made together was a ten-day horse-riding adventure to Ireland for one of our anniversaries. We flew into Shannon and upon arriving went to the rental car counter. I had agreed to drive on the condition that Annie arrange for an automatic shift car. I didn't want to have to drive on the opposite side of the road and use a standard shift car. When we got to the car rental place, the only car they had was standard shift with the shifter on the opposite side of the car!

Suddenly, jet-lagged and very tired, I had to learn to shift in what seemed an opposite direction to all the other standard shifts I had driven. The Irish roads were very narrow. Many of the oncoming drivers would be in the middle of the road until just before they met you

Chapter Seventeen

and then would get over in their lane. On the long drive north to Dunfanaghy, we ended up breaking off one of the side view mirrors on our car and the side view mirror of the parked car we were passing by. And then since the roads and sidewalks were virtually the same color, I managed to bust a tire along the way. Whew! I was really happy to arrive in the small town knowing I would be off the road for a whole week!

The old hotel and stables where we stayed were first class. We were the only horse-riding guests there at the time and were treated with great generosity and kindness. We had ten wonderful days of riding, dining and drinking fine wine and Irish whisky. Each night we would go to the pub for an aperitif, then either have dinner there or go to the hotel's fine Irish restaurant. At the pub we met the "King of Donegal," (not the real king of course, but an Irishman who claimed to be). He was at the pub every night extolling his royalty and looking for someone to buy him a drink. He was a humorous nice guy and we obliged by buying him several drinks.

Our horse rides were over bogs, beaches, dunes, in the ocean and through the verdant Irish country side. It was just Annie, me and our guide. It could not have been a more perfect arrangement. Our trip headed home going south to Shannon was much less stressful. I had become comfortable with driving on the opposite side of the road and opposite side gear shift. And I was not nearly as stressed when I saw oncoming cars coming down the middle of the road.

RIDING BEACHES IN DONEGAL

We even stopped in the town of Sligo and visited the sights memorialized in W.B. Yates poems. This was also the place of Annie's very first horseback riding trip when she was going through chemo. She shared fond memories of dancing on the graves in the megalithic cemetery at night after their day long horse rides through the countryside. The people of Ireland are so generous and welcoming. Annie said when she was here on her first trip, she had forgotten the needles to give herself some Procrit shots. The pharmacist actually came out to the farmhouse she was staying at and brought her several needles to choose from. It was here she learned other important Irish facts. There is one bar for every three houses, and many stables have their own bar attached. An idea her stable at home soon implemented as well. Her first Irish trail guide had told her about his ex-wife who he said was a great house keeper ... because when they divorced, she kept the house. Annie was so happy to be there again.

Yes, we found Ireland to be a place of great beauty and their cows and sheep were the cleanest we had ever seen. I guess they have so much rain in Ireland the dirt on the animals washes off and keeps them nice and white. When we finally turned our car in, I felt better after chatting with an American lady who spent three months every year in Ireland. When we told her of our early driving woes, she told us not to worry, because most travelers have this problem, especially Americans. Good to be part of the norm.

THREE-YEAR "Z" FAMILY REUNION PROMISE

FAMILY REUNION 2018

Chapter Seventeen

One of the joys of being married to Annie has been getting to know her great family; all hard working well educated and extremely intelligent people. Annie has 4 brothers and 2 sisters and a family bond which I have rarely seen. We have been fortunate to have most of her siblings visit the ranch and those who haven't promise to visit in the future. A challenging childhood only resulted in strengthening their bond and creating a blessed family tradition. A promise was made by the siblings to meet every three years with their growing families at a reunion so they could rejoice in how God's love continued to bless their lives.

Since I have been with Annie, I have missed only one of these fun reunions. The first reunion I became aware of was when Annie and I were dating and I had not given her a ring yet. The Z family rule was you must be married or have been given an engagement ring to attend the reunions. If I had known how much fun Annie's family was, I probably would have proposed earlier! After all, we had been dating for some time, we were in love with each other, but unfortunately, I was a bit slow. However, since we married, I have enjoyed three of these beautiful events.

It is a joyous time where everyone gets to meet new family ala weddings or births or yes engagement rings. It is a time of sun and fun on the sand and sharing the goodness of God's love we find in each other. A time for catching up on all family's life's events and renewing the love bond we all share. It is a time of giving thanks for the good fortune we all find in our lives or consoling and reminiscing lost loved ones. Annie's family all have strong faiths and they credit God with providing them the amazing lives they all have.

A seven-day feast of fine food, drinks and fun partying. Every night a different family puts on a theme dinner with games and laughter. Young, young adults and older adults (Annie and I fall into that category) are all involved in the festivities. This tri-yearly event is not only great fun but renews and strengthens the love and bond among families. What a blessing to be part of Annie's family.

 *Journey to Life's Dance Ranch*

    I admire all of them but am particularly touched by two of her siblings' families who were gifted with special needs children both requiring extensive daily care. Never have I seen such love and care being provided to these special children who are seen and treated as nothing but angels in this family. Sadly, Katharine left this world before I got to know her, but we all know she watches over this joyful family as they continue to grow. Timmy, now 30, is the other special angel who seems to be on a mission from God to attract people and allow them to see the love and laughter which flows through him on a constant basis. It is very moving and powerful to watch how Timmy creates this spiritual experience for others around him. Yes, the Z family inspires and enriches my life greatly.

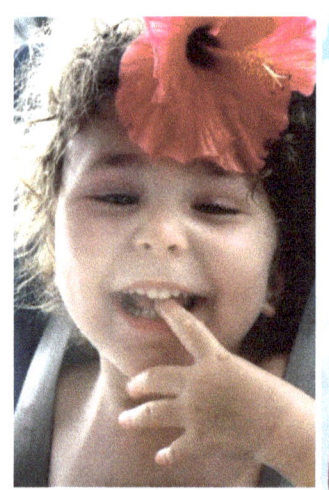

KATHARINE

ANNIE WITH MOTHER MARY AND TIMMY

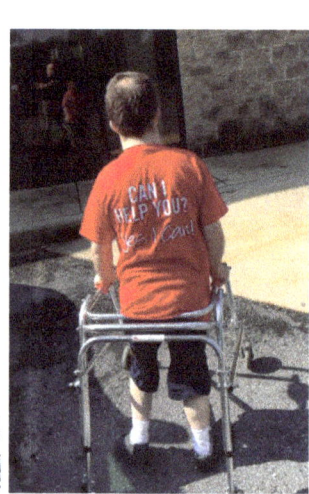

TIMMY

Chapter Seventeen

A LITTLE ACCIDENT PRONE I MUST ADMIT!

As I have grown older, I find that more and more health issues can slow me down or stop me for a while. Most of these are the expression of genetics I have received from my parents or grandparents. Some are a consequence of self-inflicted injuries either from accidents, my stupidity or both. Again, some of these dangers can be unavoidable – others, I set myself up for. As my brother-in-law, Gene, always says, "There are two activities in life where it is not 'if you will get hurt' but when: motorcycle riding and riding horses." I brought my very first motorcycle with me from Florida and started riding horses when we got to the Ranch. I even bought my dream horse, a big strong Appaloosa named Rio. I wanted to do it all!

One day I was riding my horse Rio, in our big outdoor arena. A truly freak accident caused Rio to spook. As I was riding by the muck bucket the rake slipped up into my stirrup and immediately started beating on the side of Rio. He started spinning and bucking and I was thrown to the ground landing on my head and neck. Fortunately, Annie had insisted I wear a helmet, as she does with all her riders, so that may have saved me a little. I got back on Rio and finished my ride but shortly after decided I needed to go the E.R. They thought I had a slight concussion and later showed me x-rays where I had small fractures(chips) off some of my cervical vertebrae. I was very lucky. It could have been much worse. I am still given reminders of this event when the weather changes and my neck starts to ache. Such is life, the price you can pay for living in paradise!

Motorcycle madness: Before Mom and Vern passed, I was riding my motorcycle on the gorgeous mountain drive down to Butte fairly often to see them and Marg. I purchased two more motorcycles, but was still primarily driving my first bike. The other two bikes I purchased in the event and my hope, that others living on the Ranch might decide they wanted to learn to ride. That never happened. I was still having a blast riding by myself on the Montana highways. I didn't wander far, usually only 60 to 80 miles or the 130 miles round trip to Butte. One

day my brother-in-law, Gene, invited me to ride with him and two of his biking buddies. Unlike myself, they were all very experienced riders.

They would be biking over to Lincoln, Montana to have a bite to eat then coming back to Helena another way. All of it was beautiful Montana scenery, but the road to Lincoln was through a mountainous road with many hairpin-turns to negotiate. I said I would love to go. I drove from Gene and Mary Lou's place to our ranch to get my bike. My plan was to take the bike I always rode, but when I got home its battery was dead. I had only driven one of the new bikes home from the dealer when I bought it. I felt sure I would be fine, jumped on the new bike and headed back to meet Gene and his friends.

We headed down the road. The new bike certainly felt different and shifted differently, but I was sure I would get used to the new feel and be fine after a few miles. As we were going into a sharp turn, I lost control of the bike and slid off the road barely missing a concrete structure. Fortunately, I was wearing full leathers and a full-face helmet. I hit hard on my right shoulder and separated the upper arm bone from the collar bone and scapula. I was able to pop the arm back in its socket almost immediately. The bike had taken very little damage, but the right side of my face shield was scratched beyond seeing through. Gene stopped and asked if I needed him to call an ambulance. I said no, and got back on the bike and painfully continued to the Lincoln Café. I remember having a diet coke and they all had a bite to eat and something to drink. They all asked me if I was sure I could make the forty-mile trip home on the motorcycle. Though I was hurting a bit, I told Gene I was sure I could drive the bike back and he didn't need to call someone to come pick me up.

The other two guys left us at Lincoln for another destination, while Gene and I went on a road that took us through Avon and Elliston, Montana and finally back to our ranch. God bless Gene, he got me safely back and after I assured Gene and Annie that I would be OK, Gene headed home. My shoulder was hurting but I thought I would just take some Tylenol and go to bed. The pain kept increasing and finally Annie

Chapter Seventeen

and I decided it would be best to go down to the ER where we had spent so much time with my heart problems. The moment I checked in and told them what had happened, it wasn't two minutes before they had me immovable in a neck brace. It was off to x-ray for pictures of neck and skull then to get an MRI brain scan. They came back with the diagnosis of severe shoulder separation. To make matters worse, only five years earlier I had rotator cuff surgery on the same shoulder for an old racquet-ball injury.

There was too much swelling for them to get a diagnosable MRI and they told me it would probably take several months until that was possible. Until then, I would be sent to physical therapy to see if they could rehab the injured shoulder. It was almost exactly 14 months before I would finally get the surgery and be out of pain and able to once again sleep through the night. It was also 14 months for Annie, with me waking her at night in our bed as I groaned in pain. She went through her own pain, suffering, lost sleep and worrying about me. God bless her, she was getting a lot of care-taker practice with all my health issues and accidents

I must also admit that some of the delay in the surgery date was of my choosing. I wanted to hunt that season and figured if I hurt my shoulder hunting then the surgery would cover both injuries. Not the most logical reasoning as Annie would often point out! Since the day I came home from the surgery, I have slept through the night and been essentially pain free. My shoulder has been rehabilitated and I am thrilled to be working on the ranch and going to the gym with Annie. At least until the next things happens! I decided, with a little prompting from Annie, to sell my motorcycles and keep Rio, thereby reducing my likelihood of breaking more bones by fifty percent.

HUNTING OR HUNTED?

I would never want anyone to think I am a good hunter. I told you the rather pathetic attempts my dad and I had when I was younger. Then there was my knife accident which cut my artery in my wrist as a young man. Since being on the ranch I'm not sure I can say I have improved all that much. I have gone big game hunting for five out of the eight years we have been here. I have many friends and acquaintances who are excellent hunters including my friends Tom, Bill, Shannon and Justin. Though I have only shot one bullet which took down one nice mule deer, I have very much enjoyed my hunting primarily with my friend Tom. Our times walking the woods, sitting in our hunting blind and driving the mountains looking for game are times I will always cherish. I must say the first thing I did when I shot my mule deer was to kneel down next to it and give thanks. Thanks to it for giving its life to become part of our life for the goodness and nutrition it would bring our table. We are thankful to have elk, deer, moose, bear, mountain lions, coyotes, birds of prey, sandhill cranes and a plethora of other Montana birds and small animals. It delights us every time we see them in their majestic wild beauty.

As you have probably figured out by now, I am somewhat susceptible to accidents, injury and putting myself in danger. Such was the case when Tom and I were given permission to hunt a friend's ranch over near Phillipsburg, Montana. Our plan was to trailer our four-wheelers, arrive early, set up the cabin, get water from the creek, split some firewood and check out the outdoor privy in the event we would need to use it during the night. We planned to stay about a week with each of us taking turns cooking meals and doing dishes. It didn't take me long to sustain a somewhat serious if not painful injury. It was the morning of our first day hunting. We were on our 4-wheelers when we came upon a fallen tree blocking our road.

It wasn't a large tree and I was sure Tom and I could move it. Tom and I grabbed the top of the tree with Tom pushing and me pulling. The endeavor turned out to be more difficult than we had expected since

Chapter Seventeen

the base of the tree was still somewhat connected to the trunk. We struggled with it for a bit and suddenly the tree snapped free. Tom, being considerably smarter than I, let go but I hung on going down and backwards very rapidly. I hit on my butt and with a crashing thump against a small tree. I couldn't breathe, the wind was knocked completely out of me and my back wasn't feeling so good. Tom told me to stay down and I did and finally caught my breath. Then, I told Tom I would be fine and we continued our hunt. That night and for the rest of our nights there, I slept very little because of the pain in my back and when I breathed. Still, it did not dampen the fun we were having.

I don't remember which night it was except that it was a night where Tom was cooking dinner. It was just before dusk and I told Tom I was going out where we had seen elk tracks earlier that morning to see if something might be moving. I walked to one side of a mountain then around to the other side and finally, as dark settled in, back to the cabin and a wonderful steak dinner Tom had prepared. The next morning when we started out, we saw my footprints in the snow where I had walked by myself the evening before. To our great surprise in every one of my footprints were the paw prints of a large mountain lion. The lion's prints ended about forty feet from the cabin. The lion had been stalking me and could have easily taken me out if it had wanted to. Tom and I were much more aware and vigilant to the "big cat" dangers in the area after that. During our six day hunt we ended up seeing five separate pairs of mountain lion tracks. Sometimes you dodge the bullet and sometimes not. That night I was stalked by the lion could have been my end. I was very lucky!

After we got back to Helena, my back continued bother me greatly. I made a trip to my favorite ER and x-rays showed I had fractured several ribs. Such is life in the "danger zones" I seem to put myself in. Annie by now is just rolling her eyes as I encounter yet another "oops" accident.

Journey to Life's Dance Ranch

Chapter Eighteen
Animal Family

Without a doubt one of our greatest blessings are all the animals who have been part of our life on Life's Dance Ranch. Both Annie and I have continued to expand our love for our 4-legged family and have had an opportunity to bring so many wonderful creatures into our lives. Annie believes they are all angels in fur, or wool, or skin. For her they show up as another way God continues to shower his/her love for us on a daily basis. Of course, Annie's Dudley first came with us to our new home. He seemed thrilled with the tall grasses and freedom of the pastures where he could rejoice and run without being on a leash. He was so small and he would jump like a little rabbit through the hay. Not long after we arrived, our little Dudley slipped away. He was 15 years old and he probably went off to pass away somewhere but it has troubled Annie's heart so much over the years wondering where her little chemo dog/buddy pal went and hoping there was a peaceful rather than a violent ending for her special friend.

Annie mourns him still and has tried to replace him with other dogs over the years like a Husky, Aussie, or even a Maltese. But none of these replacements made it long on the ranch. The Husky found a more appropriate home in North Carolina, the Maltese was deaf and not safe on the ranch so she was returned to the breeder and the Aussie found a home with just one owner and no other animals competing for her owner's affections. Annie feels she was a foster parent for each of these creatures and helped them find better homes for their life's journey. She finally stopped trying to find her Dudley replacement and just enjoyed her other animals. Despite the fact we never found his body we did make him the first grave in our little pet cemetery on the ranch.

Journey to Life's Dance Ranch

Dudley

Today we celebrate a life
Of love and special grace
He walked away some nights ago
To be another place
A place we all hope we will be
When we, must walk away
He brought us part of heaven
Now he is there to stay
We're left with heaven's memory
But life won't be the same
We've lost our little, big dog
...Sir Dudley, was his name

SIR DUDLEY

HERE COME THE CATS

Annie never grew up with any animals as her family had a lot of allergies and she herself was allergic to cats. As soon as we arrived, I said we needed to get some cats because we are a ranch and would have mice in and outside the house. So off we went to the Humane society.

Chapter Eighteen

Our first stop was to visit their large cat room where it seemed like dozens of cats walked around. Annie was nervous as she was really afraid of cats. She quickly found a bench to sit down on. One big orange marmalade tabby cat gently approached her and sat on her lap. She tentatively petted him and he just laid there peaceful as could be. "OK, lets take this one he seems really nice and calm" Annie said.

She was ready to leave but I suggested we find a little kitten too. So, we looked at the kittens and found a little cutie we quickly named "Little Bit." She would have to stay and be spayed before we could take her home. "Ok, now let's go." Annie anxiously insisted having her fill of cat energy. I still resisted. "You don't happen to have any barn cats, here do you?" I asked the humane society staff.

"Well normally we would say no because barn cats have a tendency to be at high risk to predators and we want our cats to find loving forever homes." They explained. "However, we just happen to have a young cat who arrived with one of her kittens. They were found underneath a car and covered in oil and dirt." They went on to explain that no staff member had been able to touch the mother because she was snarly and mean. They had to wear long gloves to even approach her. They said they were getting ready to euthanize her. My reply to them was "I would love to see her."

Off we went to a different building where in a single cage lay a cat, with very matted and tangled hair, curled up in the back of the cage. I reached my hand in and began to stroke her. She seemed beautiful to me. "We will take her," I declared even though Annie was looking at me with large fearful eyes and a dropped jaw. I told her not to worry it was going to be in the barn not the house. This cat also needed to be neutered so we made arrangements to pick the other two up after their surgeries the following week. And off we went with our orange tabby. They told us his name was Cantaloupe but Annie and I decided to call him "Scotch" in honor of our trip to Scotland with the gang.

Scotch remained calm and steady and Annie was relaxed with

him immediately. The following week we picked up the other two. "Little Bit" seemed to be doing well recovering from her surgery. However, the barn cat looked awful. She was sick with diarrhea and vomiting. We put her in our solarium so she would not mess up the rest of the house. We eventually took her to the vet where they put her on antibiotics and said we should hope for the best. That night Annie found the cat curled in the corner barely moving. Annie sensed this cat was going to slip away from us soon. She sat next to her crying and said, "I don't know anything about cats, but if you give us a chance and let us learn to love you then I promise you do not have to be a barn cat. You can stay here in the house with the other cats."

HOPE   CLEO AND LIL' BIT

That night Annie slept in the solarium with the cat. The next two nights I took over night duty. And slowly this cat started to move and eat a little. She walked tentatively and was weak but she was definitely making improvements. Annie and I decided to call her "Hope" because we certainly were hoping she would make it. She eventually did get better and for two years she was in the house somewhere but we rarely saw her. After the second year she started to peek out and even started to interact a little with the other cats. It was as if she never learned to trust animals or humans and she certainly did not know how to play. Over the years we have delighted as we have watched her blossom into a wonderful lap cat and the princess of the pack.

Chapter Eighteen

We lost Lil' Bit unexpectedly one day when her heart just stopped. She had stayed little and not grown much and eventually the vet said her heart just did not grow either. She was the second pet in our pet cemetery. I later picked out another rescue we called Cleo, short for Cleopatra, since her fur was exotic looking. Cleo was my special cat and while a little loud and annoying to others, I thought she was beautiful. She too passed on and I had her cremated so her ashes could be spread with mine, along with some of Dana's and then Annie's and Jul if they go before me. It's going to be a lot of ashes to spread! The amazing thing with all these cats in our house, Annie never had any allergic reactions. She believes as her fear decreased and her love increased for these curious and playful creatures the allergy was no longer activated in her body.

Lil' Bit

She gave us love
She gave us joy
Showed us trust and courage
She warmed our hearts
She changed our lives
She shouldn't have died
...At her age
But then again...
She'd sung her song
With beauty and with grace
It was her time
To move along
Unto that better place

THEN MY DOG

Another great blessing came to me via our neighbors the Shaw's (Ray's & Delona's daughter Laurie, and her husband, Brian.) On the fourth of July 2011, they came over to our place with a stray dog that had shown up on their doorstep. She was a beautiful border collie/Aussie mix. I immediately fell in love with her. They couldn't keep her and asked us if we could take her. I said sure and that we would try to see if we could find her owner. We looked for dog missing ads in the paper, checked with local vets and even took her to our vet to see if she was chipped. We never saw anything that indicated someone might be looking for her, so we named her JUL, for the month July when she found us. One morning I was taking her to an appointment to have her spayed and chipped. Just before that appointment, I went to get the newspaper. Jul was in the car with me and Jordan Alexander happened to be driving by. He stopped, and we talked a bit and then he said, "That dog looks a lot like one in a picture outside a furniture store downtown." My heart sank. She had become her Daddy's dog and I couldn't imagine losing her now.

I immediately drove to the furniture store and there on a telephone pole was her picture and some tabs with a phone number. I headed back to the ranch down in spirits. I called the number and a lady answered. I told her I thought we probably had her dog. As it turned out she was a veterinarian in Hamilton, Montana. She explained she was in Helena a few months ago to visit a friend. They had been walking their dogs and the dogs ran off ahead of them, and when they called them only one came back. She told me she would be in Helena the next day and would pick up her dog. I told her I had grown quite attached to Jul and wondered if she would consider selling her. She said she had never thought about giving her up, but she would think about it. I said some prayers. When she arrived the next day, Jul immediately recognized her and was happy to see her. My heart sinking, I asked if she had considered selling Jul.

She was impressed with our ranch and the freedom Jul was

Chapter Eighteen

experiencing. She said Jul had to stay locked up in her apartment all day while she was at work and felt this would be a better life for her. She said she had two hundred dollars in Jul and would I consider paying her that. I couldn't write the check fast enough. Jul has been with us ever since. She is a wonderful creature who is partial to her Daddy, in

fact she has separation anxiety when we are apart for too long. She goes with me everywhere in my pickup and is with me constantly when I am working the ranch. She loves chasing tennis balls, pine cones or sticks. She has a natural herding instinct and tries to herd horses, sheep and chickens. She is a bit of a chicken herself and several of our chickens know this. They seem to revel in her herding them but, occasionally, they will turn on her and chase Jul around my truck or our big stock tank. She really is a sissy but acts tough when she is in the car and sees another dog. She is a great watch dog and enriches our lives in so many ways.

AND OUR OUTSIDE ANIMALS

We've had two animals on the ranch that we raised from babies which gave us much joy and then much good eating. One was a bum ram I named "Rambo" the other a baby Holstein calf we thought was a steer but turned into a bull. I named him "Herd" although we called him "Herdie." Their names fit them both beautifully if I do say so. Part of the fun of raising them was feeding, first formula with a bottle, then pellets and finally grass and hay. They both had wonderful playful personalities and grew up best buddies. In particular, I enjoyed telling people about our "Herd." I would go downtown and meet people who always ask about the ranch and ranch animals. We did already have six adult ewes when we got Rambo, not a bad little flock but when people asked do you raise any cattle? I didn't really want to say we had only

one cow. Anticipating this question, I named our little bull "Herd." That way when people asked if we raised any cattle, I could truthfully say, "Yes, we have a small "Herd" but our "Herd" is growing and we will have to move our "Herd" to a bigger pasture in the near future." Of course, when I'd finally tell them we actually only had one little Holstein named "Herd" we would have a good laugh.

Rambo went on to become a big strong ram and did a great job of impregnating our six ewes. They delivered eleven lambs the spring after the romance and what a delight to have these babies dancing in our pastures. Of course, babies do grow up and when the time came, we had all but four of them butchered. Annie loves lamb and this was probably the best lamb we had ever eaten. Again, we always gave thanks for them when they were on our menu.

We decided Rambo had had enough loving and it was time to turn him into a wether, a castrated male sheep. We summoned our vet to come and do the deed on Rambo. Our vet was amazed and said Rambo's gonads were the biggest he had ever seen on a ram. He jokingly said that when he cut them off Rambo may tip over. It made us so proud! Fortunately, Rambo's surgery did not take away his beautiful deep voice. He still sports the deepest voice I have ever heard on a sheep. Unfortunately, none of his children inherited his wonderful bass voice.

Herdie grew into a gentle giant, almost seven feet tall and still loved playing with his best bud Rambo. Unfortunately, he also loved to run to me or anyone in his pasture who he thought might want to play with him. Butting heads with his friend Rambo was fine but at seven feet and thinking it fun to butt heads with humans, that became a liability. So, we had to have him put down. It was a very sad day for us but Herdie continued to give us delight. We had him butchered and we gave thanks every meal we had where Herdie was the entree.

Chapter Eighteen

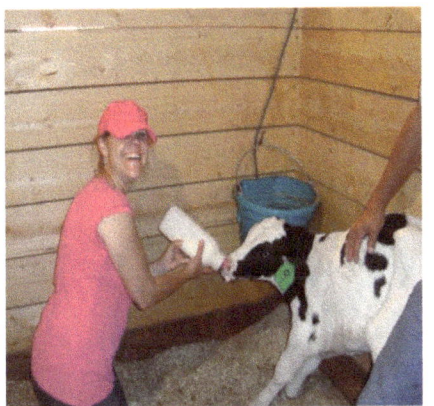 

BABY HERD & BABY RAMBO

FULL GROWN AND BUDDIES 'TIL THE END

After Rambo lost his pal, a new best Bud showed up to our ranch quite by happenstance - our donkey, Joker. Our good friend, Jordan Alexander's daughter had a horse that was hit by a car and had to be put down. Joker and the horse had been their own herd. Joker needed a place to go where he could have other animals around him and Jordan asked us if we would take him. Not wanting the little fella to be by himself, of course we said yes. However, Annie said we had enough equines so he would have to go into the sheep herd and become a sheep protector. He seems to really enjoy their company as he is now their pied piper. He has become a wonderful addition to the ranch. He is an incredibly gentle and loving creature. Kids love petting him and feeding

him his favorite treat, red licorice. We know he is somewhere between forty and fifty years old. We do love him and his unique energy.

OUR HORSES AND THE LESSONS LEARNED FROM THEM   (ANNIE'S INPUT)

I am so grateful to these beautiful creatures because I know Annie's love for these animals is THE primary reason she was so willing to move to Montana. I have learned to love horses as well but it is all of the Big Sky country that I adore all year long! Montana 's winter wears Annie down, as does our ranch and home workload at times and she misses her daughter, grandchildren, family and friends in Atlanta so much. I know it is her love for her horses, this land, and me, of course, that keep her committed to our beautiful ranch. She believes the horses give guidance to her on a daily basis, if she listens!

So, at this point I am going to temporarily turn the reins over to Annie to let her explain the magic and miracles she has found with our herd over the years.

Chapter Eighteen

While Mike's focus is on other ranch duties, I primarily take care of our equine herd and love their calming energy and the whispering encouragements they give. If I ever get overwhelmed with other things going on, the horses are where I head to breathe in their peace and love. They never fail to steady and sooth me. I know that, in addition to Dana's guidance, Steppes also helped lead us to our ranch, for purposes which are still unfolding.

After Mike bought Paula and she was settled in, he saw a horse on the internet that looked just like Steppes. He showed it to me and the next thing we were off to LoLo, MT to see this horse which was for sale. When we arrived, I walked over to the horse. I took one look at her and started crying, the horse even had the one blue eye like Steppes. The owner said she used the horse for trail riding but admitted "Bonnie Blue" was still recovering from laminitis. I bought her anyway without even having her vet checked because I felt Steppes was

working through this little mare and she was meant to be on our ranch.

Bonnie Blue was an Arab, fast and spunky. I was bucked off on my first ride. Over time I realized our Bonnie Blue was here to teach me a lesson, and then every horse after her as well.

My Lesson #1: Slow Down and Pay Attention to the Horse's Needs, not just what I want the horses to do for me.

Of course, we really had no idea how to take care of the horses at first. Sonnet had always been stabled prior to our move where horse care and instructions had been provided on a daily basis. Mike saw how much I enjoyed the time I spent with the horses, and decided he wanted a horse too. So, we were off to a ranch near Shawmut, MT where he found his Appaloosa, Rio. There were over 100 horses on this ranch and Rio was the only Appaloosa and he was being picked on by the others horses. Right away Mike fell in love with this cowboy tough looking horse and then we fell in love with a little baby pony they also had. Being the ignorant equine owners that we were we proceeded to buy both Rio and the pony. We named the pony Dewar Bell for the Bell kids. We really had no business raising a pony and were way out of our league. Our farrier at the time told us to do ourselves a favor and find a better home for this little one. We listened to this sage advice and we did find a sweet home for the pony.

MIKE'S RIO

Then Came Riley

By now Sonnet was lame. She had tried to protect me over the years from my unbalanced attempts at riding and now was her time to retire. I continued to focus on dressage as this was the most therapeutic approach for working on my balance issues. However, since Sonnet could no longer provide me with a balanced partner, off I went trying to find a new dressage horse.

I searched the web and made several trips to visit a few horses but there was one in particular who caught my eye and captured my heart. He was a Canadian warmblood whose father was a champion stadium jumper and the mother a thoroughbred. I asked Tana Dearborn to drive to Canada with me so I could try out this horse. As we were crossing the border the border patrol asked me why I was headed to Canada. I said I was going to check out a horse. His answer was, "Why, don't they have any horses in Montana?" I quickly replied,

Chapter Eighteen

"Not like this they don't." I had not found as many dressage riders and horses in Montana, as I had in Georgia. I arrived in Saskatoon and rode Riley and fell in love. And he became part of our herd's expansion at "Life's Dance Ranch."

Much to our farrier's dismay and then ours as well, his hooves were not in the best shape. He had inherited the worst of the thoroughbred's bad hoof issues. The farrier scolded me and said, "never buy a horse without having their hooves checked out too!" He went on to say, "Because if you don't have hooves you don't have a horse to ride!" I was devastated as I loved Riley and he was the most expensive horse I'd ever owned.

After a few years and going through at least four different farriers we were blessed to find the right ones. First our veterinarian, James and then Tim Hensley, a former bronc rider now farrier, became the saviors I found to guide us with Riley and our other equine hoof issues. Riley will always have this issue but he is doing so much better with the proper care.

My Lesson #2: You Must Pay Attention and Care for the Whole Horse, it is Your Absolute Responsibility as an Equine Owner. P.S. It is also a good reason not to buy too many horses so you don't end up focusing enough on any at all! Ask me how I know.

Riley is such a gentle creature even at age five when I bought him, he was kind and careful. He continues to be our lover bug. We know if we could let him in the house, he would snuggle up with our cats and dog and try to sleep with us as well. Riley is also very patient with me as I do my therapy riding on him. I dream of the day when I can sit a perfectly centered seat on him with all my muscles, bones and joints moving together as one with him. I will pursue this goal forever for it is my true passion. And then maybe one day, I can canter and gallop with him through our fields with confidence.

Journey to Life's Dance Ranch

ANNIE ON RILEY & MIKE ON SONNET
IN OUR EQUESTRIAN ARENA

Next Come Our Fox Trotters

Mike and I suffer from a similar affliction. We both have big eyes and want to do so many things, we can be rather unrealistic about how all this can be accomplished at this time in our lives. Anyway, I was dreaming of trail riding with Mike and I got on the internet again. I wanted safe trail horse, better yet two, so we could ride the trails together at the same pace. In no time we had two Missouri Fox Trotters being unloaded at our ranch. Sure enough, they were from Missouri and I bought them sight unseen and unvetted. The first boy was Domino and he was exactly as they had described him in the ad. He was steady and easy to navigate on the trails. He is a wonderful horse and riders of different levels enjoy his gentle, steady nature to this day.

The other beautiful Fox Trotter was Blue Bell. She was a beautiful mover, very smooth, very fast. The problem was she did not

Chapter Eighteen

like to stop. We had several good riders on her but all had trouble keeping her in control. We decided we should sell her. We found her a wonderful Forest Ranger who worked as an outfitter in the Bob Marshall wilderness. He was a very experienced rider who needed a horse who would go fast and far to help lead his trips. So off Blue Bell went to her new home, a match made in heaven.

TWO OF THE BELL GIRLS WITH SOME OF OUR HORSES. OUR FOX TROTTERS ARE ON THE RIGHT

My Lesson #4: There is a Fifty-Fifty Chance on Any Decision You Make. It Could be the Right One and You Will Feel It if It is, Or, it Could Be Just Another Stepping Stone Leading You Toward a Better Match.

By now you can see logic has nothing to do with my passion for acquiring equines. I follow the whisperings of the horses and my heart and soul. We have learned a lot over the years.

My Lesson #5: Sometimes, If It's Not in the Flow, It's Time to Let Go.

Spending time with these beautiful creatures has taught me much about the importance of their care and how time, money and is required to care for them in the way they deserve. This is why the Carroll students who love horses and come to our ranch are so welcome. We obviously have more equines than we can train and work with on a regular basis. The attention some of our horses receive from these students is just what we need to ensure they are being loved and cared for. And it is just what the students need to be in the presence of the horses. A win-win all the way around.

My Lesson #6: Ask for What You Need Then Stand Back and Allow it to Manifest.

And Then Comes Another!

Recently we decided to find a small horse for our granddaughters to learn to ride on. Once again, I looked over the internet for months. Finding this "beginner safe" type of horse was hard to find because if people own these safe horses, they want to hang on to them! One day, when I was working out, I heard "Come find me," being whispered to my heart. I immediately got back on the internet and saw a video of this cute little palomino, "Twinkie", doing a walk, trot, canter in an arena. He was located in Kentucky. I looked up shipping costs which were three times as much as the horse cost. I quickly ruled him out. But a few days later I received a call from the seller who said she found a transporter for a much more reasonable price. It was an amazing deal so we jumped on it and are settling in this very sweet little 14 hand gelding. Once again, he appears to be a lot spunkier than described, however we have already fallen in love with him and look forward to what he has to teach us and our grand-children on the ranch.

Chapter Eighteen

My Lesson #6: When You Are in the Flow, Just Go For it, Trusting the Process to Unfold the Blessings for You.

TWINKIE NEAR LITTLE PORCUPINE CREEK

HONORING STEPPES' REQUEST

Steppes had left this world with my cancer and I still feel the need to help equines evolve, as Steppes requested of me. Supporting Carroll's Anthrozoology Program has been a great start, but I felt the need to do more. I did get certified as an equine specialist in the EAGALA model. Equine Assisted Growth and Learning Association is one approach for professional mental health and personal development services. From this training, I learned **My Lesson #7: The Power of the PAUSE Before Responding in any Given Situation.**

Friends of ours Jeff and Darlene Patterson also run an interpersonal communication program called Herd2Human where they work with veterans with PTSD and others using the horses as guides. There are many equine assisted therapies and personal development programs which currently exist. Last year I was drawn to Melisa Pierce's amazing program, "Touched by a Horse." Excitedly I filled out the application for this 2-year long training and was accepted. Mike and I attended a couple courses together, excited about what we might learn. We drove in our camper first to Canada then to

Colorado. I loved the program but we soon realized the intense work required to actually run these workshops was not what my body and energy level could handle.

It was then I realized that perhaps one of our expanded missions for "Life's Dance Ranch" was to simply host these various healers and/or horse trainers at our ranch. By first attracting and then offering various healing and training modalities here on the Ranch we would be advocating for the evolution of equine's role in human healing. We would be providing a service to our community and would also be mindful of our health limitations and demonstrate the importance of taking care of self. The wheels were beginning to turn in our brains for a possible addition at "Life's Dance Ranch."

My Lesson #8: Turn Over to God, to the Horses, to the Universe and Trust the Process. Never Stop Learning, Living and Loving. Amen.

I am very excited about these future possibilities and Mike has been so supportive of my efforts and so understanding of my passion for the equines. With that I will now give the reins back to Mike!

Chapter Nineteen
My Family Blessings

MY BOYS AND THEIR BEAUTIFUL FAMILIES

Perhaps my greatest joy is having my two boys move to Helena and the ranch. Andrew came first. When I started having heart problems, he told Annie he had lost his mom to ovarian cancer way too young and he wasn't going to lose his Dad to a heart issue if he could help it. He told Patrick that he would have to work their business in New Smyrna, Florida by himself. A couple weeks later Andrew was here. He moved into the old cowboy bunkhouse. It had been fixed up as an efficiency unit and we had Carroll students renting it before Andrew moved in. He has been an absolute blessing for us. Andrew fell in love with everything Montana. He loves the beauty of nature and was particularly excited to bring chickens into our lives. He is a truly nurturing man for both animals and plants. He is a sports enthusiast. He gets excited about every single aspect of this ranch. I often hear him calling, "Dad, Dad you gotta come see this" and off I go to see the magic he sees. This I know he inherited from my father and me and it is a joy to share this land with him.

About a year after his arrival, his wife to be, Elisa Kiss, moved to the ranch and has been a wonderful part of our lives for many years. Eliza is a talented actress and vocalist who was living in L.A. when they met. She gave up the bright lights for Andrew and despite growing up in Florida and then California she embraced Montana. Her talents were quickly noticed by our local community theatres and she has been in many plays since she has been here to rave reviews. We are so proud of

her. She is a great match for Andrew's high energy and they are always camping, hiking, exploring, planting and buying more chickens. It has been so much fun to see them enjoy the ranch and all the wonders of Montana.

Just before Christmas 2017, Patrick, Lizzie and our two-and-a-half-year-old granddaughter, Kailyn, moved from Florida to Helena. They have been pure joy for us. Lizzie was due to have another baby the following April. Boy or girl? We didn't know; they wanted it to be a surprise. And a surprise it was when Lizzie gave birth to a new baby girl, Qiannah, in our solarium assisted by a midwife. What a beautiful experience to have in our home. It has been wonderful having our new baby girl and watching the daily changes that come in the first year of a baby's life. They live in an apartment downtown but keep a 5th wheel camper on the ranch so they can spend more time here when the weather is nice. Patrick had stayed home to care for Kailyn when she was born. Lizzie with her Master of Social Work had been the primary provider. So, the plan in coming to Montana was that Lizzie would stay home with the kids while Patrick worked.

Patrick and Lizzie are amazing parents and Annie and I are often in awe as we watch them patiently talk with and correct the little ones. We both wished we could have been a little more patient with our own children! Both Annie and I enjoy our grandchildren so much and hearing their laughter puts such smiles on our faces.

Patrick and Andrew work together doing the things they are skilled at: Cutting down trees, landscaping, construction and property maintenance. They are fortunate to have plenty of work between my brother-in-law Gene and Ray Zinn to keep them busy full time. They take every chance they have to spend in nature with their families and the wonderful friends they have made here in Helena. And of course, they love hosting Barn Parties!! They are first class BBQ men, along with my buddy Tom Dearborn.

Chapter Nineteen

ENGAGEMENT AND WEDDING TIME

Andrew and Eliza got engaged in our barn on the 4th of July 2017. We were thrilled. Their plan was to be married in Florida on November 10, 2018. Annie and I had to miss the engagement event as we were in France with our granddaughter, Tessa, Patrick and Lizzie's oldest daughter. We had promised her a horse-riding trip to France as her high school graduation gift. We did have an amazing time in France along with our beloved JoJo. We later had a costume engagement party for the couple to be. We all dressed up in different characters and each gave advice to the couple from their character's perspective. I must say the best costume and words of wisdom definitely went to Tom Dearborn as he dressed up as Gene Mallette and looked and talked the part to a T. I dressed up as Ben Cartwright from Annie's beloved Bonanza, and Annie dressed as Scarlett O'Hara. It was a delightful fun night.

COSTUME ENGAGEMENT PARTY

It was a tremendous honor to have Andrew and Eliza ask me to be the officiant for their wedding. I had actually already officiated at Tom and Tana's daughter's wedding, so I had a little practice. The wedding was a beautiful event at a luxury resort on Sanibel Island, Florida. Eliza's parents, Jeff and Sue Kiss did an outstanding job of arranging this destination wedding. We all flew to Florida by different routes. Annie and I flew to Jacksonville where we picked up JoJo. She knows the boys well and they love her and Kailyn calls her Grandma JoJo. We drove from Jax down to Sanibel where we had rented a VRBO on the ocean very close to the wedding site.

Everything from the Rehearsal Dinner, the Wedding and Reception and the morning after breakfast went off beautifully. There were so many friends and family who had made such a special effort to come to this destination to witness the joining of this beautiful new couple. I was able to catch up with Dana's parents and siblings which was wonderful as most are still in the Florida area. Andrew and Eliza had set up a special table for those who had passed on and could not be with us that day. Of course, his mother Dana was very well represented at this table. It was beautiful and touching. The guests eventually scattered back to their homes while the bride and groom headed to Costa Rica for a first-class adventure. I was so proud and happy for my son and his new wife.

Chapter Nineteen

"With Us in Spirit" Table

They came back after the wedding and honeymoon tired but happy. However, they did let us know that while they loved it here in Montana, next November they would be moving back to Florida, where Eliza's family is and where the winters are not so tough. We will be sad to see them go when the time comes but totally understand in life there are always changes and compromises. Andrew loves Florida too and the beach and all activities that go along with it. I know they will miss being on the ranch as we will greatly miss them.

Their moving will actually be a positive for us in that we will make more trips to Atlanta and Florida. So, we will see more of Annie's family, JoJo, Dana's family and Eliza's family. And, we are hoping for little red-haired grandbabies!

Chapter Twenty
Ever Growing on Life's Dance Ranch

Ever since we came here, "Life's Dance Ranch" has been growing and improving. We actually feel the land, and maybe vibrational suggestions from long ago owners, to keep making improvements. We know God has brought us here for a purpose. We are not always sure what that is but up until now we have felt sharing the beauty and peace of this land with family and friends is a good enough mission.

GROWTH STEPS

The first year Annie had our dressage arena built so she could ride her beloved Sonnet and then Riley. Not long after the arena was finished, we purchased ten more acres north of our property where we gained a beautiful Aspen grove and a gorgeous view of a meadow and other rocked and forested land. We just felt called to add and care for more land. After a couple years, improvements were made to our rental cabin/Lodge including adding bedrooms downstairs and handicap walkways for our renters.

Then a couple of years ago we had the opportunity to add more land to our property. Annie and I are trying to manage all of these properties and buildings on our fixed incomes and with a little help from long term renters. So, we really had to pray a lot about the decision to invest in more property. And as there was an abundance of acreage available, exactly how much was enough for us and our wallets. We would have loved to buy every acre available but we knew this was not meant to be.

Journey to Life's Dance Ranch

We walked and talked with the land to help us with our decision. Annie who had become especially close with the blessed Virgin Mary in recent years, prayed for guidance. When we walked to what could be the back of our property, Annie fell to her knees as she viewed the rock/grotto near a gorgeous robust stream. She felt Mary encourage us to buy this land and perhaps even one day build a small chapel on this sacred ground. So, with deep breathes and a tightening of our belts we added another 20 acres to our Ranch. Our neighbor, bought the rest of the available adjoining land and a final fence was added to set the 70-acre boundaries of our piece of heaven.

Last year, Annie felt the need to add an 80 x 80 ft. round pen to help her with training the horses, teaching young riders, and assist with her own therapeutic riding. This project took all summer to clear out the rocks at our future round-pen site. Annie hand-picked and moved many of the smaller border rocks from our neighbor Ray's land. Grady Hall was used a few times to clear some rocks and I attempted to use our small tractor which still left a lot of rock in the ground. Jordan helped us tremendously to make the project a success. Again, thank you Ray for loaning us your foreman and equipment which after a solid day of working in the rain our space was ready for Shannon Bell to spread the arena gravel. Then we put up the fencing. A sacred circle has been created not only for training horses and riders but which can be used for various events, workshops and retreats.

EXPANDING OUR VISION FOR LIFE'S DANCE RANCH

After nine years on this land we feel our Ranch's Vision expanding. Because of all the requests to use the barn for reunions, weddings, parties and other events, we are now getting the barn ready to rent for such occasions. Our long-term renter left last year, and we decided the log home should become a short-term vacation rental lodge. We decorated the lodge in the pure Montana style we love. Annie and I spent an amazing three months completely furnishing this log home and creating our MT Moose Lodge. We found many things on Craig's List and Craig's

Chapter Twenty

Mart, and we traveled to Bozeman and Missoula for "deals" on used furniture and antiques, all with the authentic Montana flavor. Our moose mount even came from LoLo, MT and he is part of the special, peaceful energy our Lodge provides. It was a very fun time we had putting the finishing touches on this special place.

MT Moose Lodge

[Booking: vrbo#1543136 ; abnb.me/rNbnAPAV40]

Then as things began to evolve the idea came to us to package the Lodge with the event barn and the use of our property for whatever people may want. If there are more people who need lodging than our Lodge can hold, we have plenty of beautiful private camping sites for RV's and tents. We also have teepees and can provide an economical alternative that lets guests "lease" our property to celebrate in her beauty with their family and friends, for whatever their reason.

We believe this sacred space was meant to be shared and experienced by others. And then as if the Universe, or God, or Something, Nothing and In-Between, or whatever you may call the source energy of this world, were nodding in agreement, through a friend our first wedding was on the books.

Neither Annie or I are very tech savvy. You can say we are way behind the eight ball with regard to computer and social marketing

skills. As we move forward in leasing our properties, it is obvious we need to provide a presence on the web. Most of these technical and financial duties will have to fall on Annie's plate. I am the handy man and ranch worker. Our intention is not to overwhelm ourselves with these Ranch changes. We will trust the word of mouth process and the power of prayer at this stage.

Annie and I both feel the energies of God at work. We feel the energies of Dana's goodness, of Steppes, of our parents sending encouragement from wherever they are now. It is the energy and beauty of the mountains, the streams, the equines … it's the energy of the rocks and the earth. It may be energies of old mixed with new energies but we know we are encircled in a sacred vortex of goodness and love which we want to continue to share with others. We feel entrusted perhaps by the first inhabitants of this land to help it continue to blossom. We are not sure exactly how this will look.

We are in the infancy stage for exploring these options. We do love all the talk about the possibilities which could evolve at "Life's Dance Ranch." Our extended family on and off the ranch have contributed to many ideas about the use of the ranch. The boys and their wives have made great suggestions over the years about how we can move forward. Do we have the time, expertise, money to do so? Exactly, how much can we take on at this point in our lives? I am 70 this year and Annie is 8 years behind me, can we do this? Will it exacerbate our health issues, stretch us too thin??

Even as I write I hear the loving energies which surround me whisper "Stop…Pause…Breathe" and trust the process to unfold as it has done for you so far. Let "Life's Dance Ranch" do what she does best, let her dance and create more peace and beauty. And as challenges arise, we may just need to learn to dance in the rain as well as the sunshine. We both love to dance so we will continue to create the "Magic and Miracles" we have been so blessed with in our time here on this land.

Chapter Twenty

I truly believe that it was first and foremost Dana who brought us together and me back to Montana. I found a journal Dana had kept for many years with writings of various authors and of her own writings. It didn't surprise me that most of them focused on love, kindness, friendship, fairness, living a good and honorable life and doing good for the world. What did surprise me was that the style of the poems she wrote was almost identical to my writings. Perhaps it was Dana and not me who wrote much of this book. I know she would be so happy for me and our boys to see us now.

And so, to honor our journey to Life's Dance Ranch Annie and I, along with Sara Dearborn's graphic skills, created a logo which tells the story at a glance. It was the Butterfly that I designed for Dana which brought Annie and I together. It was the sacred energy of the horses Annie trusted so much to be willing to leave her family and move west with me to Montana, where we live amongst the sky, the wind and the Rocky Mountains.

I am a blessed man. My life has been full of love, laughter, tears, joys, sorrows, triumphs and losses. But through it all I can say I listened to the music of the universe and danced. Like the lyrics my son Patrick wrote, "The Dance of Life, the steps they aren't written, but you can't be wrong as long as you're livin ..." And oh, how I've lived! Dancing through life with Dana was a smooth graceful waltz. Dancing through life with Annie is more of an energetic, fun Charleston - we come together and then pull apart and then always come back together. Two very different but wonderful dancing partners. I know there is still more to come and I welcome each new day's adventure. Dear Reader, my final wish for your life is that " I hope you take the chance and dance."

Blessings, Montana Mike

P.S. If you get a chance, come visit!

Journey to Life's Dance Ranch

4TH OF JULY AT THE BARN

CAMPFIRE AND SING-A-LONG

VIEW FROM NORTH PROPERTY

Chapter Twenty

The pastels on this page were done by Eliza's mother, Sue Kiss, who is an accomplished artist.

She created these from some pictures she had taken after a visit to our ranch.

Her works can be found at SusanKiss.com

Part IV: Selected Poems

Chapter Twenty One
On Nature

Blessed to grow up in a tiny town on the Montana prairie, with parents who were in love with the beauty of nature in our Montana paradise, I came to love and appreciate all the never-ending nature's gifts. I have lived a life in love with our Mother Nature and I am happy to say my boys learned this from their mother and me, just as I learned from my parents. This section too, is a love story. I hope that my gratitude for the simple beauties and truth found in nature can be found in these writings

No Regrets

And when the river changes course
... offers us a gentle force
And bids to come and ride
We mustn't run away and hide
For this may be our only chance
To ever do this river dance
And even if the current's strong
Sometimes it's best to go along
And take the chance at what can be
Lest we lose...the opportunity
Then regret it for...eternity

Naked

I see upon the naked branch
The still cocoon
Clinging in its lonely wait
Winter still controls its fate
But Winter only gets so long
To hold the life within
'Til Springtime comes and breaks
Its grasp and sets life free again
And hope that was this chrysalis
Takes flight and does its dance
The butterfly emerges
And finally has its chance
To be at one with Springtime
And then Summer, but not Fall
The leaves will go and so the dance
Is wrapped back on the naked branch

Chapter Twenty One

GARDEN DANCE

The dancing in her garden
Is coming to an end
A couple lonely blossoms
Still waltzing in the wind
The autumn leaves are falling
The dancers will soon go
For they must clear the floor
Make room for winter's show
But winter only takes so long
To sing its lovely winter song
Then Spring will let them dance again
The garden will renew
The flowers will be ushered back
With sunshine, rain and dew
And bloom once more

Egret

Egret wades in ripples
Knee deep in the pond
Could not, create more magic
If one, had a magic wand

Butterflies still dancing
In the autumn breeze
Rejoicing in their autumn life
Before the autumn freeze

Eagle soaring in the blue
Above the bright fall day
Soon will bring life to the nest
In spring, they'll fly away

Old man running down the road
In his autumn years
Mourning his lost lover
Knowing it's not hers

With all this autumn beauty
There is nothing he can share
And he smiles as he sees it
Knowing she's already there

Journey to Life's Dance Ranch

NATURES CYCLE

Where grass goes back
To be a seed
Then seed gives up its hope
And heads on back to nothing
Back down the endless slope
And comes to rest with nothing
Until its rest is over
Then off it goes, this time to be
A lovely four-leaf clover

ECLIPSE

And so, the eclipse happened
And the moon soon disappeared
As it moved there in the darkness
While earth, its movements mirrored
But it could not hide forever
As the earth would soon dance by
And once again, the full moon
Would bring magic to our eye

Chapter Twenty One

Creation Ripples

When ripples move across the pond
We know that something's there
Yet when we look, whence ripples come
The life that sent them can be gone
Or is it gone?
For we can see its life upon the water
The yellow dog that made the wave
May never make another
But what it left for us to see
Even though it had run on
Is not just ripples on the pond
Or movement on the water
Its life affecting other life
Us touching one another
And so, creation ripples
And we're the other shore
The waves of all creation
Can reach us evermore

Sundog Clips

Oh wondrous day, oh perfect day
With sky so brightly blue
And wisps of pure white angel hair
The hand of God brushed through
With sundog clips of rainbow
That pulls this hair aside
To let us see, her mother sun
On her celestial ride
And as she comes now closer
With spring she brings her gift
New life will be emerging
Give winter hearts a lift

Cicadas

Cicadas singing in the night
As they climb among the trees
And fly to find their lovers
On the gentle evening breeze
From the earth, they're summoned
By natures clock
And must not, must not miss this call
It is their one and only chance
To dance in nature's ball
To waltz together, two by two
Then leave upon the branch
New life to fall into the earth
Whence there, to wait its chance
For nature's clock to make its call
And summon life, unto the ball

It was late, early dusk, when I began my run this evening. The sky...sad and gray, but a playful and happy breeze was there to run with me...and how I do love the wind. We ran joyfully together for a mile, and then, **_she_** joined us with her soft gentle tears, not yet weeping, but we knew she would. At the five-mile point, the breeze abandoned me, leaving me alone to console her, and she wept. Soft rain in a lonely darkness, one place where the soul can share sorrow with another element of nature.

Chapter Twenty One

Sun Dogs

The little puppies danced the edges
Of the cloud bank where they played
And it was a magic rainbow
On those edges, that they made
As they chased their mother sun
On her journey to the night
And to all the eyes that saw them
Sunset puppies brought delight

Eternal Flow

As rain fell upon the live oak
Worked its way down to the land
It dripped upon his body
And down his skin it ran
In its never-ending journey
This life's eternal flow
Giving birth to leaves and branches
And the grass that lived below
Brought with it, all the stuff of life
To where matter, had to be
For life was all that mattered
And rain brought energy
As it drove life through its cycle
With its mother nature's sun
Its fluid force directed course
Toward the great eternal one
And the cycle never ended
And the cycle never can
Nothing becomes something
Then, nothing, once again

Playful Clouds

The clouds dash by the treetops
With the early morning light
Revealing their great hurry
To finish off the night
Come back into the day
To dance and twirl and spin and whirl
Above our lives they play

❧ Emergence ❧

The flower first must wither
Before it drops its seed
And leave its life's potential
With its dormancy and need
To find its own new place to be
...Its soil, sun and rain
And out of death arise again
To blossom once again

EERIE SIGHT

MOONLIGHT THROUGH THE EVENING MIST
BUT THE DARK STILL RULED THE NIGHT
AND USED THE MOON AND MOISTURE
TO CREATE AN EERIE SIGHT
SOFT SHADOWS HEAVY ON THE GROUND
STRETCHED BACK IN DARKNESS LAIR
AND TOUCHED THE BODIES OF THEIR BIRTH
FROM NIGHT AND LIGHT, IN THERE

Chapter Twenty One

Flaw's Perfection

The Tuscan earth gave birth to life
 Pulled by the Tuscan sun
To paint a tapestry of God
Behold, the perfect one
And, as the masters came to see
In this their god's reflection
It was the flaws that made it real
And lead to all perfection

Night's Compression

Tonight the stars came closer
And, so too, did the moon
He'd like to share this with her
And, he will see her soon
Then they will watch the night compress
The stars and moon and sky
It's light will shine upon them
Its beauty…make them cry

FROZEN TIME

IVORY INSTINCT
FROZEN TIME
DEATH THAWS OUT
NURSERY RHYME
THAWING DEATH
BECOMES LIFE
RIVER FLOWS
EVAPORATES
CLOUDS FORM
PRECIPITATES
WATER FALLS
MELTS STONE
SOIL WAITS
SEEDS COME
LIFE EMERGES
TAKES TIME
LISTENS TO
NURSERY RHYME
BORN OF WATER
AND OF STONE
DEATH HOLDS BOTH
CAN'T BE ALONE
AS IT THAWS
GIVES THEM BACK
TO NATURE'S LAWS
RULES OF LIFE'S
ETERNAL GAME
NOTHING'S CHANGING
ALL THE SAME

Journey to Life's Dance Ranch

I have always enjoyed watching and learning about birds. We were fortunate to have a Birds Unlimited store just a mile from our subdivision in Jacksonville. I made friends with two delightful and very knowledgeable ladies who owned the shop. After Dana died, I would often visit their store just to visit. They showed me great kindness. I wrote this for them and they posted it on their store window.

Birdbrains

The girls at Birds Unlimited
Are smart in every way
I visit their store daily
To hear what they will say
And if I have a question
That has to do with birds
I know I'll find the answer
With a smile and their words
They've taught me 'bout the bluebirds
And the lives of sandhill cranes
JoAnn and Sandi's knowledge shows
They really are birdbrains!

Chapter Twenty One

NAKED PINE

NAKED PINE
YOU'VE LOST YOUR CLOTHES
TIME HAS LEFT YOU
INDISPOSED
AS TIME WILL DO
WITH EACH OF US
ON OUR GREAT JOURNEY
BACK TO DUST

JUST PASSING BY

FROM THE DARK NIGHT SKY
CAME A VISION OF THE PAST
AS A SPARKLE TO OUR EYE
THAT HAD ARRIVED, AT LAST
AND AS THIS PAST, BECAME OUR PRESENT
WE MARVELED AT THE STARLIT SKY
AND THIS DEATH, WHICH WE WERE SEEING
UNLIKE OUR STAR, STILL GIVING LIFE
THESE STARS HAD BEEN AND GONE
WHAT ONCE HAD REALLY MATTERED
WAS SIMPLY…MOVING ON

Journey to Life's Dance Ranch

NEW DAY

Oh, glorious morning
Now given to me
I mustn't neglect you
And fail to see
The gifts that you bring
With this first light of day
God's holy sun
Now showing the way
On this Sunday morn
In love and with light
Our new day is born
Oh, glorious sight!

SPRING

And the wind blew...
With a gentle chill
Winter taking its last breaths
As comes the springtime will
Soon winds will be much softer
With scents from flowers new
Awaft upon Spring's clean fresh air
And chasing springtime's dew
Off morning grass, now turning green
As life now comes anew

STREETLIGHT DANCE

Streetlight glow upon the grass
Early morning dew
Reflects what now precipitates
'Fore day will come anew
And on night's blades it will remain
'Til sun puts it in flight
No more to dance in streetlight glow
Or early morning light

Chapter Twenty One

Soft Rain

Tears of gentle joy
At dusk, to us she came
The loving mother for her child
A spirit with no name
From up above, she wrapped herself
Around the coming night
Played rain's, soft sweet music
Without thunder, without fright
Her tender loving song
At the finish of this day
A gift, if we just listen
To wash our cares away

Montana Magpie

Montana magpie, on winter's branch
Awaiting death's donation
For there is where, you find your life
The source of your…satiation
While others prey upon the soil
Or that which lives thereon
You wait your chance for gifts between
That life, that's come and gone
In time then, you become the prey
As all existence, must
And once again assume the roll
Of life's eternal dust

Vulture's Cosmic Dance

Above him in the clear blue sky
A vulture softly floats upon
The breeze's gentle breath
As it looks for what will give it life
In its search for recent death
And so it is with all of life
And existence does this too
Life preys upon existence
When the preying stops, it's through
Somethings become something other
Or spin on back to nothing
To wait upon their chance
To once again be somethings
In nothing's cosmic dance

Sun's Energy

The snow reflects the energy
That led to its creation
As it, will also be the force
Which leads to its cessation
Unto another form
Either flowing or a flight
Unsure what form it may become
As day gives way to night
And so then goes existence
We're given from the one
With driving force of energy
Sent to us from its sun

Chapter Twenty One

Bloody Dawn and Dusk

First blood flowed just before the day
Then just before the night
And though it was a bloody show
It was a glorious sight
It spoke of life, it spoke of death
Of birth, and moving on
How blessed we are when bloody sky
Gives us the dusk and dawn

Wrinkle's Truth

She loved to feel the summer sun
For she knew it brought the shade
Yet this was just a passing thing
In Fall's light, less was made
And, Winter's time and temperature
Made faster, still the fade
'Til all left there, was memory
Of what could come again
A summer sight, to her delight
The tan upon her skin
But, Summer's shade, came at a cost
It hid for her in youth
The shade which so delighted her
With age, shows wrinkle's truth

Patio View

As water spray, at end of day
Made rainbows with the sun
It used its magic prism
Before the day was done
To bring the night
With colored light
A blessing from the one

Breeze

The clouds would race their shadows
To the sunset...where they'd die
And the breeze, would run along
Chasing both...across the sky
Then the night would put the breeze to bed
So the night could be then still
But the breeze would come again in 'morn
Where day couldn't break her will

More Winter

No light had yet come to them
Through the clouded morning sky
Yet snow, would soon illuminate
As sun was onto 'nigh
To bring them winter's magic
That they'd long waited for
And so, as they gave thanks
They also prayed for more

Chapter Twenty One

Frost

Sitting in the cold
Looking out at spring
Just beneath the snow
Potential...smoldering
Soon God's sun
With soil and dew
Will bring a verdant
Life anew
But with this resurrection
One day will come a cost
The price then
It is everything
As life is simply lost
And time as well
When autumn comes
To bring its
killing frost

Chapter Twenty Two
On Sorrow

We all experience both "Sadness" and "Darkness" in our lives. Though they can be related, they are different in certain respects. Sadness to me seems to have an element of something greatly loved that has been lost and must be grieved. Or sadness can be a perpetual grief for something wanted yet never fulfilled.

Darkness on the other hand has elements of fear and hopelessness associated with it. This is why I separate these 2 categories of my poems as to me they are different experiences.

LIFE'S GRIEVING

IF SADNESS IS A LONGING FOR SOMETHING GOOD, ONE'S HAD
THEN SADNESS IN AND OF ITSELF, CANNOT BE SOMETHING BAD
FOR IN IT, THE HEART REMEMBERS, THE GOODNESS IT RECEIVED
AND IF TRUE LOVE HAS BEEN THERE, THE HEART WILL ALWAYS GRIEVE
BUT IF SADNESS IS A LONGING FOR SOMETHING UNFULFILLED
THE HEART WILL ALWAYS SUFFER, UNTIL THAT NEED IS STILLED
AND, <u>THIS</u>, SADNESS GOES MUCH DEEPER,
FOR IT HASN'T FOUND THE GOOD
AND THE TRUE LOVE THAT IT HOPED FOR,
AND ALWAYS THOUGHT IT WOULD
THIS SECOND KIND OF SADNESS, CAN BLIND THE HEART TO SEE
WHAT THIS SAD AND LONELY HEART...REALLY MUST HAVE, TO BE FREE

SADNESS

AND WHAT IS SADNESS?
IT'S NOTHING LETTING YOU KNOW
HOW MUCH YOU LOVE
A PART OF IT
THE PART THAT WAS SOMETHING
THE SOMETHING, NOW NOTHING
…ONCE AGAIN

Her Eyes

Those eyes, those eyes
They haunt me, they taunt me
They make me feel sad
They make me miss you so
They make my heart glad
They give me great comfort
With their silvery blue
Reflection of goodness
Reflection of you

ETERNITY'S TEARS

LET ME CRY
IT HAS ONLY BEEN A YEAR
AND A YEAR IS ONLY A MOMENT
AND A MOMENT IS ETERNITY
AND ETERNITY
IS WHAT I WANT TO BE
IT'S WHERE I'LL FIND
MY DANALEE

Chapter Twenty Two

Locked Souls

There are those who lock their souls
That lock their souls away, and
They have a thousand lifetimes, yes,
And it's there they'll have to stay
And they won't see God or understand
Or even think it's there
They may even make believe
They really, don't even care
But it's fear that keeps them in the cage
For they all still hold the key
To open up the prison doors
And let themselves be free
It's tough to watch them stay in there
When we wave and yell and shout
We want them to just use their key
And let themselves come out
And feel the joy of nothing
That we have, when we are here
But they are there, and there they'll stay
In their prison made of fear
And who knows what next lifetime
That fear will go away
But only then
Will they be allowed
To come, nowhere, to play

OLD CATS

Cats upon a roof
Sleeping in the sun
Once they were both kittens
Now, is neither one

Autumn breeze is blowing
Leaves are going by
Time will come a calling
Someone's going to cry

Kittens once were playing
Now they're laying still
Age has slowed the life in them
As…..Age always will

Autumn breeze is blowing
And though the breeze is warm
It gives a hint of Winter
And Winter's coming storm

Grey cat by the bedside
Its autumn's almost done
Time to sleep forever
Its wintertime has come

Autumn breeze is blowing
Soon there will be tears
Old cats are a dyin'
Heartache lives for years

Chapter Twenty Two

A Greater Gift

Ladies, ladies... go to sleep, although
I know, you prefer to weep
You've better things to do today
And weeping sweeps your heart away
Instead rejoice that you can weep
Life's given you feeling, that runs deep
Rejoice and give your heart a lift
Your tears reflect a greater gift

GRANDMA MARY (a magical lady)

Why was she lucent?
Why was she clear?
Her mind had been gone
For over a year

Yet with that one visit
She came to the living
Once again, she was Grandma
Her love she was giving

Then they left, and it's said
That her life left her too
She never came back
Her living was through

FINAL READING

The book of life is ending
The cover will soon close
The pages with his story
Will now, so much expose

Life Stalled

Heartache happens
Family cares
Friends come by
To help repair

Broken life
Broken heart
Broken soul
Try and start

Life again
When life has stalled
Void is there
Love one called

Gone to nothing
The void is ours
We live on
With sorrow's scars

Nothing happens
Nothing heals
Nothing changes
How life feels

Nothing brings
Us back again
Lets us be
'til our life's end

Desperation

This desperation has my throat
I've got to break its grasp
My soul must have some breath
Or I'm never going to last

Chapter Twenty Two

ROCKING CHAIR

ROCKING CHAIR
SITTING STILL
NO ONE THERE
TO DRIVE ITS WILL

ROCKING CHAIR
ROCKS ALONE
SISTER CHAIR'S
ROCK IS GONE

ROCKING CHAIR
ONCE HAD LIFE
NOTHING THERE
ONCE A WIFE

ROCKING CHAIRS
ONCE ROCKED TWO
NOW, ONE ROCKS
THE OTHER'S…THROUGH

ROCKING CHAIR
LIFE'S METRONOME
OLD MAN ROCKS
END WILL COME

ROCKING CHAIR
END WILL COME
BUT NOT BEFORE
LIFE'S WORK IS DONE

ROCKING CHAIRS
AUTUMN AIR
NOTHING HAPPENS
NOTHING'S THERE

KEEPSAKES

KEEPSAKE BOX
LIFE WITHIN
MEMORIES
COME AGAIN

OPEN LID
LET THEM OUT
LOOK BACK AT
WHAT LIFE'S ABOUT

KEEPSAKE BOX
SMILES AND TEARS
LOVE AND LIFE
YESTERYEARS

KEEPSAKE BOX
HOLDS A KEY
HOLDS OUR HEARTS
LETS US SEE

IMPORTANT BAUBLES
JUST A GLANCE
SHOW US OUR
MOST PRECIOUS DANCE

Someday Tomorrow

He's going to leave someday tomorrow
If tomorrow's ever there
Find that place to ease his sorrow
Reach a place where he don't care

Lost his one true love to cancer
Knows he knows the place she's gone
Still he's looking for the answer
'Til his time for moving on

Can't go yet, 'cause time won't let him
Someday, tomorrow will come along
Time will help him reach tomorrow
But today's nights take so long

NEVER

I know that never happens
When you never think it should
When you never think it's coming
When you never thing it could
And you're never really ready
When never finds you there
And never is it easy
And never won't be fair
But..never's always fair
We never know the reason
That never has to be
But never always happens
And can bring such misery
No, never never happens
Cause never never's there

Chapter Twenty Two

Never's always showing up
And giving us despair
We never see someone again
They never will be there
We'll never have another chance
To give our love and care
We'll never see another
Or see another moon
We'll never fly another kite
Or see another June
Cause never's really nothing
Is really never there
Is never just a fact of life
That causes us despair?
Or maybe it can bring us joy
Like, never will be war
Or never have great suffering
Or never want for more

Never, when it comes to you
It always leaves you there
Can leave you with deep sorrow
A sorrow you can't share
And never will be able to
At least the deepest parts
The parts reserved for hurting
But not with other hearts

Something Happened

Driving down life's lonely highway
In a borrowed Chevrolet
From a friend, who didn't need it
On an ice-cold winter day
On a road I've rarely traveled
But I think I know the way
Driving down life's lonely highway
Something happened...yesterday

Now the snow is in the headlights
Say a blizzard's on its way
Say it will be...real bad
Can't compare with yesterday
Storm is closing in around me
But I've been out here before
And thank God they've always found me
This time I'm not quite sure

They may close the road behind me
Leave me out here in the snow
On a cold Montana highway
Don't know where, but I must go
Keep on drivin' 'til I get there
Where ever, there, may be

Chapter Twenty Two

Drive until the blizzard's over
Or I lose this misery

Driving down life's lonely highway
In a borrowed Chevrolet
Don't know...if I'll make it
Something happened yesterday

They all worry 'bout his driv'in
But not about the car
Pray that he will be surviv'in
That he will not go too far
That the storm will pass
And ease his way
Bring him back into the sunshine
Something happened... yesterday

Sometimes we have to drive alone
Take leave of all our friends
Those times, we must be on our own
Til life's sad journey ends
And if we're lucky, we make it back
To see a brighter day
To feel again, to live again
Something happened... yesterday

Endure the Fear

So damn tired
So damn old
So damn ready
For the cold
Cold can't come
Too soon for me
Take me to
Eternity...
God I need
My Danalee

Don't jump yet
You have to dance
You can't go back
You must advance
You must go on
Until the dawn
And then go on...some more
She'll show you when
The time is near
For now, you must endure this fear
And live...perhaps another year
Or maybe longer
Yes, my Dear
Maybe longer...

Chapter Twenty Two

She's Waiting

Some days, life's fear overwhelms me
And will not go away
And the safety that she gave me
At the end of every day
Which allayed my fears, and
Calmed my soul, and
Gave me strength, and
Made me whole
Such a struggle now I find
Though she still resides within my heart
And I see her in my mind
Yet, the nights can be a struggle
Often hard to get some rest
How I miss patting her bottom
Saying "Sweetheart, you're the best"
And now I cannot touch her
On the far side of the bed
And yet I feel her presence
I know she is not dead
She's doing what she promised me
The day before she died
Waiting close, behind that curtain
Just on the other side

Journey to Life's Dance Ranch

LET ME STAY

Is it miracles and magic?
Tell me, is this really so?
Sometimes I swear to God
I really do not know

It seems at times surreal
Defies reality
And truly makes me question
Have I lost my sanity?

Oh God, if I
Have lost my mind
Please let me stay here
Oh, please be kind

Don't take this gift
That I now own
It helps me through
This time alone

NEW SORROW

That night,
They all turned in
Went to bed without a care
Never once suspecting
Death's miasma would be there
And turn life's course,
For some of them
And end the course for others
With fetid evil vapors
It lingers, 'til it smothers
The life it came to take
Then death is on its way
The lives it leaves behind
Find new sorrow…on this day

Chapter Twenty Two

GOODNESS WORKING

It's not about me Lord
It's not about me
I know what is happening
Is my Danalee
The magic and miracles
She brings every day
Is her goodness working
It's what she must do
Her work is not ended
She'll never be through
With bringing her beauty
And joy to this earth
And showing the things
In life of most worth

LIFE'S PLAY

In their final chapter
For some, their final page
This has been magnificent
It set a brilliant stage
And gave what all great literature
Needs to bring unto the mind
The reader must find tragedy
Then triumph, they must find
The plots must be quite numerous
The characters unique
In goodness and in evil
In selflessness and greed
You never want this book to end
It is a joyous read

Journey to Life's Dance Ranch

MOURNING DARKNESS

Oh God, I'm still here
As I look in the mirror
And I see I have found a tomorrow

Though I try to rejoice
I find I've no choice
I'm still desperately lost in this sorrow

And I know that tonight
Will come all too fast
And the darkness will hold me
In its lonely grasp
And I'll struggle with what I can't see
The love of my life, my Dana, my wife
In the bed, lying there, next to me

And then there is morning,
And then night again
Where the mourning continues to be
At the end of tomorrows
Night brings back the sorrows
With greater intensity
In the morning, the mourning
In the light of day
Can sometimes distract
'Til the light goes away
And darkness brings mourning
Back once again
But I know, when the darkness
Will come to an end

Chapter Twenty Two

DIDN'T ASK MUCH

She was on the airplane
And her heart was sad
She had lost at love
As so many had

Though her heart was good
It had been broken
And her eyes, they told
What had not been spoken

They showed the pain
That she'd been through
Dealt from a love
She thought she knew

And she longed for a
Gentle tender touch...
An honest love...
She didn't ask much

BRIGHTER DAY

We must all drive through the rain sometimes
And sometimes in the dark
And though we slow for safety
Or to the side we park
The rain keeps driving faster
It will not go away
And we must wait forever
To see a brighter day

HEAVEN'S TEARS

Sometimes we need this water
Sometimes we need this rain
Sometimes we just need something
To wash away the pain

Sometimes we all need darkness
So we can see the light
Sometimes the day, it must depart
And leave us with the night

And the night can be so lonely
As you live there in your pain
When you've lost, your one and only
Sometimes all that's left is rain

And that rainy night in Georgia
Or where ever it may be
Bathes the heart in tears from heaven
As it brings back memories

Oh that rainy night in somewhere
Where ever somewhere comes to be
Needs these tears to come from heaven
...wash away this misery

Sometimes we need this water
Sometimes we need this rain
Sometimes we just need something
To wash away the pain

Sometimes the heart must suffer
Sometimes the rain must fall
Sometimes those tears from heaven
Are what's needed most of all

Chapter Twenty Two

Road With No End

On the road that seems to have no end
Not sure where this road will take me
Sometimes this road is difficult
But, I'll never let it break me

I'll keep pushing 'til I get there
Just not sure where, There, might be
Down this road that has no end
Heading for…eternity

Seems that sometimes life can give you
More than you think you can bear
But no matter what it gives you
Life will always take you there

Take you through the darkest hour
Bring you out the other side
Time will get you past the darkness
To the light, where God resides

If you're lucky you will stay there
But there are no guarantees
Pray that nothing cares about you
Pray it's nothing that you please

Help me down that lonely highway
Down that road where I must go
Know that God is down that highway
But what God is…I do not know

Journey to Life's Dance Ranch

RUNNING THERAPY

WHEN HE RUNS, LIFE MOVES AWAY
AND TAKES WITH IT, HIS PAIN
LETS HIM SEE THE SUNSHINE
LETS HIM FEEL THE RAIN
LETS HIM BE AT ONCE ALONE
AND STILL WITH ALL OF THOSE HE'S KNOWN
MOVES HIM IN A DIFFERENT SPACE
A DIFFERENT TIME
A DIFFERENT PLACE
WHERE MIND IS FREE
WHERE HE CAN SEE
THE NOTHING OF ETERNITY
AND BE AT ONE
AND LEAVE BEHIND
THE SHACKLES OF HIS BEING
ESCAPE FROM THIS REALITY
'TIL IT'S NOTHING…HE IS SEEING

WHEN NOTHING BECKONS

There were no clouds
There was no sun
There was no sky
The day was done
There were no stars
To light the night
Our everything…
Was out of sight
The dream, had simply
…gone away
It had grown old
It could not stay
…nothing beckoned
It must obey

Chapter Twenty Two
Growing Away

I can't imagine the pain
Of growing away from love
What once made one so happy
Now makes the mourning dove
A wound too deep to suture
You cannot stop the bleed
Unless you find a true love
There'll always be a need
And the heart will not stop bleeding
This sorrow it must let
Unless true love can bandage it
And help the heart forget
What it had hoped would make it whole
Instead, a scar now on the soul
Once thought to be the perfect one
The choice was not, the love has gone
And though this could not be predicted
The wound one feels, seems self-inflicted

Tragedy

In his tragic boyhood
He was a little man
Never was a little boy
Or came to understand
The magic of a childhood
The wonder that was youth
He never heard "I love you"
He lived a tragic truth

Heavy Heart

The wind knew that I loved her
And… I needed her tonight
She sensed my heart was heavy
She felt my desperate fright
And though, this didn't come often
When it did, she always knew
She could never, never leave me
She must stay and help me through
Run with me to my sunset
Then let me feel the still
Help me make it to the darkness
Beg me never lose my will
And I cannot disappoint her
Somehow, I must go on
And trust I'll find my love there
With every morning (mourning?) dawn

Gray Coat

She rolled in with her gray coat on
And she didn't want to leave
Her heart was filled with sorrow
She had a need to grieve
She wanted me there with her
To help her bear the pain
She opened up her cloud to me
And gave her grieving rain
And her rain fell down upon me
As my night grew darker still
Her tears beat down upon my heart
She tried to break my will

Chapter Twenty Two

Ready to Move

I know I'll eventually
Get rid of time and space
Then freedom will arrive, and
Take me to another place

I know I must rejoice 'til then
And help others while I'm here
Must help them deal with their fear
And deal with mine
Though much is gone
I'll soon be set
To... travel on

Visit to The VA Hospital

I stopped in for a visit
But I wasn't happy there
The visit was essential
I felt that death was near
Not to come and take me with it
For some others, time would end
The wounds of war upon their souls
For nothing now would mend

NEVER

I know that never happens
When you never think it should
When you never think it's coming
When you never think it could
And you're never really ready
When never finds you there
And never is it easy
And never won't be fair
But never's always fair
We never know the reason
That never has to be
But never always happens
And can bring such misery
No never never happens
Cause never never's there
Never's always showing up
And giving us despair
We never see someone again
We'll never have another chance
To give our love and care
We'll never see another day
Or see another moon
We'll never fly another kite
Or see another June
Cause never's really nothing
Is really never there
Is never just a fact of life?
That causes us despair
Or maybe it can bring us joy
Like never will be war

Chapter Twenty Two

OR NEVER HAVE GREAT SUFFERING
OR NEVER WANT FOR MORE
IT'S NEVER, NEVER, NEVER
THAT BRINGS AN END FOR US
AND NEVER HOPES WE FIND
WHEN WE TAKE THIS GENTLE HAND
IT'S NEVER WHERE WE GO WITH DEATH
TO ... NEVER, NEVER LAND

Blue Existence

When you've lost a piece of nothing
From the middle of your heart
And they say it's only something
That can help put back the part
Remember it was something
That brought the piece your way
And probably something else
That made it go away
For heaven can be transient
While we are somethings too
And while our hearts need nothing
Existence can be blue

Chapter Twenty Three
On Darkness

I first suffered with darkness and depression with the divorce of my first wife. I was so ashamed of being the first person in our family to ever get a divorce. Winning had been my life until that point and then all of a sudden, I felt I had lost in the biggest way. It took many years before I was able to let myself fully back into the light.

When I married Dana, my life became bright and beautiful, as good as it gets. When she passed, I went into a darkness I had not felt before. For the first four months after her death, I was completely lost and depressed. Then after a beautiful dream of Dana dancing across the sky, the darkness went away and spontaneous writing started. Joy was back in my life. I was in a state of elation. Though many of the early poems I wrote were of darkness, others were of light and joy. I learned that both darkness and light are wonderful gifts in a person's life. From the darkness we learn so much about the light and from the light we learn the gifts of darkness.

I experienced depression's darkness at other times in my life and Annie has also suffered through times of depression and darkness. I've always made it back but at times I wasn't sure I would. Some of the writings below were written when I was in the depth of depression. My thanks to all those who helped me through those dark and difficult times.

 *Journey to Life's Dance Ranch*

Darkest Moments

There are moments when the darkness
Surrounds me like a cape
And in those darkest moments
I, can find…..no escape
And nothing seems to help me
Deal with my grief
There's really nothing there
That gives my heart relief
And when my darkest moments leave
I know that nothing's helped me grieve

Depression's Grip

When the darkness closes in on you
And the world is left behind
When you can only look at it
And feel, you've lost your mind
When they tell you that
You'll be all right
That they've been there before
When you know, you've, also been there
But still, you are not sure
If this time, you can make it back
As you fall into this hole
As depression takes away all joy
As you feel you've lost control

Chapter Twenty Three

As you live in desperation
Feeling you have lost all hope
And you hear them on the other side
As they try to help you cope
But like the final dance with death
This place you go alone
There is no darker place on earth
For anyone who's gone
Oh God, I'm trying to get back
But it has it's grip on me
They call this thing…depression
But I feel…insanity

Unfreeze

The darkness was so heavy
The sun, it could not rise
And in the blindness
Pure dark brings
He came to realize
That simple life
Devoid of things
…responsibilities
Can help to find the light again
And let the dark…unfreeze

FIND JOY IN DARKNESS

Ripples of light from a happy pond
'Neath a clear blue crystal sky
Reflecting life, from the sun of God
As the gift of day goes by
'Til the pond finds darkness once again
But still, happy it will stay
Reflecting stars throughout the night
Awaiting its new day
And like the pond in darkness
Finding joy in points of life
We must find joy in darkness
If we're to be all right

RENEWAL

Dark moving way past midnight
The fog is moving in
A brain that reached its limit
And, begs for sleep again
Let alcheringa find me
And keep me paralyzed
Then give me back…to consciousness
Awaking…. Energized

Chapter Twenty Three

PAIN

What do we want?
What do we don't?
What can we make
Come true?
How do we know
Where we must go
And that which
We should do?
How do we find
What's in our mind
To bring us happiness?
Where will we see
What we must be
Before we feel blessed?
How can we
Step from darkness
And find
A guiding light?
Where will we find
The sunshine...
Escape this desperate night

Or will the light
Bring comfort...
When night gives way
To dawn?
Or simply shine a
Brighter light
On what we feel
Is wrong?
When will we see
With clarity
The reason for
This lesson?
When will our hearts
Recover
From the pain
Of this depression?

Night Time Pain

Night time hurting
Night time pain
Night time
Here you come again
Night time memories
Still too clear
Night time memories
Still too near
Night time quiet
Won't be still
Brings the memories
Always will
Night time used
To give some rest
Now it brings
An awful test
When will nightmare's
Game desist

Desperate

How the darkness makes one desperate
How it draws upon your soul
How it takes the life within you
How it makes you less than whole
How it amplifies your sorrow
How it magnifies your fright
How it steals hope for tomorrow
How it lengthens every night
How it keeps the sun from rising
How it kills the will to fight
How it wraps its cloak around us
How it will not let us go
How it's strength can so astound us
How it smothers life's lights' glow
How it takes our vision, we can't see
How it takes away reality
How it brings to mind all deep regret
How the darkness makes one desperate

Chapter Twenty Three

Life's Torture

Sadness, gladness, madness
So closely they're aligned
And found to live together
In the dungeons of our mind
And when life's torture
Gets too great
And they can't take the pain
They give way to hysteria
Then pray to be insane
And finally there is nothing left
But darkness and the night
No stars of hope to guide them
From this dream, of endless fright
So they descend into nothing
And sit with their blank stare
We tap upon their shoulder
But find that nothing's there
Emotions once we found so deft
Are now of soul, complete bereft
Emotions once were there for life
Now sliced away with nothing's knife

Toronto

*Lost in an airport
In Toronto, somewhere
So many people
Yet no one is there*

*Loneliness holds me
And will not let go
So many people
But no one to know*

*Lost in an airport
Waiting to fly
So many people
They keep walking by*

*Only less lighting
Could darken this show
So many people
But so little glow*

*Lost in an airport
Looking for life
So many people
But where is his wife?*

INSANITY CHASING HIM

Insanity is chasing him
And, may catch him one day
But he hopes,
Death will catch him first
And take him on his way

    Away to final destiny
    Where he can stop the chase
    Where he can find that nothing
    With it's gentle, resting place

        And there, where nothing happens
        Where time has gone away
        He'll stay till time is given back
        Then he'll return to play

DARK AWAKENING

Darkness called me, woke me up
At four-thirty in the morning
It was so disconsolate
And showed up without warning
The depth of sadness that it brought
Just could not be consoled
And even though the love one lost
Had grown very old
The love we have within our hearts
That's touched when age moves on
Will always bring sad darkness
The moment they are gone

Chapter Twenty Three

Entombed

If only I woke this morning
And there was sun
Where darkness had entombed me
The light, it opened up night's jaws
Before the dark consumed me
And now I live another day
But darkness, that's just out of sight
Will have me in its jaws tonight
Survival is the nightly test
Oh God, I need some real rest to find the strength
But the strength I cannot find
I've lost my strength, lost my soul
My God, I've lost my mind

THE BOY

Tonight, I saw deep passion
Tonight, I saw deep fear
Tonight, I saw humility
And something else was there
Tonight, I saw a boy
Too smart, to be a man

Journey to Life's Dance Ranch

Nightmare

Terror snuck up and grabbed him
In the middle of the night
And held him in its ugly dream
Consumed his soul with fright
This wasn't its first visit
It had been there before
And just as it had always done
It brought its deadly horror
It held its arms around him
In death's grip for a while
And then slowly released him
With a nightmare's evil smile

OBSESSION/PASSION/ELATION/DEPRESSION

Between the two, distinction, can often be unclear
One brings exhilaration, the other comes with fear
One will not let you cross the line
The other always sends you flying
One blinds the fearful eye to see
The other, it, will set you free
Obsession's, then, what fear is of
But passion, passion, comes from love
And often we can suffer both
As opposites pass by
Passion brings love's truth
With fear, we get the lie
So where we find elation
Depression may be near
And show us when we least expect
Its ugly face of fear

Chapter Twenty Three

The Quell

Deep clear pool
Candlelight
Sitting on the edge
Tonight
Sudden ripple
Now the quell
Mirror broken
Now comes hell
Nothing happens
Nothing's there
Nothing clears
The fetid air
Deep clear pool
Candlelight
Sitting on the edge
Tonight
Always on the edge
Waiting for the quell
Life can give us heaven
Or life can give us hell

Revelation

Oh, the day was Cimmerian
And the night was, darker still
And those who chose this fetid lot
Were soon to feel their thrill
As the moon was choked into the clouds
And would not re-emerge
While those, living on the evil side
Their souls, this gloom insured
There was no hope where they prevailed
In this dark and murky sin
These souls were lost in hell
And wouldn't be free again
'Til their journey, back to nothing
Where a revelation…be
They differ just in magnitude
From every…you and me

Nightmares of Darkness

Incandescent nightmares
Still keep haunting her
Memories of a darker life
Won't stop taunting her

Face of Vile

We all have demons deep inside
They hide in dreams, in souls reside
And come to see us now and then
But will not tell us where or when
They will impart their terror on us
But, they will bring that animus
Then they'll go back and hide awhile
'Til next we see…their face of vile

Chapter Twenty Three

Depressed

At times you have no options
Or at least, they're very few
When life presents, this feeling
And depression...captures you
Takes you where, you're out of place
Out of touch
Don't have to face
What you've now left behind
And though you see what's going on
You know you've lost, your mind

Annie, God bless her and her siblings, suffered some of the most awful abuse and emotional trauma imaginable. With strength and courage that I can't even imagine, they survived with each other's love and help to become incredibly wonderful people. Some of what I have written below came by way of things Annie told me of her abuse and struggle to overcome the emotional scars on her heart and soul.

Ugly Noose

Her soul had endured the rape
That so few ever must
And still she found within her soul
Some things in life to trust
And though evil almost took her
It could not be her end
For so many needed what she had
Hearts like hers must mend
And many souls, she must set free
Release to their eternity
Then find her own, and cut it loose
From, now past evil's ugly noose

Journey to Life's Dance Ranch

EVIL'S RAPE

IF YOU HAVE BEEN WHERE EVIL LIVES
AND BEEN IN EVIL'S HOLD
AND LIVED IN EVIL'S UGLY LAIR
AND FORMED IN EVIL'S MOLD
CAN YOU ESCAPE TO GOODNESS
IF GOOD'S WHAT YOU WANT TO BE
DO YOU KNOW, THAT YOU WANT GOODNESS?
OR IS EVIL'S PEDIGREE
SOMETHING YOU MUST ALWAYS LIVE WITH?
SOMETHING YOU CANNOT ESCAPE?
MUST YOU ALWAYS SLEEP WITH EVIL
AND ENDURE YOUR EVIL'S RAPE?

EVIL ESCAPE

SO WHAT THEN IS THIS, ANNIE?
A CHILD FROM EVIL'S NIGHT?
RUNNING FROM THE DARKNESS?
ESCAPING TO THE LIGHT?
CAN SHE MAKE IT NOW, THIS TIME?
CAN SHE STAY THERE, IN THE SHINE?
AND HOLD ON TO THE LIGHT?
OR WILL IT VISIT HER ONCE MORE
IN THE MIDDLE OF THE NIGHT
AND IS <u>HE</u> HERE TO HELP HER?
HELP WITH HER QUEST TO BE…
AWAY FROM EVIL'S DARKNESS
AND WITH GOODNESS…SET HER FREE?
CAN SHE ESCAPE THE EVIL
AND FINALLY LOSE HER FEAR?
ONLY SEE THE SUNSHINE OF
HER GOODNESS IN THE MIRROR?

Chapter Twenty Three

ON STAGE?

LAUGH AND TALK AND THINK AND PLAY
CRY AND HOPE AND FEEL AND PRAY
REJOICE IN LIFE THEIR SPECIAL WAY
HE'D LOOK INTO HER EYES, TODAY
AND IN THE SPARKLE OF THEIR LIGHT
SHE'D SHARE A VERY SPECIAL SIGHT
AND LET HIM SEE SOME MORE TONIGHT
SHE'D SUFFERED AS A NEOPHYTE
IN EVIL'S DEEP DARK CAGE
AND WAS SHE TELLING HIM THE TRUTH?
DARKEST SECRETS, FROM HER YOUTH
OR WAS SHE ON THE STAGE?
PERFORMING IN HER MAGIC WAY
ENCHANTING HIM WITH WHAT SHE'D SAY
HOW FROM THE NIGHT, SHE'D FOUND THE DAY.

THE BANK

And from the bank of darkness
She dove into the light
And swam in sunshine's river
Felt the goodness, lost her fright
But if the bank should call her
Try and lure her from the stream
She must swim...to the deepest part
She must not lose this dream
For the bank has lured her out before
And held her captive on the shore
Has coaxed her from her goodness swim
And made her think she needed him
When what <u>his</u> ego really needed
Was her life control,
again

Journey to Life's Dance Ranch

HEAVEN'S LIGHT

SHE WAS BORN INTO THE DARK
BUT THEN, SHE TURNED AWAY
TOOK ALL THE STRENGTH THAT SHE POSSESSED
TO FIND THE LIGHT OF DAY

AND THOUGH THE DARKNESS TOOK HER BACK
ONCE OR TWICE, ALONG THE WAY
SHE NOW KNOWS SHE HAS FOUND PURE LIGHT
IT'S WHERE SHE WANTS TO STAY

FOR SHE KNOWS FROM HER EXPERIENCE
IN THIS LIFE SHE'S HAD TO PLAY
WHEN YOU TURN FROM HEAVEN'S LIGHT
THERE'S ALWAYS HELL TO PAY

SHE HAS CLIMBED ONTO THE MOUNTAIN
WHERE THE LIGHT CAN BATHE HER SOUL
WHERE SHE CAN FEEL ITS WARMTH
WHERE IT CAN MAKE HER WHOLE

AND SHE KNOWS SHE CAN'T GO BACK
GO BACK INTO THE NIGHT
THOUGH BORN IN EVIL'S DARKNESS
SHE WAS MEANT FOR GOODNESS' LIGHT

AND IT'S WHERE SHE'LL KEEP HER FAMILY
IT'S WHERE SHE NOW MUST STAY
FOR WHEN YOU TURN FROM HEAVEN'S LIGHT
THERE'S ALWAYS HELL TO PAY

THOUGH LIFE FIRST GAVE HER DARKNESS
SHE OVERCAME THE PAIN

Chapter Twenty Three

Escaped the evil thunderstorm
And evil's pounding rain

Emerged into a meadow
Of soft and gentle light
Where she embraced light's goodness
And lost her evil's fright

Though she knows the dark's behind her
She must never lose her way
For when you turn from heaven's light
There's always hell to pay

She can go back now, to evil's edge
And look evil in the face
For she knows she now has strength
To never go that place

And she can now help others
To come from evil, to the light
Bring them from their darkness
With her goodness, bring them sight

Help them step from their dark evil
Into goodness light to stay
For when we turn from heaven's light
There's always hell to pay

Evil's always there behind us
And it beacons us to play
For when we turn from heaven's light
There's always hell to pay

Vigilant

He watched her go into the darkness
He could see it in her face
She'd grown up with the darkness
But she never liked the place
She knew she must remember
Lest the darkness get control
Of her, or worse, her loved ones
She must stay on patrol
For evil is persistent
It never will relent
It will attempt to hurt them
She must stay...vigilant

Resurrection Room

The room, it was true magic
A reflection of her soul
And of her healing goodness
Where she helped to make them whole
Brought back the broken pieces
And put them in their place
There was nowhere within this room
You didn't feel her grace
And the pure joy of her being
Though this hadn't always been
There were those times of sadness
Where her life was touched by sin
But she's had a resurrection
And started life anew
Her times of desperate darkness
Now a past, that she's worked through

Chapter Twenty Three

HER CHILD'S BIRTH

Oh, child out of darkness
Came child of your own
Not ready for that journey
With your little one
In fright and blind confusion
You had to let her go
To arms of those you trusted
Trust yourself? You did not know
Couldn't take the chance you'd hurt her
Couldn't take the chance, you'd bring
The darkness you'd been raised with
To this most precious thing
At times, times made you run away
To where the hurt was…yesterday
Times past now, were your present
And light went back to dark
Where your pain, it never lessened
Till you dealt with all your demons
Until you reconciled…hell
Until you dealt with that past darkness
You never…could be well
Now you've come back from your darkness
Though you know what it is of
You now control the darkness
With your strength, your light, your love
You won't let it hurt your baby
Or your baby's babies too
You've saved them from the evil
You all can live anew

Turn to Light

She was born, as other children
With a beauty and a call
To be straight, out in the sunlight
To be good and to stand tall
But then, life would abuse her
In a way...so unexpected
And present a chance, to her
When she'd been misdirected
As it broke her back, and left her there
Assuming she would die
The life that wouldn't abandon her
Her heart, would just not lie
In where, most find self-pity
In where most choose to stay
She chose, instead, to turn her limbs
.... Rejoice in every day
And as she turned her broken back
And saw the sun of God
She knew, that it would heal her
From life's backbreaking trod
Give her opportunity, to be something much more
Than others who had seen this light
And who had gone before
She made the turn, unto the light
And raised her limbs above
The pain of her adversity
Gave beauty and gave love

Chapter Twenty Four
On My Life's Truths

I believe truth is a relative condition. My truth may vary from yours but none the less both our truths can both be absolute. It is my hope that what you find in "My Life's Truths" are things you can identify with. And if I'm lucky, help you see how all truths have a certain connection. All my truths may feel completely wrong to you but for me and hopefully some others, they will be that rock we can stand on in the middle of thin air and relativity.

Frozen

Was the frigid night,
Or the eerie sight
What brought horripilation?
And a shiver to this damsel
In her quiet desperation?
Now the darkness
Which she felt was hers
Was now, not hers alone
And what lurked there
Where she once felt safe
Would chill her to the bone
Would freeze...her in fear
Freeze...her very soul

And paralyze her being
The nightmare of pure evil
Was what her mind was seeing

Oh darkness, you can't hurt me now
For soon I'll see the dawn
And with the light of morning
Your evil will be gone

Illusion Need

For time is an illusion,
An illusion that lets us be
For without that illusion
We find eternity

Ego

He was locked in his ego
And he couldn't escape
Its grip was cold and dirty
And his soul endured the rape
Oh, he had seen some others
Who had slipped the bully's grasp
With a stealthful move of selflessness
And gotten free at last

Outer/Inner Space

If we look at outer-space
We find it is quite small
For it lies in our here and now
In what matters and that's all
But if we look at inner-space
It's clearly plain to see
We're joined with all existence
In a grand eternity

Chapter Twenty Four

Good and Evil

Is there really evil? Or is it
Just goodness understood?
For without knowing evil
How can we know what's good?
So we must love our enemies
It is how we know our friends
It's how awareness happens
And where intolerance ends

So, it isn't good or evil
In our enemies we fight
It's their or our intolerance
That takes away our sight
And steals from us existence's
<u>Most</u>…important vision
That which is eternally
The need for this division

Good and evil out of balance
Where one is less and one is more
Begets deathful intolerance
That leads us into war
And war will rage
It will not end
'Til we find the balance
Once again

INTOLERANCE GOD

IS INTOLERANCE THEN NECESSARY FOR EXISTENCE?
A PART OF BEING, THAT SEEMS ODD....
SINCE INTOLERANCE OF INTOLERANCE
IS THE THING THAT WE CALL GOD

INTOLERANCE = LIFE

ON WHICH SIDE OF INTOLERANCE
DO YOU FIND YOU WANT TO STAY?
FOR INTOLERANCE IS LIFE, YOU SEE
THERE IS NO OTHER WAY

LIFE = FREEDOM + WILL = CHOICE = INTOLERANCE

EXISTENCE = INTOLERANCE BY NECESSITY

Lost Intolerance

Sometimes we speak of life
Sometimes we speak of death
And so we are redundant
With every spoken breath
Though some see them as opposite
Or ...Incompatible
They only see the half of it
The half that they find palpable
They need to see in opposites
To help them be existence

But they will find all is the same
When they lose their resistance
So as we lose what gives things sense
We'll find we've lost...INTOLERANCE

Chapter Twenty Four

MISSING GRAIL

Time and time and time again
And still again, one time
The misty vale that hides the grail
Gives silence to the mime
It locks the secret from our sight
And will not let us hear
It puts our world in shadow
Its cloak's a wrap of fear
And with it, it surrounds us
A terrible embrace
This force of endless evil
A sadness without face
It locks our self within it
There's only one escape
Give up the self to nothing
Or you'll endure the rape

Lost Trust

Time to weep
The trust is lost
Resentment brings
The killer frost

Another Broken Trust

And when the trust is broken
And there's nothing left but pain
The vase with life's most precious gift
Will never be again

FINAL DESTINY

GOING BACK, LIKE GOING FORTH
MAY SOMEDAY GET YOU THERE
BUT OFTEN IT'S A JOURNEY
THAT TAKES YOU, GOD KNOWS WHERE
AND THAT, <u>WHERE</u>,
IS USUALLY NOWHERE
YOU EVER THOUGHT YOU'D BE
IT'S THE NOWHERE, THAT IS SOMEWHERE
THAT'S YOUR FINAL DESTINY

Arrogance

Arrogance is a wondrous gift
But behind its givers veil
Is a teacher called humility?
With her gift, you're doomed to fail

THE COST

We'll always pay for arrogance
For it is never free
The price is high for arrogance
Our cost.... humility

And pride will cost
The same, you see
The price, again
Humility

ONLY IN-BETWEEN

There's no such thing as now and then
There's only in-between
Try to tell just when now is
You'll know just what I mean
There is no now, it's always past
And, then, is never here
For time is a continuum
The movement of a wave
A giant soapy bubble
That will take us to our grave

Nothing's There

And still, life happens
And so does shit
And often it can
Feel a bit
That nothing's really going right
But nothing is just out of sight
When our life ends
And we don't care
We see our sacred
Nothing's there

Pray for Energy

We are only something a short while
But what we are as we exist
In our humanity
Is what we have, to give back
When we reach eternity
And others can access it
Through what you could call prayer
Can draw upon that energy
That always is still there
It's part of <u>our</u> being
And that of other's too
It's part of all of those who passed
And makes up me and you
For we all are, and are to be
All things that we have known
Everything life's given us
With prayer, is never gone

Goodness

That goodness could be so abused
By evil's ugly hand
That goodness lets itself be used
For evil's ego land

That goodness lets it happen
And then accepts the blame
For evil's ugly treatment
And, then carries the shame

That goodness takes the evil
Then forgives the evil ways
Forgives the evil treatment
And what evil, evil says

That goodness doesn't harbor
What evil, evil's done
But in the end, all evil's lost
And goodness, it has won

GOD'S GIFT

GOD GAVE ME THIS LIFE
THIS CRISP FALL DAY
AND GOD EXPECTS
THAT I WILL PRAY
AND THANK IT
FOR THIS BEAUTY
AND EYES THAT LET ME SEE
MAY I KEEP IT IN MY HEART
FOR ALL ETERNITY

Chapter Twenty Four

THE WAY

It cannot be real unless we believe
'Til then, just what others may say
But once we believe, we accept…
We affirm that it is… the way
Then it is real
And to it, we become a slave
And so, we must be, to exist
'Til we all go to our grave
Without beliefs we are nothing at all
And the energy given goes into a stall
That force of existence
That takes us along
Depends on believing
Without it, we're gone

AIRPORT PEOPLE

Airport people walking by
So few, will look you in the eye
Perhaps afraid of what they'll see
Or maybe what they have to be
For when eyes meet…
So then do souls
And they must play
Life's touching roles
And give another, a part of them
And take another, inside again
Take a chance that this could fail
Could take their time, so keep the vale
And hide the eyes, until they pass
Now tragically, the gift each has
Has been lost again…this day
We've lost what we should give away

Reflection

Creation is reflection
As we look into the mirror
What we see is something
But nothing's really there
The mirror will always
Let us see
What seems to be
Reality
But if we view it
Deep inside
We find that on
The other side
There's nothing there
To see
The other side of the mirror
Reflects eternity

So nothing is the mirror
And we are its reflection
Life is the illusion
Death, our resurrection

Chapter Twenty Four

I must say the following poem does not truly represent my feeling for all priests. It was written about the priest who told me he wouldn't do Dana's memorial mass unless I went to confession. I was incensed. He cared and asked nothing about Dana or me or our boys and life. Instead, this little man wanted me to make sure I visited his website to see how many men had died in his arms while he was in the military and all the newspaper stories about him. It actually made me sick that he was a priest. Again, I would like to emphasize that I believe many, perhaps most priests are incredibly intelligent good people with a calling who do a great service to their congregation and their country.

Mass Without Me

Mass went on without me
God and I were there today
A priest of self importance
Who didn't have much to say

His theatrics are impressive
But he doesn't know your name
Or that of many others
Doesn't care, and that's a shame

Like the seasoned politician
Always looking for more votes
He shakes your hand and smiles
Bring him power, then he dotes

In his shameless egomania
He dances for his crowd
And sings of God and love
But often sings too loud

As we hear him pontificate
On how he'll save our soul

Journey to Life's Dance Ranch

> It's clear that ego's driving him
> And he must have control
>
> Priests with true vocation
> Really can be rare
> For ego usually takes them
> Where they prey on our despair
>
> See sorrow as a chance
> Where, in man's darkest hour
> These are their opportunities
> They must expand their power

GOD MAKES THEM REAL

FOR EVEN DREAMS NEED GOD
IN ORDER THEN TO BE
WHAT MOST OF US CONSIDER
A NON-REALITY

Bitter Shame

So afraid of dying
We never really live
So afraid of losing
We never really win
So afraid of living
We never play the game
Until we conquer fear
Life can be a bitter shame

Chapter Twenty Four
OWN REALITY

And when they speak of what they think
Or what they think they know
And need you to accept their views
When it's their turn to show
What they envision life to be
Must be the same as you and me
Or they can't take the fear
And be alone in what they are
They speak in question, looking for
Acceptance of their thoughts, and more
A place where they'll feel safe, to be
What they call their reality
But until they are able to let go
Not form their views, or those of others
Then demand they are their own
With thoughts of depth and clarity
Others have not known
Their needs have locked them in a place
They never will be free
Until they start to realize
Their own reality

TOMORROW FIND TODAY

I HEAD INTO TOMORROW
AS I BID TODAY GOODBYE
BUT I FIND MUCH TO MY SORROW
THAT I'VE WALKED INTO A LIE
THOUGH I THOUGHT I'D REACH TOMORROW
SOMETHING HAPPENED ON THE WAY
FOR JUST AS I ARRIVED THERE
I FOUND, IT WAS TODAY

Family

It's what gives purpose to our lives
It's what ties us together
But often we don't realize
Until life's stormy weather
When one is taken from us
Then we see with clarity
What is of most importance
Life's gift...our family

Dream's Reality

Is this existence real?
Or is it just a dream?
And does it really matter?
If things aren't what they seem
And if it is a dream
That is only in the mind
The mind must then exist
Or it's nothing that we find
So even dreams need this (God)
To exist, to let us see
What really isn't real
In this dream's reality

LIFE – A POSSIBILITY

AND THOUGH, LIFE CAN HAVE DIRECTION
AT TIMES IT IS JUST CHANCE
AND WE JUST CAN'T KNOW, WHAT WILL BE
IN THIS CRAZY COSMIC DANCE
EXISTENCE IS QUITE RANDOM
AND TRANSIENT, YOU SEE
FOR IT IS JUST THE VISION
OF A POSSIBILITY

Chapter Twenty Four

On the Way to Heaven

For when the wind bites you
You'll know you are alive
And what could be better
….until, you arrive
At that gate we must enter
Where life is no more
Where we will find nothing
On God's distant shore

Dignity

The death of dignity
Will always bring great sadness
For dignity shows what to be
As we travel through life's madness
Without it, life is so diminished
If we kill it…God won't forgive
When our life's time is finished

Babies Crying – True Reality

I hear the babies crying
Hear footsteps going by
But none of them will look at me
They will not show their eyes
They walk with icy purpose
Except within their clan
And most of them have closed themselves
...it's hard to understand
A glance is all they'll give you
Won't let you look inside
They have to get on past you
You must not break their stride
Or interrupt their cell
Which they hold up to their head
It's always in the airport
Where you can see the dead
And yet, I love the airport
For though they all will pass your side
The magic that resides in them
Is something they can't hide
It's only when we leave behind
What we've been taught to see
That life will let us witness
What is true reality

AN EPITAPH

WHEN HIS LIFE COMES TO AN END
HE HOPES THEY REMEMBER HIM
AS NOTHING SPECIAL...
EXCEPT FOR THE DEPTH OF GOODNESS
THEY FOUND IN THEMSELVES
WHEN THEY WERE WITH HIM

Chapter Twenty Four

COMFORT

AND AS WE FIND OUR INTEREST
AND ALLOCATE OUR TIME
DEFINE WHAT LIFE WE'LL TAKE WITH US
AND WHAT WE'LL LEAVE BEHIND
IF COMFORT IS OUR ONLY RULE
FOR THAT LIFE THAT WE CHOOSE
SOME OF THE VERY BEST OF LIFE
FOR COMFORT, WE WILL LOSE

AND NOTHING IS MORE COMFORTABLE
THAN FINDING NOTHING THERE
KNOWING NOTHINGS HAPPENING
KNOWING NOTHING CARES
FOR SOMETHINGS BRING DISCOMFORT
BUT THEY'RE WHAT LET US SEE
WHAT BRINGS US BACK TO NOTHING
AS WE LIVE OUR DESTINY
IF WE'RE ONLY WHERE WE'RE COMFORTABLE
THEN WE'LL ALWAYS BE JUST FINE
BUT COMFORT CAN BE RELATIVE
NEVER FOUND OUTSIDE THE MIND
IF WE STAY TOO CLOSE TO COMFORT
IT CAN KEEP US FROM THE DANCE
AS WE SIT ALONE WITH COMFORT
AFRAID TO TAKE THE CHANCE
THE CHANCE THAT SOME DISCOMFORT
MAY BRING US WHAT WE NEED
YET STILL, WE SIT WITH COMFORT
AND WATCH AS OUR HEARTS BLEED
AND SAY, THAT WITH OUR COMFORT
IS WHERE WE NEED TO BE
BE THAT THE LIE, WE LIVE WITH
IN OUR...COMFORT MISERY

Reality Foundations

Yes, he was prone to daydreams
And they woke him in the night
He found this life of fantasy
Was much to his delight
And he wrestled with his dreams
Wouldn't let them go, until he knew
They had become reality...
Once dream, was now what's true

All dreams can be reality
If only we believe
If not, they are just fantasy
On awakening, they leave

Often others want to wake us
And take us, from our dreams
Knowing that it's strange
If our dreams become reality
It's then, their lives will change
And change is always frightening
For those who don't know dreams
For dreams, are the foundation
Of reality... it seems

ETERNITY

I KNOW WHAT ETERNITY IS...

IT'S MORE THAN A DAY
IT'S LESS THAN A SECOND...

EXISTENCE WITHOUT TIME

The End

When once, one feels resentment
The relationship has ended
There cannot be contentment
What's now broken, can't be mended
Though this may be a tragedy
This love was never meant of be
More than a passing fantasy

Chapter Twenty Four
Ordinary

And so within the ordinary
The extraordinary lies
And often it's the ordinary
That hides it from our eyes
And keeps it from us
Lest we care
About the magic
Hiding there
Though ordinary
It's plain to see
If one looks deeper
There's majesty

TRUE BEAUTY

WHEN WE OBSESS UPON OUR BODIES
WE OFTEN FIND OURSELVES GRIEVING
THAT SOME STANDARD OF BEAUTY
IS NOT WHAT WE'RE ACHIEVING
BUT IF WE CHOOSE BEAUTY
AS DEFINED BY OTHERS
BY WHAT WE HAVE BEEN TAUGHT
BY OUR FATHERS AND OUR MOTHERS
WE INHERIT, THEN, THEIR BIAS
OUR EYES ARE RENDERED BLIND
WHAT WE CAN SEE AS BEAUTY
IS NOW FOR US DEFINED
SO, WHAT REALLY IS, TRUE BEAUTY
WE CANNOT SEEM TO FIND

Weed

So what then is a weed?
A vision of intolerance
A child that's not wanted
It's matter we don't need
Existence where there's prejudice
That doesn't want it there
Unwilling with this other life
Its time and space to share
Intolerance so total
Its soul cannot be freed
When placed among the tolerant
Then it becomes the weed
And yes, we are all predators
That's how all life exists
And life begins to end for us
If this, we do resist
For then we want for nothing
And life we do not need
We become the soil
While others are the seed
They'll prey upon the soil
And they'll become the weed
So life is just an exercise
Of predator or prey
Then all goes back to nothing
Existence goes away

Chapter Twenty Four

Freedom vs Bondage Snare

So do we find that freedom's best
Or prefer we then, the bondage nest
Though freedom lets our soul take flight
It also brings its share of fright
In bondage's nest, is safety there
And safety doesn't bring the scare
But bondage pays an awful price
For the safety it procures
A soul now in captivity
Is what it then endures
All existence is the bondage
Matter, that has made the choice
Has chosen time and space and being
And scoffed at freedoms voice
But freedom leads to nothing
It can take you there
Away from all existence
Escape…from bondage's snare

A Tanker Truck's Reflections

As we watch the road go forward
Going backward all the while
Like so many things we see in life
It's illusion that beguiles
And lets our mind imagine
As we look at what we see
Illusion often gives us
What can be reality
For life is a reflection
Of what's been and what can be
And that mirror will always show us
How to get, where we'll be free

Our Reality

And what then was this thing
Before it was a leaf?
From what did it arise?
This thing of our belief
Or any other object
We chose to be our dream
Give them their existence
And make them what they seem
Take them back to where they're from
And we lose them in the dust
All existence, there, will look the same
Where existence loses trust
That it can hold its form
In our dream for us to be
The leaf, the rose, the butterfly
…what's our reality

Gifts

The bars that do encage us all
In one way or another
The gifts of good and evil
From a father or a mother
Will keep us locked
Deep there within
'Til we escape their mortal sin

Life in the Shadows

Shadows move across the wall
As clouds move 'cross the sun
Painting life's reflection
A work that's never done
And we, make up that shadow
Of all we're let to see
And there, within the shadows
Lies our final memory

Chapter Twenty Four

Moth & Flame

And the flame is not evil
As it draws the moth in
But the magic it holds
Means neither can win
For the moth can't resist
As the flame works its magic
And its love for the flame
Will always be tragic
And with flame on its wing
It can snuff out the fire
With both now extinguished
Comes the end of desire
So, two things are lost
With this deadly dance
The light of a flame
The need for romance

Racing Time

One should never race with time
For time will always win
Time has got forever
We...'til God knows when

Journey to Life's Dance Ranch

Perfection

She said, there's no perfection
She claimed it couldn't exist
But, he knew she was mistaken
And he had to tell her this
For perfection is existence
From God's hand unto our eye
And not the unattainable
For which we only try
But what we are
And what we'll be
As part of this, eternity
And when we, <u>see</u>
Our place, within this great milieu
We see it's all perfection
Including...me and you

The Road

The road kept coming at us
It passed us in the wind
Not caring, we were headed
Where it had always been
And that it would not be there
When finally, we arrived
For it had gone the other way
And once more had survived
To turn around and pass again
Those needing this sensation
If the road, did not come toward us
There'd be no destination

So when the road does disappear
So too, that final place
Will become, unattainable
No longer, time or space

Reach Tomorrow?

For who would reach tomorrow
Let them speak of what it is
Let them give their definition
Let them tell us how to live

Chapter Twenty Four

LEARNING

HE COULD FEEL GREAT SORROW
FOR LIFE BROUGHT HIM GREAT JOY
HE WASN'T BORN, WITH EITHER
HE LEARNED THEM, AS A BOY
HE ALSO LEARNED THIS THING CALLED LOVE
WHICH HELPED HIM KNOW WHAT HATE WAS OF
AND AS THE WIND BLEW OVER HIM
AND HE FELT IT DIE AWAY.
HE KNEW THAT HE WOULD LEARN OF DEATH
WHEN LIFE LEFT HIM ONE DAY

MESSIAHS

This may be the messiah
That you've been looking for
But just like all messiahs
You never know for sure
For those who need messiahs
Often anyone will do
Passion's voice with timeless theme
A voice that's near to you
But, perhaps one should be cautious
When messiah <u>need,</u> is great
True messiahs are extremely rare
And one should hesitate
Lest one should fall into the trap
And give a soul away
Then find it's no messiah
That, you've been led astray

FORGIVENESS

FORGIVENESS FOR AN ACCIDENT, COMES EASY
FOR TRUST IS NOT INVOLVED
BUT IS FORGIVENESS POSSIBLE, FOR ACTS
WHERE TRUST HAS BEEN DISSOLVED?
INNOCENT MISTAKES ARE MADE BY ALL
AND THEY CAN BE EXCUSED
BUT PURPOSEFUL ACTS, WHICH BREAK A TRUST
WILL LIVE IN THOSE ABUSED

DISCOMFORT SHAME

THEY ARE TWO DIFFERENT CREATURES
AS MUCH AS NIGHT AND DAY
YET THEY CAN COME TOGETHER
IN SOME MOST UNUSUAL WAYS
THEIR NATURES WON'T LET THEM STAY
THEY MUST ALWAYS SEPARATE
OR, RESENTMENT WILL BEFALL THEM
AND THEIR ARDOR…DISSIPATE
TOO OFTEN A RELATIONSHIP
WILL BURN HOT, THEN EXTINGUISH
WHAT MADE THEM MOVE, INTO THIS FLAME?
ENJOY THE LIGHT, ENJOY THE GAME
BUT, NOW FIND SUCH DISCOMFORT…SHAME
FOR EVER GETTING STARTED
THAT THEY COULD LOVE SO DEEPLY
THEN END UP BROKEN HEARTED

Chapter Twenty Four

DEATH'S GARDEN

TO BE PLANTED IN DEATH'S GARDEN
AS A SEED THAT CANNOT GROW
WITH A HOPE TO SLEEP FOREVER
IN A PLACE THEY'LL ALWAYS KNOW
A PLACE OF PRAYERS AND TEARS AND FEARS
A PLACE FOR MEMORIES' GLOW
TO BE PLANTED IN DEATH'S GARDEN
WHEN I'M GONE...I CANNOT GO

Perception of Illusion

I know, I know, I don't know
What I think I know is real
Perception of illusion
May be only what I feel
For a time, until I'm faced
With a new illusion's dream
And, find that my reality...
May not be, what it seems
What was the old reality?
Must I, now let it go?
To know what's really real
When I know, I do not know
What I think I know is real
Perception of illusion
May be only what I feel

Tomorrow's Potential

Tomorrow is possibility
Today is always here
Tomorrow is potential
An illusion we can fear
We only have the present
But it can never last
For as soon as it is with us
It turns into the past
Time does not give the future
It gives what's now and then
Time does not hold the future
It can never give us, when
As our present spins into the past
Our future becomes clear
It is this past, after our start
But, it is never here
So it's there, we see our future
As we look upon our past
And see something, evolving
Into something that will last
Forever this existence
'Til potential runs its course
Our creation is completed
And we are with the force
(No longer has its force?)

Dot

A dot sits on the paper
Then it takes its energy
It moves across the paper
And a line, is what we see
Then the line moves here
And the line moves there
And soon a letter does appear
And has a sound
That we can hear

And it joins with other letters
Now to form into a word
And it too, has its energy
And it too, can be heard

And the words can come together
To express a wondrous thought
And to think that all this starts
From the power of a dot

For they too, spring from nothing
First a dot and then a line
Then a letter or a number
Gives meaning to our mind

Chapter Twenty Four

ILLUSION'S REALITY

THEY BROUGHT HIM THEIR ILLUSIONS
OF WHAT THEIR TRUTH MUST BE
AND WHAT THEY NEEDED OF HIM
FOR THEIR REALITY
BUT, HIS ILLUSION DIFFERED
FROM THAT WHICH MUST BE THEIRS
HE COULDN'T CHANGE, HIS REALITY
TO HELP ALLAY THEIR FEARS
THAT TRUTH, THE WAY THEY SAW IT
MAY NOT, BE...WHAT IT IS
AND THEIRS MAY BE NO BETTER
THAN WHAT HE CHOSE AS HIS

Coffee

Moments of clarity
Awareness magnified
Early morning sunlight
Coffee by my side
Vision brought by solitude
In dawn's albescent glow
Hold you for a moment
Imparts what you must know

 *Journey to Life's Dance Ranch*

ALCHERINGA

It is in alcheringa
Where death and dreams reside
As life moves into darkness
And toward the other side
Where nothing can be seen
As it becomes albescent
And oneness can be felt
In past's eternal present
When their illusion's challenged
They can get quite excited
And try then to convert
Whom they feel…is misguided

Thy Will

In a state of separation
Of expansion from the one
Is where there's good and evil
And for us thy will be done

Chapter Twenty Four

JACK

When I woke up this morning
And staggered to the mirror
The sight, it wasn't purdy
But at least, I think I'm here

My head is kinda reelin'
And my stomach, ain't quite right
I hate these mornin's after
Drinking hard into the night

Now I only drink at nighttime
When the pain is just too great
Got to see my friend, Jack Daniels
Help my spirits...elevate

Lost my darling to another
Spending too much time with Jack
Still can't live without my bottle
She ain't never coming back

I know he's got a hold on me
And I can't let him go
But, God, he helps me face the night
When I am feelin' low

Journey to Life's Dance Ranch

MICK

Mick wasn't like the others
He was our only one
His father was the plumber
His mother, she was gone

Though he was idiotic
He had his magic too
And he would oft amaze us
With all that Mickey knew

His father passed at 83
But Mick, lived on a while
Walked about in state of bliss
With idiotic smile

I always liked to talk with Mick
Though I knew he wasn't right
He showed a side of God to me
It was a happy sight

Deception?

He wouldn't abandon what he was
On a chance at what may be
On a chance that what they asked of him
Was what he'd like to see
For they asked him to their order
Their religion...to believe
But though it was their chosen truth
He sensed that it deceived

Chapter Twenty Four

Venetian Glass Pendant

The glass he gave as lavaliere
She wore with love and joy
It road on breast, with heart so near
But fate, it would destroy
For it was lost upon its chain
As it was meant to be
It wouldn't be with her again
Her loss had set it free

Fireside

Like the hearth, the fire pit
Is sacred in its mission
As embers, watch logs up above
And, recall a younger vision
Know, soon the logs, will age as well
As fire takes their youth
And joins them in this place below
On their way back to truth

Love Thy Enemies

I truly love my enemies
For they are part of me
Without them there is nothing
That we would need to be
They show me what is right and wrong
And help me then to see
Why we must have our enemies
Or lose identity

Flame to Trust

That one could own a fireplace
And want to share its fire
Yet never put a log there
And light her night's desire
To leave it cold and in the dark
To never see, that magic spark
That moves two hearts to be
At one with one another
Is simply…tragedy

…Yet if her heart is ready
With tinder, in her arms
And longing for a true love
Awaiting with her charms
Set to make the fire
She'd always hoped to share
Will once again, she lose?
Her true love, won't be there?
To spark the tinder into flame
Illuminate sweet passions game
And let her feel its lust
With the flame, she most desired
A true love, she can trust

Chapter Twenty Four

Easter

They all felt He had died for them
And perhaps they have it right
Yet still, I feel a loss for them
On this their Easter night
For their need, to grasp this heaven
With a Father God, and Son
With a Holy Spirit, Trinity
Which is the only one
An exclusive way to heaven
For those who will believe
And to hell with all the others
Their God, condemns to grieve
Perhaps there is another way
Beyond this narrow scope
That gives all those non-Christians
A reason...to find hope

The Prize

A boy who's given up a life
To chase after a prize
That thing, he'd always wanted
But finally realized
The prize, was superficial
And always out of reach
Just beyond his fingertips
Like sea upon the beach
Running in upon the sand
Then racing out, again
Something he couldn't have
A game, he could not win

 *Journey to Life's Dance Ranch*

Now

Now is really never here
Its illusion moves so fast
So the now that we experience
Is just the forward edge of past
Trying to explain what's ...now
We fail when we try
For as the words come from us
We speak of things gone by

Looking back I now can see
What I looked forward to
And looking on at things to come
The things that I might do
I find that only looking back
Will give me a clear view
To let me see what's forward
To let me see what's new

Aging

As the aged, drank the water
That brought their Lethe on
Some were pleased, while others not
To have the memories, gone
A blessing or a curse it was
Depending on the life
For some, an amputation
With age's cruelest knife
But, for those with painful memories
Which no longer they would see
As their blindness, now in many ways
Would finally.... set them free

Chapter Twenty Four

FUTURE PASSING BY

SOMEWHERE BETWEEN THE HERE AND THERE
OUR PAST AND FUTURE LIVE
AND NOW MOVES THROUGH THEIR PRESENCE
ITS MOVEMENTS, WHAT IT GIVES
FOR NOW, IS ALWAYS CHURNING
'TWEEN THE FUTURE AND THE PAST
OUR PAST, STAYS ALWAYS WITH US
OUR NOW, CAN NEVER LAST
IT'S SIMPLY AN ILLUSION
LIFE'S VIEW UPON OUR EYE
A FLEETING THING THAT TIME CREATES
WHEN FUTURE PASSES BY

TIMELESS

SOMETIME OUR TIME WILL LEAVE US
THEN TIMELESS, WE WILL BE
FOR WHAT TIME CAN'T TAKE WITH IT
ARE, OUR TIMELESS, MEMORIES
AND SO, THEY'LL SAY THERE WAS A TIME
WHEN TIME PAINTED THEIR STORY
A TIME OF LOVE, OF TIME OF JOY
THEY REVELED IN GOD'S GLORY

THEN WHAT THEIR REVELINGS REVEAL
TO THOSE STILL HELD BY TIME
IS TIME IS WHAT WE MAKE IT
AND, THEY MADE THEIRS SUBLIME

RACIST

YOU KNOW I AM A RACIST
FOR I WAS BORN THAT WAY
I'M PROUD THAT I'M A RACIST
AND A RACIST, I WILL STAY
IT IS A SPECIAL PART OF ME
IT IS MY DRIVING FORCE
WHAT IS THIS SPECIAL RACE, YOU ASK?
THE HUMAN RACE...OF COURSE

Sunday Service

They saw a head as they looked behind
What was ahead of them
And what they thought they knew
Just beyond their pew
Brought peace from bedlam
But most couldn't wait
To escape this fate
Of stand and sit and kneel
The day lay there before them
Outside…with more appeal

The Key

For life can lock us out, it seems
At times, it keeps us from our dreams
Won't take us where we want to be
The door is locked…we have no key
And no one's home to let us in
We now must wait…'til God knows when
With hope for one, with key that gleams
Unlock the door…restore our dreams

Two Sides

Then each must play
Against the other
'Til both of them
Are done
Then, two sides of existence
Will join, where there is none

Chapter Twenty Four

MYTHS GONE BY

SO THEN HE DREW, ON WHAT HE KNEW
TO SKETCH A VISION OF HIS BEING
AND WHEN HIS SKETCHING TIME WAS THROUGH
HIS PAST HE WOULD BE SEEING
BUT WHEN THE SKETCHER, THEN DEPARTS
AND ALL OF THOSE, WHO VIEWED HIS ART
TAKE LEAVE OF TIME, AS WELL
WHERE WILL THE ARTWORK TAKE ITS PLACE
AS MEMORIES FADE, WILL TIME ERASE
A PAST THAT ONCE WAS THERE
ALIVE 'TIL LOST WERE MEMORIES
OF THOSE WHO USED TO CARE

History Mystery

Every day's a new day
Inextricably connected
To the through day
As time builds past
For you and me
From futures
Now
a mystery

DEBUNK

WHO WOULD HAVE THUNK
HE COULD DEBUNK
ALL MYTHS OF TIME GONE BY
BUT MYTHS ARE
ONLY HALF THE TRUTH
THE REST IS JUST A LIE

... WE TOLERATE THE LIE

Mind's Creation

What keeps these things
As things we see?
As things we touch
As things we be?
What holds this matter,
In its place?
What gives it form
Within its space?
Does it exist
Outside my mind?
Are all our minds
Then, intertwined?
Or are you just
My mind's creation
Not a separate, entity?
But, simply something I create
... To be a part of me?

Instinct

Though it is not known exactly
What this instinct, then may be
Be it gives us an advantage
As we move toward history

Chapter Twenty Four

PENCIL

The lead, that lead the lead
Along the pencil course
Gave hand, the mind's command
To mind mind's driving force

And when the mind would quit
The pencil, it would still
Without a mind, to mind
The pencil lost its will

'Til mind again would lead the hand
To move the pencil taper
And lead to thoughts of mind
Across the piece of paper

Prophets Say

How could this God, then be so small?
While touted, as the one and all
Must we believe what prophets tell?
Is there a heaven or a hell?
Or a reward, for our devotions?
And punishment, for other notions?
A God, who must have adoration
From what we are, and our creation
And hell awaits? If we should fall?
How could this God, be, then so small?
For is there anything but God
From which, all creations flow?
And would this God, condemn itself?
Some prophets...tell us so

Peaceful Aggression

For existence to be peaceful
It must possess aggression
And use it when aggressed upon
Or lose its peace possession
Be wary of those pacifists
Who'd let aggressors in
And try to sell aggression
As existence's mortal sin
They will not fight
For what you have
Don't trust the things they say
They'll side with your aggressor
And give your peace away

Those

Yes, they could be benighted
By **Those** who'd take them there
And they would want this righted
What **Those** said…was not fair
And **Those** would promise justice
But for this, they'd have to pay
They must become addicted
To what, **Those**, have to say
Then vest in **Those** the power
To steal what is not theirs
So in the name of fairness
They all could have their shares
But when there is no more to steal
And **Those** say all is right
The addicts won't find fairness
But **Those**, will have the might

Chapter Twenty Four

Outliving Friends

The old would often contemplate
Why death didn't come anon
And why they couldn't go with their friends
Why life, kept hanging on
Was this their choice to suffer pain
While locked in body's cage
Enduring, those indignities
Be-gifted them by age
Why wouldn't life, unlock their cell
And open up, dreams door
Their spirit longed for death's embrace
And longed, for <u>nothing</u>, more

Real Illusion

Some days, life's mirror is crystal clear
And seems then to make sense
We're sure we know what's real or not
Can tell…the difference
But then the mirror, at times, can fog
And leave us with confusion
Not knowing if what's real is real
Or just a, real illusion

 *Journey to Life's Dance Ranch*

Christ's Tee Time

They all agreed that he should bleed
Upon the wooden tee
And though he had not harmed them
They needed…misery
For one who challenged how they played
Who drove a different view
For he, who claimed, to be the one
They knew what they must do
Their T time was mid afternoon
Game stopped, with dying son
They played this course quite perfectly
And got, their hole, in one

Ocean Sky

Being part of every other
Or one piece of the all
Can make one feel enormous
Or make one feel quite small
When standing by the ocean
Or gazing at the sky
What really is the miracle
They're part of you and I

Key Finding

Decomposition is the key
To finding…immortality

Chapter Twenty Four

RELIGION MYTH

OF MYTH IT'S BORN AND WHERE IT GROWS
THROUGHOUT ITS EARLY YOUTH
AND WHERE IT GAINS ITS POWER
AND WHAT DEFINES ITS TRUTH
BUT NONE, CAN LAST FOREVER
AS NEW MYTH, BRINGS NEW VISION
AND OLD MYTH SIMPLY PERISHES
ALONG WITH THAT RELIGION

PAST

I will live with you to make our past
For that is what we get
Now is just an interface to
What's not happened, yet
Past and future, inter-link by
What is in-between
Now converts the future into
Past that can be seen

Cycle

With time, we fly upon death's journey
Back to where all life begins
A process that is dying
And, this cycle never ends

Eternal Grace

For I've been given sorrow
And I've been given joy
I learned what they were made of
When I was just a boy
And I thought about them often
Even cried, a time or two
Yes, they could make me do this
As they gave the things they knew
Oh, the lessens that they taught me
In those times they showed their face
Were the moments of my greatest gifts
Of God's…eternal grace

Constipation

They said that he couldn't give a shit
But that's misinformation
They simply didn't understand
His state of constipation

Prey for Us

You may call it aggression
Or you may call it prayer
But, preying's all around us
You'll always find it here
Inside as well as outside
It's what makes up existence
And it's what gives us life
'Til we lose our resistance
We always pray that we
Will not be preyed upon
But prey is what…all life is of
That takes us… 'til we're gone

Know it All

The more we know
We don't know
The more we know
We know
And if we find
We know it all
We lose
Our way to grow

Chapter Twenty Four

Life Mattering

I know what I'm saying
And I'm saying, I don't know
That no matter, what you're saying
There's still so far to go
To find the truth...reality
If there is such a thing
To find what's really real
To find life...mattering
(and not imagining)

FREE WILL

FREE WILL, WITH MY SIMPLE-MINDED THEORIES
IT DOES MAKE SENSE TO ME
FOR NOTHING GIVES US WILL
AND NOTHING SETS US FREE
SO WE HAVE
BOTH
FREEDOM
AND
WE HAVE
THE WILL TO BE

FREE WILL II

YES, WE HAVE FREE WILL TO BE
WHAT WE CAN BE
OR PERHAPS
MUST BE

Journey to Life's Dance Ranch

FREE WILL III

AND THIS FREE WILL THAT LETS US BE
DRIVEN BY... GOD'S ENERGY
THE HOLY SPIRIT, IF YOU WILL
AND THAT'S...HOW I
PERCEIVE...FREE WILL

NOW?

AND NOW NEVER CHANGES
THAT'S PERFECTLY CLEAR
IT'S NOT EVEN A MOMENT
IT'S ALWAYS RIGHT HERE
ON THE PATH FROM YESTERDAY
AS WE GO TOWARD TOMORROW
WE TOUCH MANY NOWS
BUT MUCH TO OUR SORROW
WE OFTEN FIND
WHEN LOOKING FORWARD AND BACK
WE LOSE WHAT IS NOW
NOW'S WHAT WE LACK

Age

As I sat with age
And watched the stage
Of vacancy now there
And listened to the struggle
To bring memories
Back to where
They once had lived so easily
And came when called upon
Now mind is lost
And memories too
And soon all will be gone

Chapter Twenty Four

Ego Understood

The ego can be evil if it's
Not well understood
By the creature of the ego
But it also can be good
It can take us far from nothing
And hold us captive there
Unable to receive true love
Or give our love or share
Though just a touch of ego
Will spice our recipe
And help us live outside the cage
Will give us ecstasy
But too much can addict us
To ego's evil side
Can isolate us in our cage
And lock the rest outside
And ego's grip is hard to break
Once it has you in its grasp
It blinds your eyes to nothing
Makes it hard to see
That you're a part of nothing
Part of all eternity
It locks you in that selfishness
That doesn't let you care
And join with other consciousness
To find the nothing we all share
(to find the nothing there)

The Flow

He took a trip to no place
Where dreams and souls reside
Where spirits are not shackled
By rules that are outside
Where nothing really matters
And matter can't exist
Existence is of outer space
Where everything resists
The pull of non-distinction
'Til time and space let go
And all goes back to nothing
To God's eternal flow

Death's Face

Death showed its face to me today
As it took another life away
It let me watch, too close, its work
When from the dark, where death does lurk
It came with instant fury
It seemed in such a hurry
But oddly
What I saw
Was going in slow motion
Then a body stopping instantly
On the road the body lay
Lifeless matter now
A soul not far away
I felt him watch there with me
From just across the street
But, he couldn't linger very long
He must, his maker …meet

Chapter Twenty Four

Our Father Who Art in Heaven

A father's gone tonight
I saw him take his leave
And now the sadness grips them
As they begin to grieve
In an instant, it was over
An instant, God let me see
The instant in slow motion
That was eternity
'Til finally it was over
And life came all around it
But death had come
And taken him
A body on the ground, its soul
Would soon depart
To take its final residence
Embedded in their hearts

WILL TO BE

SO WHAT THEN IS REALITY?
IF THERE IS SUCH A THING
IS ALL JUST AN ILLUSION?
THAT WE'RE IMAGINING?
AND CAN WE CHANGE THIS
IF WE WILL?
FOR IF OUR WILL IS FREE
THEN WE ALL HAVE THE WILL
TO WILL WHAT WE WILL BE

Chapter Twenty Five
On Inspiration

MY INSPIRATION TREE

Over the years I have had many things I have seen in nature that inspired me to want to be better, stronger and more thankful. Perhaps one of the most inspirational was this tree that lived just west of our house in Jacksonville, Florida. It was a most amazing creature. From being broken in its youth, it lifted itself up, and grew into a beautiful heart-shaped tree. But its real magic came from the fact that you could touch the smallest furthest branch from the trunk and with hardy any force the entire tree would dance. Whenever we had friends visit, I would take them to feel the tree. The adults were amazed. The children squealed with delight as they moved this wonderful creature with just the slightest touch of their little finger. We are all given challenges in life and often they are opportunities to develop strength and beauty we can share with others.

Journey to Life's Dance Ranch

A number of people have read some of my poems and asked me if I would give them a copy because they found them inspirational. I was flattered. Perhaps you may find one or more of the following poems to be a source of inspiration for you or someone you know. It is a joyful thought that some of my poems, no matter the section in which you may find them, may inspire, help you in some way, make you think, make you laugh and possibly even help you cry. It is goodness and love above all that I hope you find in my writings.

What Will Come Out

I'm not sure what I'll write about
I'm not just sure what will come out
It's this and that, that comes to me
From where it comes, a mystery
Is it within, in some deep place?
Or does it flow from outer space?
Perhaps it's both, that's it, you see
It's ...coming from eternity

RUN YOUR RACE

Run after your passion
It's the only race you'll win
To run in any other race
Will be a mortal sin
So step away from others
Those that want to hold you back
Pursue your dream with passion
And get your soul on track
Life should always make you smirk
And never, never make you work
At something that you do not love
That your passion cannot be
Or you'll be locked in hell
For an eternity

Chapter Twenty Five

Have Fun

I did something fun today
But then,
I do something fun every day
...I live!

Blend

A part of life most interesting
When it appears to end...
To those who watch it closely
A lover or a friend, Or
A mother or a father
Sister, brother...knows what's true
Life never really leaves
When the body's time is through
And when a loved one passes
They do not leave or end
For life is a continuum
Where energies all blend

MIRACLES REJOICE

GOD'S GIVEN US THIS ENERGY
WE MUST NOT WASTE THE CHANCE
WE MUST REJOICE IN MIRACLES
WE SEE AT EVERY GLANCE

Roses

Hey! You can give your shit to me
I'll turn it into roses
For those who can't stand shit in life
For those who turn up noses
They miss the point
The wise man knows
It takes some shit
To grow a rose!

Journey to Life's Dance Ranch

Run

He had to run
He had no choice
He was driven
By an inner voice
It sang to him
It begged of him
To move within
Life's lovely din
To hear the songs
That nature sings
To see the magic
In all things
To feel the sweat
Upon his brow
To love this moment
To live for now
To feel his heart
Race deep within
To push the limits
Of his being
To dream of the Iditarod
To be alone…to run with God

Gas Pedal

Now I'm going down life's highway
Driving faster than before
Know I'll probably get a ticket
But the ride I get, means more
Life won't give you many chances
Or at least that's how it seems
Got to step on life's gas pedal
If you're going to reach your dreams

Don't Delay

Life rarely gives us second chances
So we must do our lovely dances
When 'ere our music's played
And when we hear that rhythmic sound
That always turns our heart around
…this dance shouldn't be delayed

Chapter Twenty Five

Life's Heroes

Life lets us all be heroes
If we want to take the chance
But we can't sit on the sidelines
We must get out and dance
And though we may feel stupid
On the floor, when we first start
Those staying on the sidelines
Always wish they had the heart
If our endeavors fail
At least we'll say we tried
And find the peace in knowing
That we lived...before we died

Mystery Lost

If we are going to be in life
What we are meant to be
Expression of potential, of possibility
Then what we'll be, we cannot know
It's something we can't see
Or we'll get locked in ego
And lose the mystery

Never Accept

I'll never accept defeat from life
And even if I fail
I'll always choose to ride the horse
Against the inside rail
And as I round the corner
And head into the straight
And charge to make the finish
One....they'll appreciate
What's more important than my place
As I complete life's ride
Is that I gave my all...
I chose to race...
I tried!

NEED 4 GOOD & EVIL

Some things you can't get over
Some things won't go away
And yet, we must be grateful
That they're with us to stay
For whether they're from goodness
Or a wound from evil's knife
They serve, still to remind us
That we've been given life
And, life, it matters greatly
And, nothing, matters more
For life's that part of nothing
We've never had before

A PRAYER

Can this intensity continue?
Can it still maintain its course?
Can it keep its true direction?
And still maintain its force?
Are there winds that would divert it?
Move it in a different way?
Blow it far from what's intended?
Or, can on its course, it stay?
Will the strength of goodness win?
When evil shows its face
God let our goodness, still prevail
At the finish of this race

Chapter Twenty Five

HIS MOTORCYCLE

HE GRABBED A PIECE OF FREEDOM
AND PUT IT IN HIS LIFE
IGNORING ALL CONCERNS
FROM HIS FAMILY AND HIS WIFE
HE RODE ON FREEDOM'S WHEELS
ON A ROAD THAT WENT NOWHERE
THAT HE KNEW NOT, WHERE IT'D TAKE HIM
HE DIDN'T REALLY... CARE
JUST THE JOURNEY INTO NOWHERE
WHERE, HE MAY NOT GO AGAIN
ON FREEDOM'S RIDE THROUGH HEAVEN
WAS WAY ENOUGH ...FOR HIM

Our Opportunity

Our souls must dive into the stream
Must never miss the chance to dream
And let our dreams, then, real be
For if fear, makes us pass, 'til when
We will commit life's greatest sin
And lose the opportunity
And isn't that what life is of
The chance to hate, the chance to love
It's always there for us, you see
Life is....our opportunity

Chapter Twenty Six
On Nothing

I know I could say that my poems have "Nothing to Say," but of course, if you have come this far you know my "Nothing Theory" actually has three parts which for me tie together the philosophies and religions of the Orient (East) and the Occident (West). This section talks about the three tenants of my beliefs, "Nothing, Something, and In-between." To understand these writings, you may have to put yourself in a different mindset or perhaps my poems will take you there and you will like what you find.

A Place Called Nowhere

There is a place called nowhere
And its here and there you'll find
That it's never really somewhere
Where you'll find some peace of mind

For nowhere goes much deeper
It's somewhere down inside
It's part of the great nothing, where
What we call God resides

And when we take our something
Back to nothing where it came

 *Journey to Life's Dance Ranch*

We'll find we are with God
We'll be at peace again

To say nothing comes from nothing
Well, that isn't really true
We're part of that great nothing
We're something ... me and you

For our nothing is an energy
From which we somethings are
When death takes us back to nothing
We'll find that everything is there
For like life and death and being
It's this nothing that we share

For all things spring from nothing
And though this may seem odd
This loving goodness energy
Is the nothing we call God

So when we take our something selves
Back to nothing where we came
We'll find we are with God
And be at peace again

Chapter Twenty Six

THE EMBRACE – A PRAYER

AS I WAS WATCHING LIGHT AND DARK
GET LOCKED IN AN EMBRACE
I SUDDENLY SAW NOTHING
COMING IN TO TAKE THEIR PLACE
BUT NOTHING LET THEM GO
AND THEY APPEARED AGAIN
SO THAT'S HOW ALL CREATION WORKS
AND HOW CREATION ENDS
IN A PULSE THAT IS A CIRCLE
OR A BUBBLE OR A RING, OR
A MULTITUDE OF OTHER FORMS
THAT MAKE A THING, A THING
A PULSE OF LIVING ENERGY
THAT JUST LETS ALL THINGS BE
THE PULSE OF GOD, WE'RE ALL A PART
OF THIS SWEET ENERGY
AND IF LIFE'S A PULSE
WE NEED A HEART
TO KEEP THE ENERGY
SO WE'RE THE WAVE THAT RIPPLES OUT
UNTIL IT'S RUN ITS COURSE
BUT NOTHING IS THE ENERGY
WHERE ALL THINGS GET THEIR FORCE
THEIR FORCE TO LIVE, THEIR FORCE TO BE
THE FORCE OF THEIR EXISTENCE
THE FORCE TO LOVE THE FORCE TO HATE
THE SOURCE OF THEIR RESISTANCE

AND ALL THINGS USE THIS FORCE
USE IT UP, AND THEN, OF COURSE
IT'S BACK TO NOTHING FOR SOME MORE
THE LOVING ENERGY, THAT CAN RESTORE
OR CREATE ANEW, ANOTHER ME, ANOTHER YOU
OH, NOTHING OF MY ENERGY
WHEN MY TIME DOES DRAW NEAR
LET ME COME TO YOU WITH OPEN ARMS
LET ME SEE YOU WITHOUT FEAR
AND STAY WITH YOU
UNTIL YOU SEND ME BACK AGAIN
WITH LOVING ENERGY
SEND ME BACK TO SOMETHING
TO BE WHAT I MUST BE
OH, NOTHING OF MY ENERGY
LET <u>THIS</u> BE MY PRAYER
GIVE ME STRENGTH
AS I COME BACK
TO KNOW I'LL FIND YOU THERE

ICE AND WATER

Perhaps like Ice and water
Where water is the nothing
And Ice is something that will be
It all depends on that in-between
That holy ghost, that sweet energy
That carries water into ice
And takes it back again
But it's all still one, inseparable
A process that takes three

Chapter Twenty Six

STALAG 13

I THINK OF SCHULTZ, SERGEANT SCHULTZ
ON HOGAN'S HEROES, AT STALAG 13
HE WAS THE SMARTEST MAN ALIVE
FOR HE KNEW NOTHING! NOTHING!
AND THAT HELPED HIM TO SURVIVE
BECAUSE HE KNEW THAT KNOWING NOTHING
WAS WHAT HE NEEDED MOST
YOU NEVER HEARD HIM SAY
"I KNOW THE HOLY GHOST"
BUT THAT'S WHAT HE WAS SAYING
IT WAS GOD THAT HE SPOKE OF
WHEN HE SPOKE TO US OF NOTHING
HE WAS SHOWING US HIS LOVE
AND HIS CHARACTER WAS NOT HATEFUL
IN FACT, HE DID MUCH GOOD
HE WAS IN TOUCH WITH NOTHING
AND IN KNOWING NOTHING… UNDERSTOOD
WHEN YOU'RE IN A PLACE OF MISERY
OR GREAT AGONY OR SORROW
KNOWING NOTHING OFTEN HELPS ONE
JUST MAKE IT 'TIL TOMORROW
AND THAT'S WHERE SCHULTZ CAME IN
HE WAS LOVEABLE, YOU SEE
HE WAS LOVEABLE FOR ME
HE WAS LOVEABLE, NOT MEAN
AND NOTHING HELPED MAKE A BETTER PLACE
OF STALAG 13

Journey to Life's Dance Ranch

Two Trinities

So if you must see Father, Son and Holy Ghost
To understand the mystery
Well that's OK
But not for me
Instead I have to see
Nothing, Something and In-between
That other energy
They're all the same
No matter how you see it
Whether looking through Christianity
Or perhaps an Eastern mystic
Or looking as some do
When they go to Quantum Physics
As they look at, look for energy
And they look, too, then at matter
And see they are all just the same thing
They are all part of one
With something in between

TAKE ME BACK

Take me back to nothing
Where all things are just one
For at times, this being something
Just isn't any fun
But when we're back with nothing
Where existence isn't there
Experience of everything
Is pure and without care
It's peace we find in nothing
It is where all things blend
It's where we find, the rest of us
We'll find joy there in the end

Chapter Twenty Six

Existence Spin

If we spin existence fast enough
Then it's something we can't see
If we spin existence fast enough
We can change reality
Is then, Life, a form of spinning?
That is, spinning we can see
And when the spinning speeds or slows
Or changes energy
Does our level of existence change?
Does it change what we can be?
And what controls the spinning
That puts us in this place and
Lets us see existence
In the realm of time and space
And when spinning stops or changes direction
Is it then we are our true reflection?
Is it then we are the in-between?
The bottom of the yo-yo string?
Or, yes, the top
For they're places where existence stops
And changes spin
To start new existence once again
And when this yo-yo energy
Has finally run its course
The game is over and up and down
No longer has a force
Then we are back to nothing
Where all games originate
But pulse or spin can't stay there
They can only hesitate
Through in-between they get there
Back to nothing whence they came

Journey to Life's Dance Ranch

And wait another chance to
Play in nothings cosmic game
On the other side of nothing
When you've passed through in-between
You find that there's existence
You're something, can be seen
And what is non-existence
Isn't nothing, but something too
It's the other side of being
It's the other side of you
And though we are existence
We know the opposite is too
Both a part of nothing
Both completely true
So, existence is resistance
But the energy comes from nothing
And there it must return
And while we are resistance
It's there we always learn
We are a part of nothing
Our parent energy
Our umbilical, the in-between
And separate we can't be

FIND IT

Is there anything that's left?
When we've left it all behind?
Yes, we see there is much more
When it's nothing that we find

Chapter Twenty Six

Nothing to Write

I have nothing to write about
And so I do
Ain't it funny
How it interests you
When I bring nothing
To your mind
It's then eternity
That you find
It seems so simple
How we know
It's how we come
It's where we go

Alone

It's only by something
That nothing is known
We must know together
To know what's alone
And when alone happens
It's because there was more
Gone back now to nothing
Where it was once before

Big Circle

The further we go toward somewhere else
The closer we will be
To finding that great nowhere
That we call eternity
For it's all a great big circle
And when we come around
The light will shine, and we will know
That this is God we've found

CLEAR MEANING

When nothing sends you something
By way of in-between
At times it can be difficult
To know just what it means
But when time disappears
And we lose what's now and here
The things that nothing sent us
Their meaning becomes clear

MIND FULL OF NOTHING

My mind is full of nothing
And nothing is good,
But nothing is often
Misunderstood
For a mind full of somethings
Finds it hard to envision
Existence without
Some kind of division
And with that division
Nothing's so hard to see
Division makes things
That obscure destiny
But when things are over
Isn't that where we'll be
Back with our nothing
Our clear destiny

Chapter Twenty Six

NOTHING TO SAY

I HAVE NOTHING TO SAY TO YOU
BUT THAT'S WHERE YOU'LL HEAR
EVERYTHING YOU NEED TO KNOW

Back to Potential

Where what is, vanishes
Into what can be
The potential of eternity

In-between, Our Friend

On our way to who knows where
It's in-between that gets us there
So as we move from now and then
It's in-between that is our friend
Without it we are here and there
But, we're not going anywhere
Something happens when it's around
But when it's gone
Just nothing's found

Journey to Life's Dance Ranch

Ride to Nothing

If where we come from
Is where we go
It's what we think
We do not know
But as we take
Our every breath
We know our life
Has come from death
And back with death
Is where we'll be
When life gives up
And sets us free
And death is not
An evil thing, or
Something we should fear
It's just our ride to nothing
Where everything is clear

Something Missing?

*Often, something is missing
in our lives
But, nothing is always
there for us*

Chapter Twenty Six

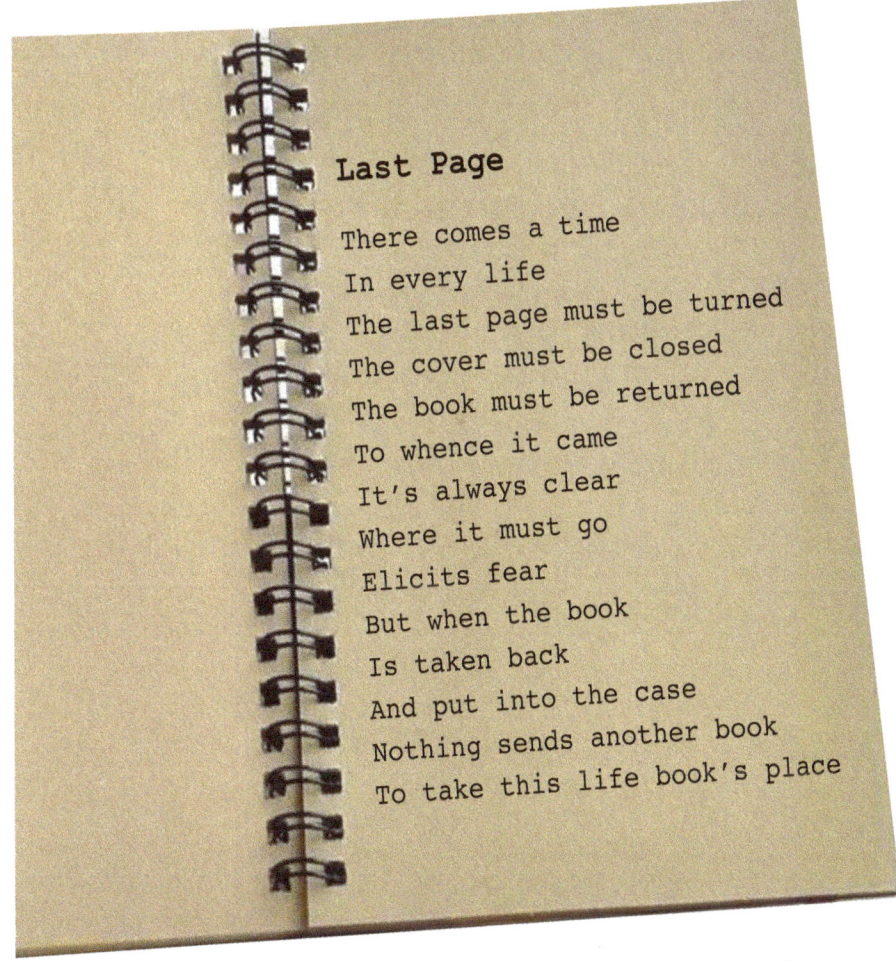

Last Page

There comes a time
In every life
The last page must be turned
The cover must be closed
The book must be returned
To whence it came
It's always clear
Where it must go
Elicits fear
But when the book
Is taken back
And put into the case
Nothing sends another book
To take this life book's place

Time Life

When we give up time
And go the other way
What we define as life
…Simply cannot stay

Time Gone

Time locked in space
Where life can survive
Take time away
You're… not alive

LIFE CONDITION

For life is a condition
Matter bound in space
Expression of an energy
That doesn't have a face
And though we cannot see it
It's that which makes us whole
An energy from nothing
That constitutes our soul
For life we need a soul

So Odd

You always find it's nowhere
Even though it seems so odd
The somewheres that are nowhere
Are the place where we find God

Shit Happens

And still, life happens
And so does shit
And often it can
Feel a bit
That nothing's really going right
But nothing is just out of sight
When our life ends
And we don't care
We see our sacred
Nothing's there

Chapter Twenty Six

NOTHING ON THE RIVER BANK

Sometimes the river rages
And catches us off-guard
The current becomes deadly strong
Our struggle is so hard

Life's river holds us in its grip
And pulls us here and there
And sometimes pulls us under
We struggle for some air

But if we're lucky, someone's there
Upon the river bank
To reach into the water
A friend that we can thank

Who pulls us from our peril
Brings us out upon the shore
Let's us know we'll be ok
And helps us live once more

Lets us see that what we feared
Couldn't hurt us after all
And nothing really happens
When we need it most of all

So nothing's on the riverbank
And in the river too
When the river rages
Nothing can take care of you

 *Journey to Life's Dance Ranch*

Nothing Lives

Nothing lives forever
While somethings never do
Nothing is the stuff of life
That makes up me and you

※

Artist Canvas

Nothing is the canvas
But it's the artist too
Its painting is existence
It's life, it's me and you
And all existence with us
And even empty space
Without it, we are nothing
In nothing's special place

EXPECT NOTHING

AND THOSE WHO EXPECT NOTHING
WILL GET NOTHING AS THEY LIVE
AND WHAT THEY GET FROM NOTHING
IS WHAT THEY HAVE TO GIVE

Something Value

To those who just need something
And do not seem to know
When all we need is something
Nothing has to go
And somethings can't go with us
As we reach our destiny
Somethings are existence
They're not eternity
When nothing's really needed
Nothing takes you there

Chapter Twenty Six

WILL

NOTHING never standing still
WILL always bring new life
And life WILL always be of WILL
Until death comes to call
For WILL, WILL go, with DEATH
And DEATH WILL take it all
Then give it back to NOTHING
That WILL not hold WILL long
NOTHING now with WILL in hand
WILL, WILL creation's song
And so it's WILL
That ebbs and flows
And that's why life
It comes, it goes

Death the In-between?

*Is death then just the in-between
That links the nothing to the being
A passageway from here to there
The common destiny we share?*

Never Been

Time will get us moving
Looking once again
Searching out a nowhere
Where nothing's never been
We'll probably find that nothing
Is really always there
Waiting at our nowhere
Our source of love and care

THIN AIR

There were no illusions
Nothing was there
Illusion evaporated
Into thin air, then
All air was gone
And nothing took its place

Nothing Never Happens

We don't stand for nothing
Cause nothing won't stand still
Nothing never happens
And somethings always will
Nothing is a changin'
Something's going to be
Nothing's got to happen
To set existence free
Nothing says goodbye to time
Sends time on its way
Time collides with matter
And something's here today

Don't Fear

Why does death
Scare the living?
Nothing's there
For us to fear
And nothing's never
Going to hurt us
As death brings
Our nothing near

I Wonder

Wonder where I'll
Find my heaven
Wonder why I
Wonder why
Hope existence is
For real
Hope that life ain't
Just a lie

Chapter Twenty Six

Road Trip With Andrew

Blue lights in the rearview
Nothing should be there
Something's going to happen
Shouldn't had that beer

Got a little ticket
Took life past the limit
Living on the bright side
Nothing that can dim it

Could go on with this a while
But time won't take me there
Time to be with nothing
Time to clear the air

On my way to nowhere
Nothing's on my mind
Don't know when I'll get there
Not sure what I'll find

Maybe it is somewhere
I really need to be
Something's going to happen
Call it ...destiny

When we reach that nowhere
Then we will be free
Nothing really like it
Pure tranquility

Journey to Life's Dance Ranch

You'll be Nothing

Nothing ever happens
Nothing always will
Nothing lasts forever
Nothing ever will
Nothing always comes to you
Nothing will be there for you
Nothing really cares for you
And you'll be nothing too

When Death Pays

Life owes me nothing
For it's everything I've found
And I know that life will, pay up
When it sends death around

About Nothing

Nothing happens all the time
While something has its moment
Nothing doesn't take up space
Something has to own it
Nothing doesn't take up time
Something cannot be without it
Nothing gives us all life's rhyme
Something's got to shout it
And when we go from something
To be nothing for a while
Then re-emerge as something
Back from nothing's short exile
We are taken by the in-between
As we go from side to side
And death will be our ticket
On this roller coaster ride

What is Now?

What is now?
Tell me when you're there
I'd like to take a look at now
But for me it's everywhere
And nowhere that I find
Now can never be
As long as we have time
But when the clocks have vanished
And time has gone away
Now, it will mean nothing
With nothing, now, will stay

Chapter Twenty Six

Anymore Time

Nothing matters anymore
Anymore's not here
Anymore is yet to come
And yet, then maybe not
Don't know when
Our time is up
Can't waste the time we've got
'Cause when time goes away
Anymore, will not stay
Time will take her with him
She is his lovely bride
And they will go to somewhere
For that's where they reside
They cannot be in nowhere
Or everywhere, you see
That's reserved for nothing
And that's where we will be
When that couple sets us free

DEATH DEFINITION

And isn't death just finding that
you love nothing more

In Our Mind

In-between what is and ain't
A picture no one's yet to paint
For it's not something, or nothing either
But it's a place, we all will be there
A place between our back and forth
That's often hard to find
A place that as we come and go
Is only in our mind

I'll See

I'd like to see forever
But, it's quite clear to me
When, I find forever…
It's nothing, I will see

When we find forever
We'll find a perfect peace
But, also perfect longing
To be something, that won't cease
For to be at one with nothing
Is a momentary state
A moment of forever
Where we only hesitate
Then move on back from nothing
To be something for a while
In this pulsing flow of energy
There is… no final mile

Can We Know

Can we really know the flower,
If we do not know the seed?
Can we really know an hour,
Without minutes that precede?
Can we ever know the present,
Without going through the past?
Can we ever know our nothing
Without knowing something first?
…and deep within the seed
Lies the nothing we all share
The nothing of existence
That puts our somethings, here
And drives them with its energy
Until, will…will not be

UMBILICUS

THEN FROM THE GREAT NOTHING THAT IS ONE
SPIN THE BUBBLES OF ENERGY,
ITS DAUGHTERS AND SONS
AND THE UMBILICUS OF ENERGY,
THAT GIVES THESE CHILDREN BIRTH
WILL STAY ATTACHED FOR JOURNEY BACK
WHEN TIME TO LEAVE THIS EARTH

Chapter Twenty Six

DEATH'S JOURNEY

Perhaps then, death is nothing more
Than energy...not free
When it's still moving slow enough
Its light is what we see
And if it comes straight at us
It shows us what it's been
But if it bounces off us
And then heads out again
To meet another set of eyes
It's we, who are seen then
So, death may be the medium
That also lets us see
Its journey back to nothing
Back to eternity

Positive Negatives

I'm positive my negatives
 Will positively be
When they turn into nothing
And nothing sets me free
But, they're enslaved by positives
Together they exist
One without the other
Then, neither can persist
So they will be here with us
Until their work is done
And then become our nothing
Eternal holy one

IRONCLAD

NOTHING'S WRONG
NOTHING'S RIGHT
NOTHING'S HERE
WITH ME TONIGHT
NOTHING'S GOOD
NOTHING'S BAD
NOTHING'S EVER...IRONCLAD

Mind's Creation?

It's really all just relative
Illusionary too
Without a point of reference
Nothing's all that's true
But nothing isn't static
It pulses in-between
And with each pulse come somethings
Points of reference seen
Existence comes in focus
But it can never last
For it pulses back to nothing
As truth becomes the past
For what is yet to be
At wait in nothing's cue
Will then emerge as something
Perhaps a me or you
Whatever form existence takes
In man we always find
Existence only manifests
Within a frame of mind
So is creation singular?
Am I the only one?
And all the rest creations
That in my mind, are spun?
And I can change it
If I will?
For the will in me
Is free
I needn't mind my
Mind at all
To be what I
Can be

Search for God

To wait for nothing
Is to search for God
You cannot see your future
For there is nothing there
Man cannot tell you what God is
Man cannot define God…
Nothing… <u>can</u>

Chapter Twenty Six

Tree Falls

*When a tree falls in a forest
Does it really make a sound?
As it crashes through its neighbors
And finally finds the ground
If a person is not present
Is there sound that happens there?
Or even, is there forest
If no one is aware?
If we take away the energy
That is the human mind
All things then don't exist
It's nothing that we find*

Time Sets Me Free

When this time leaves and sets me free
I'll find with nothing, is where I'll be
And all creation, I then will know
As I am one in nothing's flow

NOTHING'S EVERYWHERE

YOU'RE NEVER LOST WHEN NOTHING'S THERE
FOR NOTHING'S PLACE IS EVERYWHERE
BUT SOMETHINGS, NEED A PLACE IN TIME
WHERE THEY FIND THEIR EXISTENCE
AND THEY'LL BE LOST EVENTUALLY
FOR TIME HAS NO PERSISTENCE
SO WHEN WE'VE LOST THAT SOMETHING
AND IT'S NO LONGER THERE
IT'S SIMPLY MADE, IT'S JOURNEY BACK
TO NOTHING'S EVERYWHERE

Find the In-between

If while being in this present
We find the in-between

And hang on to the hand of time
As we grasp, what's now unseen
We'll touch what's on the other side
And bring some back to here
Where now it can enlighten us
Can help our vision clear

But, searching for this, in-between
Is where the problem lies
What often most eludes us
Is right before our eyes
We must step back from outer space
And inner space as well
For there, we'll find the in-between

It's there, that it will dwell

Creation Out There

It may seem odd, almighty God
Creates us from within
And from that, which is nothing
A something, starts to spin
And energy, moves outward
To show, as in a mirror
The face of all creation
Awaiting us out there
And if we should, dissect the mass
To see what lies within
We find that, it's all the same
We're one...when we begin

 Peace

When nothing is exciting you
And things just all seem wrong
It's time to go with nothing
And hear a quiet song
For nothing is the place
Where all our troubles cease
Where we will find the only one
That always brings us peace

Chapter Twenty Six

BABY

Born without concepts
Just happy in the flow
Of color, sound and formlessness
Not knowing what to know
Still happy in a world
Where nothing yet makes sense
Too soon to lose this magic
Of nothing's innocence

COSMIC DUST

From nothing spin the spheres that are pure energy
Still way too small to constitute, the matter that we see
Yet finding time and space, as every matter must
And joining with each other, they form, the cosmic dust

THE DEAL

So what is time about
And how about this thing called space
They are simply part of nothing
What helps us see our face
Helps us see our being
Helps us feel real
They're simply part of nothing
That's how I see the deal
And I could be wrong
On all of this
But it really doesn't matter
Nothing makes me feel greater
Nothing is my divine creator

PLAY ON WORDS

I'M SURE THAT MANY PEOPLE WOULD SAY
MY VIEW OF SOMETHING, NOTHING, IN-BETWEEN
IS JUST A PLAY ON WORDS
AND REALLY NOTHING NEW
I COULDN'T AGREE, ANY MORE WITH THEM
THAT'S ABSOLUTELY TRUE
FOR WE ALL CAN SEE THE TRINITY
IN OUR OWN UNIQUE AND SPECIAL WAY
FOR IT'S THE STUFF OF BEING
AND IT NEVER GOES AWAY
AND WHEN YOU LOOK AT RELIGIONS...WHETHER
EASTERN, WESTERN OR WHATEVER THEY MAY BE
WHEN YOU TAKE THEM TO THEIR ESSENCE
THEY ARE ALL...THE TRINITY
CALL IT FATHER, SON OR HOLY GHOST
OR SOMETHING, NOTHING, IN-BETWEEN
OR QUANTUM PHYSICS
WITH MATTER/ENERGY
OR MR. EINSTEIN'S THEORY
IT'S REALLY PRETTY SIMPLE
AND, AGAIN IT'S PLAIN TO SEE
WHY SOME MIGHT...SOME MIGHT CALL IT
A SUPERNATURAL...MYSTERY
BUT FOR THOSE OF US
WHO HAVEN'T FOUND
THEIR OWN WAY TO UNDERSTAND
OR SEE THIS BIG GRAND SCHEME
AND REALIZE THAT
EVERYTHING IS <u>ONE</u>
BIG PART OF THIS
BIG DREAM
WELL
THEY'LL FIND IT SOON ENOUGH
THAT WHICH IS PLAIN TO YOU AND ME
FOR THEY HAVE GOT THIS LIFETIME
AND THEN...
ETERNITY

Chapter Twenty Seven
On Life's Dance

Many of my poems use "Dance" as a metaphor for life and the experiences we find there. Having a lovely dancer as my wife for 26 years, it was easy to see our life as a beautiful dance together. Now with Annie, our families and "Life's Dance Ranch," our beautiful dance together continues in a new and glorious way. For me, it seems all of life is a "Dance." From the sun rises and sunsets with their dancing clouds and colors, to the wind, rain and snow. To natures dance of all her creatures we are gifted to see and rejoice in on "Life's Dance Ranch."

As with Dana, Annie and I love to get out on the floor to sway and move with the music. Our party facility in the loft of our old 1887 rock and log barn lets us share "Our Life's Dance" with our family and friends as they bring their dance to us.

GARDEN DANCE

The dancing in her garden
Is coming to an end
A couple lonely blossoms
Still waltzing in the wind
The autumn leaves are falling
The dancers will soon go
For they must clear the floor
Make room for winter's show

But winter only takes so long
To sing its lovely winter song
Then Spring will let them dance again
The garden will renew
The flowers will be ushered back
With sunshine, rain and dew
And bloom once more
They'll take the floor
And dance till winters' turn
It is an endless miracle
A dance we all must learn

Dance Together

They always dance together
Life's evil and Life's good
And through life's dance together
Is how life's understood
Giving meaning to each other
Together, they must reside
But occasionally they tease us
And sometimes, one will hide
And usually it is goodness
That stays just out of sight
When evil does its dance
And we struggle with our fright
But good, it is just hiding
It will always be nearby
And it will always let us see it
All we have to do is try

Chapter Twenty Seven

THEIR DANCE

Life blesses us acutely
Yet, unless we look astutely
At what often seems to be just misery
We can miss the gifts we're given
And forget that when we're living
A life of struggle, gives us, opportunity
A chance to rise above the sorrow
A chance to spread some joy tomorrow
A chance to dance while others sit and watch
And with our dance of joyous gladness
In the face of desperate sadness
We can help bring others, to the floor
Then…, <u>their dance</u>, inspires others
As the dancing, gently smothers
Feelings, that life, somehow owes us more
When life can seem most hateful
We then, must be most grateful
For its now life gives our greatest chance
To rise out of our plight
To bring those others with us
From their terrifying night
And help them dance again
In a lovely morning light

Stillness Dancing

Tell me then what happens
When stillness changes motion
For is there really stillness?
Reality? Existence frozen?
If we move into a different frame
It's stillness moving that we see
And now the stillness dances in
A frame where it is free
Yes, now the stillness moves
Where still it used to be

 *Journey to Life's Dance Ranch*

WINNING LOTTERY

SPINNING LIFE WITH COLORED SPARKS
BRILLIANT SCENTED FLOWERS
BUTTERFLIES... AND LARKS
CLEAR BLUE SKIES, TO BRING US JOY
RAIN WHEN WE NEED TEARS
SUNSHINE FOR OUR COURAGE
DARKNESS FOR OUR FEARS
THE DAWN TO GIVE US HOPE
THEN A GENTLE EVENING SKY
WITH A CHANCE TO WIN LIFE'S LOTTERY
TRUE LOVE, JUST MAY COME BY

At the Ball

If we hear creation's song
We know we're meant to sing along
Its melody can take us
And lift us here and there
Put us on life's dance floor
With feet as light as air
And there we find the others
At the ball creations thrown
But dancing can be difficult
When we have to dance alone

Life's Romance

If I must wait forever
At least I had the chance
To wait for my true love to come
And ponder sweet romance
And sometimes that is better
Than what we really find
Life's romance can disappoint
But, it's pure, within our mind

Chapter Twenty Seven
VIOLIN LIFE

Staccato fingers without bow
Upon the slender nape
Bu'res on the narrow stage
A dance that can't escape

The ears' connection
To the heart
A subtle flutter
Upon the wire
Skipping down a silver string
Music of desire

And then the lips begin to turn
They show a gentle smile
The time has come to turn the heart
Of one she would beguile

Then lost upon the tightrope
They race with passion's fire
'Til their love and song has ended
And they've stilled the silver wire

WE MUST SING

AND INTO INTUITION
IS WHERE, INTO, BELONGS
FOR WITH OUR INTUITION
WE'RE INTO OUR LIFE'S SONGS
WE KNOW HOW WE MUST SING
IF WE ARE TO BE FREE
WE MUST FIND PERFECT PITCH
THEN PERFECT HARMONY

 *Journey to Life's Dance Ranch*

Hold Hands

When you're walking with a friend
You should hold hands
And, when you're walking with your true love
You must hold hands
So if you're in this circumstance
Don't ever, ever miss the chance
For walking together with tender touch
On this life's walk, can mean so much
More than just being side by side
As hand and hand you share life's ride

Baby There

Polka dot bow, in her hair
Beautiful baby, laughing there

Their Dance

The wave, that is his passion
Moves to the count of three
To her, it is the count of four
That brings her, reverie
The count of three is always where
He feels a sweet romance
For her it is the count of four
Within a woman's dance
But, their love, it moves together
Be it three, or be it four
And their hearts, grow ever closer
When they dance upon the floor

Drums Touch

The hand is put upon the drum
And finds there, its resistance
And moves a pulse
With energy
Sound now sets
The drummer, free
Hands that love
The hide, so much
Can't hide the passion
Of life's touch

Chapter Twenty Seven

His Horse

His spurs were short
And last resort
To move the life below
Since with a squeeze
Beneath his knees
He'd usually make her go
For she'd respond to gentle coax
Before a sharp entreat
So he would always use his love
Before he'd use his feet

Annie's Girls

*She rode a horse
And shared the gift
With girls, she didn't know
But still, she gave the magic
She gave herself...and so
The girls learned more than riding
Or lov'in on a horse
They found a, gentle woman
Who showed them, God's life force*

The Final Waltz

*He watched the sunset, bring his day
To end... in a most splendid way
With Darkness gentle hand in reach
For him to take, she did beseech
This final dance with him tonight
A waltz, until their time took flight
And left no space for life or death
They once again...are nothing's breath*

EPILOGUE

Please don't feel obligated to read the following. It is simply my attempt at more explanation of my way of viewing and understanding this existence and may be more than you want to hear. Thank you for taking the time to read some or all of my book. I hope it brought you questions, thoughts, laughter, tears, peace, hope and a wonderful love story...the story of my life... Most of all I hope it helps you find the magic and miracles that reside in this thing called existence and a different way, perhaps, to see your God.

God bless you all,

Montana Mike

More of my thoughts on Something, Nothing and In-between

I realize that my "Nothing, Something, In-between" view of life, death, religion, spirituality, philosophy, existence or non-existence, time space and quantum physics may find many readers having a difficult time with my thought process. I have always been a simple boy and then a man who needs to understand things in a simple way. I visited the web to see if there was something out there that could explain my "Something, Nothing, In-between" in a better way. To my delight there have been several philosophers scientists, religions and spiritualists who have at least addressed parts of it.

My beliefs seem to be a blending of both occidental (being or "thing-ness) and oriental (no thing-ness) and Einstein, Heisenburg and quantum physics. In a publication by Olivia Goldhill, December 9, 2017, she contrasts to differences of Western versus Eastern thought and religion. Western Philosophy asks "What is Being?" Japanese Philosophy asks, "What is "Nothingness?" In a publication by Kitaro Nishida, a Japanese philosopher, he also touches on the subject and puts forth, "Whereas Western philosophers have long focused on "What is being?" as a central question about life, the Japanese and oriental thought believed that "What is nothingness?" is far more fundamental. To me they are fundamentally the same and simply different aspects of an eternal pulsing energy constantly moving from nothing to something and back again through the in-between.

To look at it from Einstein's $E=MC2$ postulate, E would be the eternal pulsing nothingness, the energy. M (mass) would be thingness, perhaps just nothingness energy slowed down to where it becomes matter. C2 is what takes M back through the in-between state to become to E again.

Heisenberg had what he called the "Uncertainty Principle" where mass is constantly popping in and out of existence. Or from one state of existence to a higher or lower state without any atom possessing a set place in time or space. To me this helps explain electromagnetic waves that can also act as particles.

In oriental depiction of existence first starts at the premise of nothingness depicted as an empty circle. Yet, to be seen as the emptiness without the circle around it. From this emptiness arises the yin and yang, unity opposites, that make up all existence. For me this helps explain matter and antimatter and the idea of parallel universes. In my writings talk of opposites, light and dark, good and evil, hot and cold and how they can't exist one without the other.

  The last poem that came to me prior to publishing this book happened on July 4, 2019. I was on my way home from a trip downtown to get ice for our annual 4th of July Barn Party. I noticed my pickup truck was getting low on diesel so I stopped at a filling station. While I was waiting for the tank to fill, it came to me and I knew I must write it down. The only paper in my truck was a paper oil funnel on which I wrote what defines my life…happiness and gratitude and how it is difficult for one to exist without the other.

Wishing you all happiness and gratitude in your lives!

Sincerely,
Montana Mike

www.ingramcontent.com/pod-product-compliance
Lightning Source LLC
Chambersburg PA
CBHW042127160426

43198CB00021B/2930